Physis

Good Wife Gollop's compendium of events presenting New Historical Evidence of how it was that God Saved the King.

Remembered by

Beloved Marshall Elm.

I will set down a tale. It may be history, it may be only a legend, a tradition. It may have happened, it may not have happened. But it could have happened…

Mark Twain.

Think outside the boundaries of permissible thought and dare to say things that no one else will say.

Howard Zinn.

Cherchez la femme, pardieu ! Cherchez la femme !

Alexandre Dumas.

Glastonbury 2024

This was going to be my year. I turned 50 and had finally got round to writing something that I hoped would be good enough to publish. I'd been inspired to write a story and was so excited about it, it was as if it had a life of its own. I borrowed a fancy device to compile all the words together and was so pleased with myself when it evolved into something like a book ! I'd always wanted to write one but now, having researched, written and rewritten, I understand why it takes so long. I'd started taking the little device out with me so that every spare moment I could add to it or edit it, everywhere I went my story came too.

One particular day, it may have been a Monday, my writing streak was at an all time high, I knew this because I transferred my precious tale to a writing app so that I had a word count and a progress report, enabling me to inform anyone that would stand still long enough that I was a writer and I was writing a book. I'd been asked via a friend of a friend to help out in a small trippy hippy clothes shop at the top of Glastonbury High street. I thought I'd have plenty of time to attend to my story as I didn't expect the shop to be busy but it was and I had a steady stream of customers who constantly interrupted my writing. I politely assisted those looking for gifts or seeking to try things on but as soon as they left I was right back immersed in my story. On this particular day it was weathery, the skies were heavy with rain and the wind was biting. I was settled in the shop corner with the device and my mind set on editing.

Suddenly the cursor began misbehaving and jumping about making my editing very difficult as I just could not control it. I found myself becoming impatient with the device while trying to be welcoming to the steady stream of customers. I wasn't expecting so many people to brave the weather but this particular day, they did, the shop was weirdly busy and I was distracted. There was so much happening at once, I couldn't understand what was making the cursor do that, it had never jumped about like that before. Quite suddenly a burly man with a round head and a spiky looking face came stealthily into the shop and surprised me. He came towards me, kind of menacingly and commanded my attention. I quickly placed the device under the counter and although I felt uneasy about him I greeted him with a smile asking if I could help him. "I'm looking for a book." He said in a deep voice, thumping his hands on the counter. I looked around the rows of tightly packed colourful dresses, saris, scarves and coats and wanted to say, 'this is a clothes shop sir', but I didn't. "I'm so sorry we don't seem to have any at the moment." I smiled. "Not to worry," he grinned, showing his smoke stained teeth, before turning and leaving almost as quickly as he'd arrived. I shook my head at how laughable it was to be asking for a book in what was clearly and quite obviously a clothes shop. I sat back down and pulled the device out from under the counter to return to my passion, but it had gone ! Not the device, the words, every last one had disappeared ! I began frantically tapping, searching the device, surely 123K words can't just disappear ! The overwhelming feeling of loss and absolute despair enveloped me as I desperately tried to retrieve and restore, I began picking it up and putting it back down then frantically pacing around, how could this be ? Where had it gone ? Had I really just lost three years worth of writing. I wanted to scream but then another customer came in, a sweet young chap who was looking for a gift for his pregnant girlfriend so I politely guided him around the trousers with stretchy waists. (The wonderful thing about retail is people come not just to buy but often just to talk or to tell you who they're buying for or where they once saw something similar. In the few weeks I'd been helping out there I'd heard all sorts of family stories and tales of far flung holidays, one chap even showed me his photographs of a recent trip to the Gambia.)

I smiled at the customers but I wasn't listening, I was mourning, deeply disappointed and hollow. I closed up the shop after a record day of sales, but a day of total loss for me, I was bereft, it was as if those characters that I'd come to love had all left me. I locked the door and wandered aimlessly down the High street in the now heavy rain. The reflection of the lights flickered in the puddles as I clumsily waded through. I felt hopeless, I had no other copies, no backup, how could I begin again ? I was so proud of it, so pleased with myself, I couldn't hold back the tears any longer.

"Now, now dear, things can't be that bad ?" I stopped my snivelling and turned to see where the comforting voice came from. The street was empty apart from a heap of what looked like blankets tucked into the corner of the Old Tribunal steps. I could just make out the twinkle of eyes from a tiny face wrapped up against the cold. I stopped crying instantly, for it was true, whatever I was upset about was nowhere near as bad as trying to keep dry on a cold stone step. A tiny weathered hand cleared the blankets from a tiny wrinkled face as I reached into my pocket for some change and asked if I could get them anything.

"Are you speaking to me dear ?" The gentle voice made its way to my ears above the flashes of traffic that flew past, whipping up the fallen leaves.

I looked about, there was no one else to be seen which didn't surprise me, it was a dreadful day to be out, even more so to be sat on the floor. Suddenly without thinking I found myself reaching out, offering my hand. A silken hand clasped hold of mine and with the lightness of a dancer the blankets lifted themselves off of the stone steps and dusted themselves down.

"I'd be delighted to come with you my dear and I know just the place, follow me," without my realising I'd invited them, the blankets led me a few paces further down the street to the George and Pilgrims a 15th Century Inn that oozes old world charm, like the Tribunal it is a magnificent reminder of the towns medieval history, the only difference being the pub was open. The George was as empty as the streets but the fires were blazing and the barmen there were welcoming and pleased to see us. It was then the fragile weather worn heap of dusty rags turned into a lady. With elegance and poise she made her way across the flagstone floors to a seat by the window as I followed on in amazement. A gentleman came over to set the table for us and he did so without saying a word. He nodded to the lady who, while uncovering herself nodded back in greeting. "Thank you Paul," she said in her clear and comforting voice. As she began taking off her several hats and scarves, I saw more of her face which although wrinkled, looked powder soft and her eyes sparkled showing she was still very much full of life.

"Can I get you a drink ?" I offered.

She smiled, " Paul knows what I have, he'll bring it for us."

Almost as soon as she spoke the waiter appeared with a tray holding a steaming teapot and two cups, she motioned for 'Paul' to set things about us which he deftly did.

"It's a herbal tea," she said. "Will you join me ?"

"Ok, why not, yes please," I said, slightly surprised at how she had brought me in out of the cold and ordered for both of us. Paul poured the steaming hot tea into perfectly dainty cups and saucers, then nodded politely to the lady again and left. With the crackle of the fire sending shadows upon the dimly lit tapestry covered walls, it was all starting to feel quite magical.

"They know you here I take it ?" I asked.

"Oh yes dear, I've been here a very long time," she giggled. There was something so sprightly about her that defied her aged appearance. She finally finished unwrapping herself then let out a sigh of satisfaction.

"Now, let me look at you," she ran her eyes all over me as if reading my future. "Wonderful, now tell me my dear ? What brings you back this way, on such a day ?" The winds began howling around the ancient architecture as the rain lashed and thrummed against the stained glass window.

"Me ? Oh it's a long story, what led you to be sitting out in it ?" I said absently, but I was sure I saw a flash in her eyes as she answered,

"I was waiting for you dear."

I laughed, how I loved Glastonbury, you never know what might happen in this town.

"And why's that ?"

"Well …it's been so long since I've seen you ?"

"I think you might have me mixed up with someone else." I said, kindly so as not to offend her. "I'm not sure we've met before." She looked surprised and instantly returned to the fragile old lady persona I'd seen outside.

"But ... you do remember me ... don't you ?" she looked at me, searching in my eyes, then shook her head as if confused. Perhaps she'd come into the shop I thought.

"Oh yes," I said slowly. "I remember now, of course, how silly of me, yes we've met before, forgive me, only so much space on the hard drive." I tapped my head not wanting to upset her and immediately her sparkle returned. Nut job, I thought to myself, we'll have a quick something then I'll say my goodbyes and scarper. Two bowls of soup were delivered in the swift and silent way 'Paul' was so obviously adept at, I thanked him as he nodded and left us.

"Excuse me Sir ?" I called, stopping him in his tracks, "Is this Vegan ?" Paul turned and smiled, "Naturally," he replied as he bowed, then went on his way. The old dear was delighted and clasped her hands together radiating such joy it was as if a plate of jewels had been set before her. I thought the old girl must be starving, poor thing. I helped myself to one of the hot bread rolls that were delivered in a neat little basket complementing the meal, forgetting that neither of us had actually ordered it, it did however smell and look equally appealing. "Shall we ?" I asked as I took my silver spoon out of its napkin cloak and tucked in. Wow ! What an explosion of flavours, textures and deliciousness, the likes I'd never known. The old lady was still in rapture at the sight and smell of the bowl before her, "try some," I encouraged, " it's very good."

"Yes, it is, isn't it ? It's a very old recipe," she said smiling, slowly picking up her spoon to gently dip in. I finished well before my companion, who elegantly savoured every mouthful. Sitting back in the chair, full and satisfied, I looked out onto the High street as flashes of lightning followed by the crack of thunder made me mightily glad to be inside.

"So," I offered, attempting to chit chat. The old lady seemed lost in a world of her own and didn't respond at all until she finished her soup, then sitting back she locked eyes with me as she wiped her mouth gently with the cloth napkin. "So..?" She replied. As we slipped back into silence, I looked at my imaginary watch.

"So... I suppose I ought to be off," I suggested, although I didn't really want to leave the warmth of the pub and head out into the brunt of the awful weather.

"Off ? Where ? Out there ? That's silly, you've only just brought me in," she laughed, as I felt myself blushing. "Come now, where's your sense of humour, I'm not trying to shame you dear," she smiled. "Talk with me, what made you want to offer the likes of me a kindness ?" I raised my eyes as I wasn't really sure I had, I just remembered thinking it was a harsh day for someone to be sitting outside.

"Then I'll tell you, shall I ? It was your heart, your heart that led you to me and us in here, you have a good one. You always have had, you may have forgotten me but I remember you my dear." She flashed a smile at me as she picked up her tea cup and drank the last of it. As if by magic our waiter, Paul, silently reappeared to clean away the bowls and refresh our drinks. I was astonished, firstly by the words she had just said and by the way the waiter moved around her quite effortlessly. I thanked Paul and lifted my cup, my mouth suddenly felt dry as I questioned myself. "Oh don't go getting all your head," she remarked without looking at me. "Unnecessary fuss, that is, just be still and be content with where we are, right here, right now." I tried to smile, she was right I was all in my head, the creeping feelings of absurdity wouldn't leave me alone, were they feelings or were they thoughts ?

"Ah, well at least you know the difference dear, they're not always your thoughts you know ? The things that leap into your head, but your heart and your feelings, well they're a different kettle of fish," she replied as if hearing me. Now things really were becoming absurd. "Just breathe dear, take a breath, funny isn't it how ignorant we are of our breath. Why don't you tell me about yourself dear ? What upset you ? What were you so sad about ?"

"Well,I ... I guess... it was because I lost something," I stammered. "Something I'd written, I'm a writer, or rather I liked to think I was but, I've just lost it all," I sighed.

"Lost it all ?"

"Yes, the book I've been working on ...for the past three years, it somehow disappeared ? Maybe I pressed something or I don't know, but what I do know is, it's all gone."

"Oh I see, so that's why you were tearful ?"

"Yes," I whimpered, trying not to cry again.

"Ah, don't worry my dear, nothing is ever lost, what was it you were writing about ?"

"I suppose it was mostly about the English Civil War, well more about the King really, the monarchy, the republic. At least I was trying to write about it, but it's really tricky to find the truth as there's so much conflicting evidence so I didn't really want to focus too much on the war, but rather on the time."

"Ah, did you now ? It's a funny thing, time, it's not really what you think it is. Don't expect there's many alive today who know how to use time properly. As for that so called republic. Pah ! Terrible business. It took all the magic out of everything. You've heard folk say, 'the victors write the books' I take it ? Yet people still believe that rubbish, there's no wonder none of them can agree, probably because it's all propaganda and lies. It was as rife back then, as it is today, they rewrote the history books to suit themselves just like every other dictatorship. Sorry dear, it still irks me, I am listening, let's get back to your story, so tell me ?"

"I don't know, one minute I was happily tapping away, on this little laptop here, when I noticed the thing that flashes up when you type, the cursor. It was jumping about which was strange and then, the whole story, every word just vanished."

"Vanished, just like that ? Where were you when it vanished ?"

"Yes, vanished …just like that. I've been helping out in a shop at the top of the High street."

"You've been writing when you should have been working ?"

"Well yes, but,"

"Unfocused and uncommitted, not really the kind of energy you want to give to a story, is it dear ?"

My eyes grew wide as the embarrassment rose up within me. I hadn't thought of it like that, but she was right, I was always trying to do lots of things at once.

"Remember, dear you haven't done anything bad, I'm not trying to shame you. Guilt and shame now that's another great gift from that republic we're still trying to shake off. Let yourself off the hook, only good people feel guilt, because them bad ones, they don't care ! I'll be happy to try and help you unravel the knots you've tied yourself in, now then, what else happened, when you were or when you should have been working ?"

"Well, it was just a regular day really, I wasn't expecting it to be so busy but it was with lots of happy customers who were pretty friendly and chatty. Oh, hold on there was one weird guy, he came in asking for a book, which is ridiculous as it's quite obviously a clothes shop, I mean I hang half the stock outside in the morning so you can't really miss it."

"Ah, but we may have missed something dear. So someone came into your shop and asked for something that wouldn't obviously be kept there. Hmmm and then what dear ? Think back, try to remember everything."

"He was just an ordinary guy, a bit older, stocky, round head with dark bags under his eyes, unshaved. He made me jump though as he came straight over and asked or rather told me he was looking for a book."

"Ah, so it was a Roundhead that came in and said he was looking for a book, how interesting."

"Yes, he was quite forceful, leaned over the counter at me and then, when I said we didn't have any he promptly left."

"And so did your book ?"

"Well, yes and so did my book !" I had a sudden flash of clarity seeing an image of the man smiling while taking off with my book. It was ridiculous but also blindingly obvious, it blew all my senses, although it still made none.

"You must remember where you are dear, this is the sacred Isle of Ancient Avalon, we are at the very heart of all Albion."

My mind was spinning, searching for the rational, the real, what did she mean ?

"Have you heard of the Quantum field, dear ?" She asked very matter of factly.

I shook my head in disbelief, where on earth was she going with this.

"Or is it Quantum Photon Entanglement ? Actually dear I'm not sure what science is calling it these days, but as I understand it, it means that things can be connected no matter how far apart they are or what lies between them, like time or space."

My jaw dropped but I had nothing to say and certainly no answer to offer her.

"Let me try and make it clearer for you my dear, perhaps something or someone from another space in time has or is connected to or with you and you've opened up the door. You see dear, there are certain ... Let's say events that cut so deep into the soul, the very fabric of agreed upon timelines of our so called history that it causes a glitch... a blemish.. a wart.. a crevice...or perhaps an opportunity. You said you were at the top of the High street, yes ? Maybe you've tapped into something there, some energy or a portal that you've unlocked, awakened with your writing, or you may have hit upon something that's been hidden in time and in tales. Perhaps it's time for that truth to emerge and there will always be those that wish for the truth to remain hidden. Or maybe you'd simply written it wrong, maybe there was more to the story you were telling. Tell me about it."

I coughed to clear my throat and my thoughts as I began slowly.

"Well ...it started off as a story about a madhouse, they were the forerunners of those amazing asylums that sprung up everywhere in the 1700's. You see, my Mother was a psychiatric nurse and worked at a magnificent one that even had a ballroom, so they've always intrigued me. I mean where did all those mad people suddenly come from ? I'm fascinated by them, those huge incredible and often beautiful sprawling estates that were so kindly constructed for the insane. ! Then I discovered that one of the first madhouses in 1656, was here in Glastonbury, would you believe ? So I started looking into the time and what was happening in England in 1656 and well it was pretty bleak. The Regicide, the republic, but there's always a bigger picture, isn't there ? For starters there's King James, he's portrayed very unkindly throughout history apparently just because of how Charles Dickens described him ! We're then led to believe that King Charles started the Civil wars but I don't think he did. I think he was set up, cornered, it seemed obvious to me that there was more of a connection with the Thirty years war, it was one of the most destructive conflicts in Europe, that strangely King James' didn't join in with, even though his daughter was married to the King of Bohemia. There was certainly something magical happening in that part of the world, a wonderful cultural renaissance that was then brutally crushed by the Catholic Church, in much the same way as what happened to the Cathars in Southern France in the 1200's. It's interesting that the witch-hunts began in that part of the world too, I feel it's all connected, I mean I know everything is connected but these events all brought about the same level of Catholic reaction, genocide ! Although it wasn't the Catholics that led to the death of King Charles, it was the puritans, a fun bunch, it was pretty obvious they had it in for him all along. I read somewhere that the Catholic Church, at that time, was using any and all unscrupulous methods to control Europe, even going so far as to support opposing religious groups, like the puritans, to divide and conquer. You can't believe everything you read I know but I always felt sorry for King Charles, it was frightful what happened to him."

"Ah, wasn't it ? Yes it's sad that history has been so unkind to the Stuart's, makes you wonder why that is, doesn't it ? Even today people still say the most outrageous and unkind things about them. Treacherous but clever how they, whoever they might be, always discredit the truth, stops people looking for it. Anyways dear, a madhouse you say, right here in Glastonbury well I never. Well that does sound interesting but you have to be careful with history books, they can be so dull can't they ? All those dates and names, like a soup full of ingredients but lacking any flavour, all that conflict, does nothing but spoil the appetite and upset the tummy if you ask me. What's the true purpose of all those wars and who would we be without them ? Without that version of history we persist in force feeding ourselves with, I wonder who would we be ? No dear, love is what we want. A nice romance to give us tingles, a story that dares us to believe in the power of true love above all else. Doesn't that sound better ? Tastes far better than all those battles, bullets and gunpowder too I'd fancy. Hmmm and as luck would have it, I happen to be known for telling such tales, so I may be able to help you, let's see if between us we can bring forth a story, a love story, a tale worthy of telling."

"I would love that, I'd love to hear a story." I smiled at the old girl as I got myself comfortable in my chair, looking into her sparkly eyes I had the feeling that I was right where I was meant to be and that something extraordinary was about to happen.

"Well you haven't come here to be ordinary ?" She winked. Now she had my full attention, I blinked and wondered if she could see into my head and read my mind. She smiled at me, making me feel relaxed and at ease, comfortable and calm. There was something about the cosy, yesteryear atmosphere of the old Inn, the crackling fire and the rhythmic rain on the windows that lulled me like a babe. Paul grinned mischievously over at us as he stoked up the fire sending a swirl of smoke and sparkles up the chimney. The old lady's voice was mesmerising, my eyelids grew heavy, I really was very comfortable.

Once upon a time, for all good stories start that way ...

Beyond the Northwinds and there was an island divided into three parts with a smaller island at its side, a fortunate, blessed and abundant land filled with wonder and opportunities. The old Queen Elizabeth, who had ruled the southern lands alone had passed to the Elysian fields and bequeathed her crown to a cousin, a King in his own right, a steward of the highlands. He was of course James Stuart and the lands we speak of became known as The United Kingdom of Great Britain. Now, only he could have done this, only he could have united the lands this way, the old Queen had been well advised by Dr Dee, who had spent a great deal of time with the alchemists in Bohemia, where James's daughter would later be Queen. It was a time of miraculous opportunity, great magic and unity.

King James with his rare and restless mind was an exceptionally clever man. He was raised from a very young age by nobles as his father had died in mysterious circumstances and his mother had her head removed by the very Queen whose crown he now accepted. Taking his beloved family and his court to rule the United Kingdom from London, he amused himself with pageants and Parliament, doing his utmost best to seek and keep peace in his Kingdom.

Life was good until Prince Henry Fredrick, the heir to all his hopes, sadly and cruelly left this world leaving a gaping hole in the heart of the King and everyone who knew of him. He was poisoned at the wedding party of his sister, which meant someone within the palace had betrayed them all. King James was devastated, he dismissed Henry's entire court and hid himself away. He trusted no one but his courtier, who he later elevated to a Duke, the only man he dared to have any faith in. Especially when his other favourite and trusted ally was unforgivably entangled in some terrible murder. Now all his hopes rested upon his second son, Charles, who was thrown upon the world stage as the future heir.

Our story is of a baby girl, born to members of King James court who had made the journey south with him. The father, a captain of the horse and the mother a lavender to Queen Anne. They named their baby Jane and she grew into a fine and bonny lass. The family lived in Mews not far from the palace, with the back of their house leading to St James park, a prime spot for a young girl to see all the comings and goings of court especially as her father would be leading the horse. Oblivious to the pressing needs of their duties, young Jane demanded her parents attention and from her father she usually got it. He was a tall, strong man with a kind smile that was always singing or whistling a tune. He had a funny way of making his eyebrows dance that delighted the young girl as he lifted her into his arms or upon a horse. If Jane wasn't running errands for her mother or skipping the back streets of Westminster she was waiting for her father to lead the King's horses past their house. Jane's father was a good and loyal man who saw to it that his family were well provided for, happiest doing his duties for the King whatever they would be. He took great care of the horses, stables and yards and with a nod he would have a coach and four together and ready at a moment's notice. He was also trusted to travel in the King's name, accompanying Royalty across Europe and was highly regarded by the King who by far prized loyalty as the greatest quality and Jane's father William, was as we've said a loyal Kingsman.

In time, King James decided on a rather grand return to Scotland and entrusted Jane's father with the honour of organising this event. Jane watched in awe as the court put every effort into preparing for the long and arduous journey and waited a whole summer for her father's return. She had missed him terribly, they all had, the house was so very empty without him. Her longing for him took her sparkle away as she focused every bit of her attention on the empty road that led out to Charing Cross. Unbeknownst to her this absence was to prepare her for an even greater one. Kicking the heels of her bare feet against the wall she patiently waited, never tiring of looking for the man who loved her the most. Then she heard it, the familiar calls and clips of hooves and the rattle of wagons as the magnificent Royal procession returned and rolled into the mews. Jane was bubbling over with joy at the very thought of seeing her father again. There was such a swell of celebration as loved ones poured into the streets to be reunited with shouts of thanks that the King had returned safely. Jane felt enormous pride that her father had been party to it all, 'God save the King,' rang out in welcome to them that had made this epic journey and returned safe, well and by all accounts divinely protected. Jane's eyes darted about the throng of loved ones in search of her father. She soon spied him securing a horse so she nimbly skipped around the busy folk who were moving like parts to a well oiled machine and threw herself at his legs, tightly, much like a cat. William swung around and scooped his beloved daughter up into his strong arms, swirling her through the air. Her tumbling locks of Scot red hair flew around her beautiful face as she giggled, laughed and cried all at once. Jane, deliriously happy, wrapped her arms around his neck as he took great strides making his way home to see his wife and new born son. He gave thanks and said a gentle prayer, pulling his dear wife to him and held them all in his great arms and wept. The six merciless months abroad and on the road had taken their toll and changed him. He was exhausted, withered, worn and trampled. The memory of that day holding on to her father, of his whiskers and waxy hands that were surprisingly smooth for such a hard working man, would stay with Jane her whole life.

Alas, the joy was not to last. Jane was too young to understand and too happy to realise something was amiss when her father quite suddenly was no longer there. One day he just didn't come home again and poor Jane was quite bewildered by her mother, who would fall to the floor sobbing, overcome with grief. Jane would sit patiently outside their house with her eyes fixed upon the Charing road, waiting for him. When likewise her young brothers were suddenly no longer there, she felt sure they must be with father and felt somewhat envious that he hadn't come for her, where was he ? Whenever Jane heard the familiar sounds of shouts or the clip clopping of horses and wagons she would scan every face looking for those dancing eyes and whiskers. Everyone always waved to her for she was well known and well loved in the Scot's community and everyone knew she waited patiently for her father to return but no one had the heart to break it to the big eyed, red haired girl that so politely and sweetly acknowledged them all.

Jane continued to ignore the obvious until the day she was forced to face reality when her Mother announced she was to remarry ! James Maxwell, of the King's bedchamber had brought the light back into her Mother's eyes. It was awkward for Jane at first but she soon settled seeing her Mother happy and smiling again. James Maxwell, had known and respected Jane's father and was well placed and respected at court himself. He loved Jane's mother and wished to take care of them and Jane believed him. She would however always be a Ryder, her fathers daughter.

Days passed and quietly turned into months, then years as Jane watched a great many events sail past her sat upon her wall, her prime seat and view to all the great and good goings on in Westminster.

The funeral of the Queen was a terribly sad episode in their lives, especially for Jane's mother, who had been in her household her entire time in London. King James, who never fully recovered from the loss of their son Prince Henry, was grief stricken when his wife died suddenly and it wasn't long before the heartbroken King joined her in everlasting peace. The feeling of loss was total, for James had been a good King and the Scot's had all thrived upon his patronage. The King had made such a difference to the lives of everyone living in these fortunate isles and he had changed the face of England forever. Jane had a great deal of respect for him, he had always been kind to her and had always been a part of their lives, she would miss him. The coronation of King Charles brought a wave of much needed rejoicing and none could have been more jubilant than Jane's family and neighbours. What a spectacle, what hope, what joy. King Charles, chose himself a new court, with none of his elder brother's former servants, which obviously greatly upset them all. Much to their annoyance and that of Parliament the King kept his counsel with the Duke of Buckingham. The Duke was a gentleman, one of those rare individuals that define charisma and inevitably invoke jealousies.

King Charles took a dainty French princess for his wife and they were a lively couple. Queen Henrietta was the daughter of Henry, the Good King and her mother Marie was a Medici, making her a great granddaughter of the formidable Caterina Sforza. The Royal couple were great patrons of all things beautiful and commissioned the most wonderful works of art and masques, breathtaking sensations of allegorical performance. These were often performed by the Queens men, who were the finest acting troupe of the time. A raw assemble of poets, musicians and playwrights who were always ready and able to whip a crowd into hysteria with each performance far exceeding the last. Thanks mostly to the flawless mind of Inigo Jones, the Queens architect and set designer extraordinaire, he constructed such feats of mythical magic, one couldn't help but be amazed. Often the King and Queen would take great pleasure in performing themselves with a great many Lords and Ladies taking parts as well. It was as if Ancient Greece and all their Gods were brought to life, once more opening the gates to Hyperborea. King Charles and his Queen took great satisfaction from these opulent performances and Jane would always find a way, either on tip toe or through a slightly opened door, to appreciate and experience the wonderment. The Royal court were well aware of her and played along so as not to embarrass the girl for they knew she enjoyed the sneaking and creeping about almost as much as the performance. She thrilled and found joy in every tiny exquisite detail, amazed at what wizardry could do this. The stage would be filled with magical coloured lights and moving scenery, often with real tamed animals. Jane never ceased to be amazed and enthralled by it all, especially the actors who performed so perfectly. There was one young actor in particular, a rather captivating and handsome embodiment of beauty that bedazzled her. There was something otherworldly that happened to Jane whenever he spoke or sang in his gentle whispering voice. Inexperienced with men, she was unsure what began fluttering, sparkling and fizzing inside her whenever she set her eyes upon him but she liked it. He seemed to reach into the very depths of her when she was unaware she had any depths at all. He would captivate the audience, then perfectly bow all the way to the floor while the crowd erupted into rapturous applause, none more appreciative than Jane who at this point couldn't help but reveal herself and clapped until her hands were sore. He would graciously bow again, then sweep off the stage leaving poor Jane gasping for breath.

The masques became more elaborate and more astonishing with each and every performance. Of course this meant there were many rehearsals and after parties, wild eruptions of joy and pleasure that Jane would peer into, silently watching these explosions of sensation from behind curtains with her heart racing. The actors, dancers and musicians would continue their revels till morning light, a swirl of decadent passion writhing in sweat and kisses, leaving the poor girl intoxicated by the heat of their sheer energy.

Jane lived in anticipation for these masques and was beside herself for weeks when she knew one was on the horizon. She filled her head with thoughts of the handsome stranger. Gossiping with the maids somehow bringing every conversation round to discuss him. She'd soon discovered he was part of The Queens men, the great company of actors who enjoyed the generous patronage of Queen Henrietta and of Queen Anne before her. Jane was not surprised they were considered the very best actors in London.

This gilded world was tragically shattered by the untimely exit of the handsome Duke of Buckingham, George Villiers, whose heartbreaking night time torch lit funeral floated silently past Jane's wall. Apparently he'd come off worse in a bar room brawl in Portsmouth, but the whispers of the court and more than likely the truth of the matter, was that he was assassinated on orders of the French Cardinal Richelieu. The wicked Cardinal, who was envious of the Duke's dalliances with the French Queen, had been driven mad by jealousy. It was rumoured that he plotted the Duke's demise with none other than that famed and despicable harlot, Milady De Winter.

King Charles was devastated, as indeed was everyone that had ever had the good fortune to be in the Duke's company. He truly illuminated all of life and his loss was felt for a very long time. The poor King, the court and the whole Westminster were as if cast adrift. Parliament however, rather despicably, saw some benefits in the Duke's departure and moved in like vultures upon the grieving King, who understandably, dismissed them all again.

It was around this time that Jane's stepfather was appointed Black Rod, a senior officer in the House of Lords and responsible for all the major ceremonial events in Westminster, which also made him fabulously wealthy. It meant Jane and her siblings had the luxury of freedom and for Jane that freedom meant masques, riding horses through the parks and heaths or whiling away hours sat high upon a wall, daydreaming, watching life and clouds drift by. Jane was accustomed to the company of Royalty, Bishops, Lords and Ladies, they all came to or past the house making their way to the Palace or to the Tower, but she was unaware of parliament or their thoughts regarding anything. Jane thought it was probably for the best as the news her stepfather would tell of parliament were dark tales of treachery, thuggery and insult which often angered and frustrated him.

Much like every household with girls of a certain age, there soon came whisperings of weddings and husbands and although Jane tried hard to ignore them, she instinctively knew they were directed at her. These whispers were persistent and grew louder until Jane was forced to acknowledge her parent's interests in her future.

"You can't carry on like this," Jane's mother threw over her shoulder as she busied herself in their kitchen.

"Like what ?" Offered Jane, nonchalantly.

"On your own, there's talk, you know, most girls your age are married by now and have bairns of their own." Jane's family had never lost their Scottishness despite years of living in London.

"But Mother, I'm still not sure that's what I want."

"Oh not this again, not sure of what you want ? You're mighty sure of what you don't want aren't you Lassie ? And who you don't want, your fathers fast running out of ideas for a suitor for you."

"Good, I've told you I don't want a suitor, I want someone to love me madly, I want to be so deeply in love that the heavens open and angels rejoice." Jane would often drift off into poetry holding the image of the actor in her mind. She had long since discovered his name was James and she liked to say his name over and over. Now she was older she no longer hid away from the grand masques, she took great pride in accepting a part in them, any and every part offered to her, she revelled in every bit of them from the ceiling to the floor.

"I'd like a husband," piped up Jane's younger sister.

"Oh don't worry dear heart, ma and pa will soon find you one," Jane replied, sarcastically.

Her Mother huffed.

"You must want something more for yourself Jane, you must want a family of your own, something other than…" said her Mother impatiently.

"Other than what ?"

"Well, other than drifting around here, laying upon that wall, those plays."

"Masques," Jane corrected as her Mother huffed again

"Those… masques then, it's them that fill your head with all that crazy talk, poetry and nonsense," Jane's Mother threw her hands in the air.

Jane gasped and pulled in her chin in disgust.

"Nonsense ? Crazy talk ? I'll tell you what crazy talk is Mother, it's thinking that I want nothing more than to marry some lifeless dullard or that I'll happily accept what no one else wants, some inept that wishes nothing more for me than baring his children ... and embroidery... probably."

"Nothing wrong with embroidery," remarked her Mother, half smiling. "You can't keep turning them away Jane, you're a fine looking girl and you'd make a fair family if you'd only give one of them suitors your fathers found a chance."

"Mother ! Those ...suitors, care nothing for me, my heart or my dreams. I feel frozen at the very thought of it. Am I to settle for being nothing more than a broodmare and that be it, my lot in life ? To me that is crazy talk, because I see nothing wrong in wanting my life to be filled with love."

Jane drifted into heavy sighs and her favourite pastime of daydreaming, in which James would take her in his arms and they would dance as if in tune with all of existence.

Her Mother meanwhile would shake her head in that familiar way of disbelief at her eldest daughter with a hope that her younger children hadn't caught the madness their sister was so clearly inflicted with. She took a deep breath and sighed, "what am I to do with you ?"

"Nothing Mother, absolutely nothing, let me be." With that Jane jumped up and grabbed a chunk of bread from the side, twirling out of the kitchen and kissing her mother goodbye. "I'm going to find Elizabeth. Please don't worry about me Mother, I am fine just as I am, free."

Elizabeth was a laundress like Jane's Mother had been and was Jane's very best friend in all the world. Elizabeth hadn't the luxury of a wealthy family so worked hard but happily. She was most happy when Jane waltzed in with her wide eyes, big dreams and tall tales. The girls never grew tired of their what if stories and would heartily laugh at their own fairy tales. Most of all Elizabeth liked to be kept up to date with the preparations of whatever masque was to be performed, listening intently to Jane's ramblings about James which if we are honest, was always where the conversation pointed.

"Jane," shrieked Elizabeth when she caught sight of her friend. "I wasn't sure I'd be seeing you today, I'm almost finished so I'll be free to walk with you, if you're not on your way elsewhere that is?" Elizabeth asked with the air of hope in her voice.

"No silly, I've come especially and only to see you, so yes please I'd love for us to walk."

Elizabeth finished her chore and hung up her apron asking permission to leave from the other laundress present, the other older lady waved to both girls, calling out, "lovely to see Jane, give my regards to your mother won't you and don't you be too long Lizzy."

"I will and I won't," chimed the girls laughing together as they swept out of the door holding each other's arms and already in full gossip.

"So tell me, tell me everything," Elizabeth was always eager to hear Jane's news, of Westminster, the world, but mostly the masques. She delighted in hearing all about these ridiculously flamboyant events that Jane always wound herself into. Apparently this latest Masque was to be the most fantastic yet and Jane had savoured and memorised every last detail.

"Honestly Lizzy, I'm breathless just thinking about it, it will be magnificent, magical, almost unbelievable. I hardly know where to start, it's to be led by the King's Marshall and his men all bearing torches, all the way from the Strand with over a hundred men behind them all dressed in silver and gold …lace, I think. Then, there comes two music chariots, the first carrying the lutenists dressed as priests and Sybil's while the second brings the singers who strike picturesque poses in costumes representing the celestial gods, you know, such as Venus and Mars, then comes the boys all dressed up as birds, honestly Lizzy I swear you've never seen anything so wild, so enchanting, the costumes are so rich and fantastic. Then there comes the main actors in four more magnificent chariots each drawn by four horses that are dressed in gold and silver and crimson cloths with huge red and white feathers and each chariot bearing a flaming torch and that's just the procession ! It's to be called …The Triumph of Peace, isn't it marvellous ?" Jane loved the way these words rang inside her, she thought them so wonderfully well put together. "The Triumph of Peace," she said again and slowly so as to accentuate every syllable. Elizabeth loved the way Jane got so excited vividly retelling her tales, she was a natural storyteller. Always of course, building and setting the scene for James, conjuring an image of someone so handsome, so courteous, so chivalrous he was like a god in their mind. Elizabeth had never met him but then in all honesty neither had Jane, but she could hardly contain her adolescent adoration, recalling the beauty, the colour, the decor, the animals and the wonderful scenery and the god like James and delighted in sharing every detail with her friend as it brought it all back to life for her.

"And then ?" Breathed Elizabeth, quite literally at the edge of her seat.

"And then dear Lizzy," laughed Jane, eyes wild with excitement.

"There, before your eyes is a magical forest, so real, so enchanting you can almost smell the pine. The spirits of Peace, Law and Justice descend to honour our King and all those before him as the moon sets, then in plumes of mist, there he is ! As if by magic, which it probably is, he just appears, in a cloud of smoke, poof !" Jane moved around the bench and draped herself across it acting out James's every move, with great flair she threw her hand up and over her head, bringing her hand down slowly over her eyes.

"And then ?" Elizabeth began salivating as Jane went on.

"He," Jane looked about her and whispered, "He, who sparkles and shines under the moonlight, he is the bringer of the morning and …he is naked as a babe !"

Her friend shrieked, blushed and raised her hand to cover her pleased smile, "naked ... really ?"

"Well, yes," said Jane, swallowing as she devoured the memory of the moment. "Certainly to his waist."

"To his waist ?" Elizabeth echoed.

"Yes," the girls locked eyes as Jane went on.

"Suddenly, there are flashes of lightning, as Confidence, Opinion and Fancy appear, along with the feathermakers wife but…but the smoke clears, it is he, that commands your eyes for you can see his most perfect outline of his manly, muscular body shimmering from head to toe with his eyes like jewels," Elizabeth nodded enthusiastically encouraging her friend, "and then ?"

Both girls sat in silence with the images dancing in their minds.

"Well dear heart," Jane breathed, with a wicked smile and no sense of apology."I could hardly think straight after that. My eyes were fixed upon him, his beautiful skin, I mean, I could see all the …way …down," Jane ran her finger seductively and slowly down her front, "to his..."

"No, no, no this is too much," laughed Elizabeth, her eyes like saucers and her mind a whirl. Jane fell about laughing, "but ..don't stop there," said Elizabeth, pulling her friend up, "tell me, I have to know, to his what ?" She looked into Jane's eyes and they burst out in giggles again. It was while they were in this feverish state that the old lavender appeared and called Elizabeth back to her duties, which brought them back to their senses as if waking them from a magical dream.

They both heaved a heavy sigh, "until tomorrow then ?" Mused Jane.

"Oh no, you can't ? You can't leave me lost like this, tell me the end, tell me, what happens next, you must." Elizabeth took hold of her friend's hand making Jane laugh harder.

"Please, please, I am aching to know, the suspense might kill me."

"Oh and what a wonderful way to die," quipped Jane, fast as lightning.

"Oh Ginny Ryder, you are a tease, I do wish I didn't love you quite so much."

"As I love you Lizzy, that is why I shall save the best until tomorrow, anticipation is everything, it is the way of the theatre."

"ELIZABETH !"

"Oh, I'm coming, I'm coming," the girls embraced, composed themselves and straightened their skirts, Elizabeth going one way and Jane the other.

That evening's rehearsal exploded into the wildest revelry Jane had ever seen. There was something so different about everyone, their spirits seemed exalted. Jane was very much a part of things by day but by night she usually stowed away and watched the others enjoy themselves. She was beyond surprised when one of the dancers, perhaps it was Faith, uncovered her hiding place and pulled her from the shadows to join them in their celebrations. Although nervous Jane couldn't resist the temptation to follow the elegant hand that pulled and guided her into the dance. Within moments she was caught in the music and found herself moving in ways she had never dared before, nor had she felt the thrill of being so dangerously close to strangers. She enthusiastically whirled her way through the arms of many deliciously amorous dalliances. Faces, colours, music all became a haze, she felt euphoric, unable to contain her happiness neither did she want to, this feeling of absolute liberty electrified her. The heady mixture of exotic perfumes and plumes of smoke stoked her awareness as the music played to the rhythm of her heart, she was so completely enthralled and never wanted it to stop. Having watched these folk enjoying themselves this way she never dared to imagine that she too could reach such heights of ecstasy. Yet here she was in the very middle of the revels dizzy with wonder, beaming like a sunflower in full bloom. She floated through the throng of beautiful people caressing her as if in a dream, the free flowing wine dripping from her mouth as she gleefully accepted everything that was pressed to her lips. She felt so at ease as if she belonged amongst this company of exuberant romantics. The flaming torches cast bewitching shadows upon the walls that fired her imagination as her senses succumbed to the wine and feverish excitement. It felt like a dream when the whole room began spinning as she was deliriously twirled through the arms of lovers, eventually causing her to stumble and trip through a curtain. Everything slowed as if she was falling through time and space, landing with a bump upon a sumptuous velvet cushion that sent sparkles of dust flying through the air like stars, causing her to laugh in rapturous joy.

The company erupted into rowdy whoops and calls as she had landed quite unexpectedly next to the man she admired the most. James, who was blindfolded, inebriated and deep in the throes of passion with another, turned and roared with laughter too.

"Well, well, well, what do we have here ? A gift from the heavens ? A nymph, a sprite, a wildling ? It appears a little bird has flown into my nest."

Jane, recognising his voice at once turned slowly to face him. Awestruck, her eyes grew wide and she gulped the air, far too stunned to speak. He had taken her breath away, again, only this time she was next to him with his face dangerously close to hers, she felt sure she must be dreaming for she could hardly believe it. She dared not breathe or move an inch in case the spell was broken. She dissolved into his embrace as he wrapped his arm around her like a cloud, whisking her all the way up to heaven for now she could see only him and hear nothing but the sound of his voice.

He laughed, "come little bird, sing for me, oh are you a shy little bird ? A silent bird ? Do I know of any ? Would you then allow me to boldly coax your voice, your sweet song with a kiss ?" He tenderly teased his fingers down her arm until he found her hand and gently kissed it, then placing her hand upon her chest he blindly ran his hand up and over her arm to sweep the strands of her hair that covered her peachy cheek, no doubt feeling the heat from it, then delicately he stroked her lips.

Jane's eyes widened as her whole body quivered. Could this really be happening ?

"Do you know who I am ?" Jane whimpered, desperately wanting him to know who she was, to remove his mask and see her, truly see her and want her as much as she wanted him. After what felt like an age he whispered softly into her ear.

"Who else could have flown into my arms ? If you're not a little bird then you must be an angel or perhaps you're a fairy, who flew in upon fairy dust, the queen of fairies ?" She shivered as a feeling of bliss washed over her. "No," she giggled, as he moved his hand, tenderly tracing the curve of her body.

"Then sweet thing, I would certainly like to know you." he said, taking more of an interest in his acquisition. He went to remove his mask only for Jane to stop him and gently recover his eyes. She had a fleeting thought he might not want her if he was to see her or maybe he had expected her to be someone else and she couldn't bear the thought of his rejection or disappointment now. As if hearing her thoughts and keeping his face very close to her, he whispered, "Hush now, sweet thing, do not give into fearful thoughts, it takes away our joy. I implore you to let only love keep a dwelling place within you. Isn't it love that we all want ? To love and be loved." His words poured over her like honey. Feeling the heat from his breath and the warmth of his skin, Jane couldn't contain her feelings any longer, she was blissfully overcome with excited anticipation. He untangled himself from the other lover, who had until recently held his attention and he fixed his focus fully upon Jane who was trembling at his touch.

"I have loved no one else, I am already yours," she whispered, much to his delight, he smiled and laughed wickedly as he took command of her body in ways she had never known. As the softness of his lips met hers, she felt the surge of pure pleasure running through her veins and pulsating through every part of her being, never had she tasted anything so divine.

As their kiss became more passionate, the former lover gayly drew the curtain around them and left to rejoin the party. Jane was now lost in the realms of fantasy helplessly adrift upon the very essence of the actor who took her all the way to womanhood in the most pleasing ways possible. She surrendered to him fully, squealing with delight as he lifted her skirts. He gently ran his hand up her thighs, parting her legs while softly kissing her neck and took her breath away as he thrust himself into her again and again, setting every part of her being alight.

Jane awoke in a haze of love, wrapped in the arms of James who had just made all her wildest dreams come true. He was even more perfectly handsome when sleeping, especially when sleeping so close to her. She was deliriously happy and only became aware the party was still in full swing when the curtain was abruptly torn open and many arms and faces appeared to heave her idol from his slumber and back into their pleasure. Jane at once became timid and shrunk back hoping no one saw her as James was passed more wine and disappeared into the sea of revelry. Jane suddenly felt the need to leave and quickly, she slipped off the bed, under the curtains and out of the door without looking back.

Dancing all the way home she was mystified, replaying the evening's events over and over in her mind, had it really happened ? She knew she was still dizzy from drink, not that she could blame the wine, for the songs, the throngs, the folk and the music had all equally seduced and consumed her. She couldn't help but laugh to herself as she fell into bed and would spend a good deal of the next morning in delirious disbelief.

"Lizzy, you won't believe it because I can hardly believe it myself, I've been aching to tell you, oh, but Lizzy I hardly know where to start."

"At the beginning silly," laughed her long time friend, seeing the joy all about her face.

"Well... Last night, something truly wonderful and totally magical happened... to me. It's so exciting, it's unbelievable, but I truly hope it happened because nothing else fills my mind. I wanted it so much that I can't believe it, does that make sense ?"

"None at all ! Oh out with Jane, what on earth happened ?"

"Well I think ...he kissed me."

"You think ?"

"Well, yes... I think ...I think so, although the very thought of it all makes me shiver with delight and I dare not believe it. I'm so afraid of my thoughts, afraid of how I feel, I've convinced myself it must have all been just a dream ... a wonderful, wild ... and totally wicked dream."

"A dream ?"

"Yes, I know it makes no sense but I am caught between the realms of what is real and what isn't. You see, I'm not wholly sure, sometimes I think I am and then ...

well it all seemed so perfect, so colourful... so extraordinary, I so want to believe it...but then it frightens me and I feel it far safer to believe I must have dreamt it."

"Jane, you're making no sense, slow down."

"Ok, I'll try, last night, I was discovered, actually I was invited to join them all after the rehearsal by Faith I think and I found myself in the middle of the most wonderful merrymaking, dancing, drinking and well, then I sort of fell into him and ...he kissed my hand, well, he didn't actually know it was me and he was in the arms of another... but,"

"In the arms of another ?"

"Yes, to begin with ...but then the other girl left, you see... I stumbled upon them when they were behind this curtain, he was in a fancy mask, laid upon this luxurious velvet bed that was filled with stars..."

"Who was ?"

"James, of course who else would make me so delirious but the handsome and oh so perfect James of the Queens men ? The object of all my desires and dreams, who takes my breath away and makes my heart beat so fast I feel I may explode."

"He kissed you ?"

"He did Lizzy, it's true I swear it, well it's certainly true what I'm telling you, but whether it happened in this reality or was in the realm of dreams at this moment I'm not entirely sure, you see he took me in his arms, he put his finger to my lips and whispered in my ear ...he stroked my skin...he played with my hair ...and ..."

"And ?" Demanded Elizabeth, excitedly.

"Lizzy," Jane lowered her voice looking about her making sure no one else could hear.

"Lizzy, I think ...I do believe ... I want to believe, actually I'm pretty sure that last night I gave myself to him."

"You did what ?"

"Oh you heard me," giggled Jane.

"Jane ! Have you lost your senses ?" Elizabeth whispered in disbelief.

"Yes dear heart, every last one," Jane and Elizabeth looked at each other and burst into girlish laughter.

"Good God, you never stop surprising me, you must tell me everything."

Jane drifted off into the dream of the evening as she passionately recalled to her friend all the things she dared to remember. Elizabeth cast her friend a concerned glance, for she had heard tales of the Queens men, how they toyed with many adoring women and how they were never shy of affection.

"Jane, you've been obsessed with this man for so long he's driven you mad I tell you. Whether you dreamt or not he's got under your skin that's for sure, just you be careful...that's all ...he's probably got many young girls like you giving themselves to him and I wouldn't want you to be heartbroken. It's one thing to want something, quite another when you get it ! Don't go getting any fancy ideas about him that's all ... and don't go flinging yourself at him ... if you haven't already that is."

"How would I know such things, how he felt, how he smelt, how he tasted, if it was just a dream ? But it feels so unreal, I mean, oh I don't even know what I mean. It was the most incredible feeling I have ever experienced. Never have I known or imagined such things Lizzy but I am slightly embarrassed as I didn't wholly reveal myself, to his eyes at least. The room was so full of people, to him well, I suppose I could have been anyone, but to me, he is the king of my heart." Jane sighed.

The weeks flew by until it was the final rehearsal before the grand performance of 'The Triumph of Peace' that would cascade through the streets of Westminster. As usual Jane, who had been given the part of a minor nymph, was there shyly adoring James from the wings. She desperately wanted him to see her, to notice her, to speak to her, but he never did, he was totally immersed in his art. Jane felt rejected and tried to convince herself that she didn't want to see or even know about the final rehearsal party but she found herself in her usual hiding place all the same. Although this time it felt completely different to the last one she had been exposed to. There was an edginess that kept everyone's demeanour sharp and she felt uncomfortable just being there. It didn't seem at all welcoming, Jane timidly cast her eyes about looking for James, she had seen very little of him these past weeks with the production taking up so much of everyone's time and attention. Even Lizzy was busier than usual. Jane sighed at her stupidity and was just about to leave when James burst through the doors with a bottle in hand and two scantily clad goddesses clinging to his arms, swaying under their charms and kisses as they led him to the velvet bed that Jane remembered. Her heart sank as she watched one of the goddesses, who she thought in the dim torch light resembled Charity, put her finger to her lips requesting silence and then in a flourish drew the curtain about them as the company erupted into rampant laughter and they undoubtedly fell into passion. Jane slumped in despair, she felt ridiculous, heart broken and embarrassed. She had hoped that he might be looking for her or alone at least but now those hopes were in pieces along with her heart, but then why would he have been looking for her ? How stupid to think he knew she existed or even cared ? He wouldn't have remembered her anyway, she was just another girl on his bed. He clearly had a steady stream of willing lovers, he was a terribly handsome man and these were virtues no less. Jane berated herself for her stupidity, for thinking of him, for being there and for believing it all to be anything other than an intoxicated dream, she sulked home to cry herself to sleep.

The day of the great masque finally came, the whole of Westminster was ablaze with flaming torches and a fine crowd gathered to witness the sumptuous extravaganza. The air was filled with excited anticipation as if waiting for the vault of heaven to be opened. What a display it was, more astounding and breathtakingly wonderful than even Jane had dared to imagine. It naturally delighted the King and Queen who were so enchanted, they asked the company to parade it all again so they might enjoy it a second time. Never had Jane seen anything so magnificent.

The spirit of the spectacular that had bedazzled the streets of London lingered in the ethers for weeks, leaving the people somehow magically altered. There was a swell of such happiness around Whitehall, the people were going about their business in the joyous mood of celebration. Jane however was sullen, she spent a great deal of time hiding her hurt, sighing, crying and furious at her own foolishness. She tried not to think about James and she certainly didn't want to talk about husbands with her Mother, so she hid herself away.

It was in these weeks of solitude that Jane's body began to change, swelling about her tummy and breast, her Mother soon noticed even though Jane tried hard to hide her obvious blossoming.

"Who is he ? Or rather, who was he ?"

"Mother !"

"Darling girl, everything about you has changed. You've been an emotional wreck sulking around the house. It's not like you, these past weeks have been unbearable… for all of us. I know heartbreak when I see it and I know when a maid is carrying a child. Look at you, besides that you've not had your menses. Which my dear, is a bit of a give away."

Jane looked up at her Mother with her huge doe eyes about to burst with tears.

"Oh Mother, what am I to do ?"

"Well, there's only one thing for you to do, you've got to get married and quick, your father won't have any disgrace brought to his door."

"What do you mean ?" Jane sobbed

"You know exactly what I mean, you'll have to accept one of the suitors your father brings and sooner rather than later."

Jane was beyond miserable, burdened by the weight of her situation, swamped in melancholy and hopelessness. Even her own family were despairing at what to do with her and just when she thought things couldn't get any worse, she was summoned to the kitchen.

"Yes Father ?" Said Jane, surprised as it was not often that her stepfather would be seated in the kitchen. Jane cast her eyes about to see that all eyes were settled upon her, her sisters were clinging to their mother who stood firmly behind her husband.

"Am I in trouble, father ?" She asked innocently, blushing at the thought of her misdemeanours.

"No, no," smiled her stepfather raising his hands, "far from it lass, I have some good news for you...come..." Jane, who was now suspicious, followed her stepfather's gaze and looked up at her Mother who was smiling in an all knowing, I tried to warn you, way.

"Yes Father ?"

"There's someone I'd like you to meet."

Oh no... Jane suddenly had the sinking feeling that she was about to walk into something or more than likely, someone, unwanted.

"This is Sir Thomas Whorwood and his son Broome. Gentleman, this is my stepdaughter, Jane."

Jane was immediately uneasy and uncomfortable in the obviousness of what was a foot, these men had clearly come to propose and by the looks of it, her family were in agreement. Jane couldn't hide the shock on her face but she curtsied for she had impeccable manners. She suddenly felt hot and dizzy, as if she might faint, oblivious to what they were saying, all that rang through her head was, 'what sort of name is Broome ?'

It was just as she thought by the end of their visit Jane was betrothed, with plans to be put forth immediately. All very, matter of factly and business like which only highlighted what Jane already suspected, her stepfather had made some sort of deal with these people and she was nothing more than a bargaining tool. She was horrified, disgusted by the way everything had just been settled so swiftly without her saying a word.

Broome was a stupid looking clumsy chap who was round in face and body and if we were honest slightly shorter than Jane in height and slightly younger in years, it really was a badly put together package. He had eyes that were deeply set into his fat little face and try as she might Jane could not find one thing pleasing about him. Thankfully, he also had said very little as the deal was hammered out between the fathers, he just eyed Jane as if buying a ham or a clutch of birds. Jane looked mostly at the floor, she was indignant as her Mother brought them all tea seeming quite pleased about it all, Jane couldn't bear to look at any of them. The men shook hands sealing the deal, making Jane wince, how could they ?

And so it was that the life of Jane Ryder took an abrupt turn. Wedding preparations took over the carefree days she had once known and the impending fear of a very different life engulfed her. It became apparent that Sir Thomas was indebted to Jane's father for large sums of money and Jane's forthcoming nuptials were part of the repayment deal, how romantic. Jane could not be comforted, she cried continuously, dreading the prospect of being torn away from her beloved Westminster and dumped in some hideous backwater with that fat oaf, lumbering about all over her. For a long while she was distraught.

"Jane, you must pull yourself together."

"Must I Mother, must I ? It's easy for you to say, you are not the one who is being bundled off with those …those people, rather than them paying back their loan ! How did I come into the bargain ? How did this happen ? " Jane glared.

"Hush now, you and I know too well how this happened, it's your own doing, you needed a husband and fast. This one, well he may be daft enough to believe your child to be his but you'll have to be comely towards him and quick. I have encouraged your father to hasten the wedding plans and he's in total agreement. Yes, you're right Sir Thomas does owe your father a lot of money but what else do you think there is for you if you stay here ? The shame of it, unwed and with a child. What sort of life do you think there will be for you ? Or your bairn ? I tell you this for nothing your father would abandon you, much like the baby's father has. This is the best possible outcome, for it suits us all. Your stepfather had graciously agreed to a healthy dowry which will see you all alright, Sir Thomas will have his loan cancelled and what's his name ? …Broome ? He'll have you as his wife, you will become a lady and you'll have a house and money to raise your child."

"But mother, it's all a lie, I'll be forced to live a lie. I'll be lying to him ... to myself …I don't love that man, or want him." Jane shook her head in anguish.

"Not yet, but you may come to love him, when you see the way he cares for you and your child. He may turn out to be an excellent husband and father, if you just give him a chance, many men have taken care of children that are not theirs by blood, it's the raising of a child that makes for a real father. Besides, you've been rolling around this house in misery for longer than is good for you, you can't carry on like this. Snap out of it, you've always been such a difficult child, picky, disagreeable, not compliant like your wee sisters. They'd be happy and silent with any decisions that were made for their best interests and trust me Jane that's all we're doing, we're trying to help you. Your heads in the clouds as usual but you can't keep ignoring what's happening here. Soon you'll begin to show, then what ? As it is you've a country house that comes with this man and Oxford's not so far away, come on lass you're stronger than this."

Alas, Jane doubted her strength, she doubted everything.

♕

Her wedding day came round far sooner than Jane had hoped, sadly no great calamity had stopped the looming nuptials. Jane's thoughts were fixed upon James, hoping he might arrive in one of those flaming chariots to rescue her from this awful situation. She felt so hopeless, she shouldn't be feeling this wretched on her wedding day, surely ? Jane stared down at her feet, unable to look her Mother in the eye as she dressed and fussed over her. She clearly only wanted the best for her daughter but Jane knew that this wasn't it. Her stepfather, who was a busy man, was eager to hurry it all along as he was meant to be at Hampton Court by the afternoon, he had other things on his mind and it showed. Jane's sisters were all paraded out in their finest dresses although they wanted to be chasing the butterflies about the lanes and gardens. Everyone in Jane's party clearly had somewhere else they would have much rather have been that day.

After a particularly uncomfortable and hasty ride in Jane's stepfather's carriage they all arrived slightly shaken at St Faiths church in the bright autumn sunshine. Jane was quite literally dragged into the church upon her busy stepfather's arm, closely followed by her Mother and sisters who struggled to keep up. The light from the windows cast dreamy hues as Jane made her way up the altar, she hoped it was all a dream and that she would soon wake up in her bed in Westminster. There were no smiles, no joy and no friends, just an eerie silence broken only by Sir Thomas's coughing and wheezing. He looked as uncomfortable as Jane felt, with his stern wife next to him muttering, chastising him for breathing ! Having been abruptly delivered in front of the man she was due to marry, Jane sighed heavily at the sight of him in his ugly oversized suit. She stood clutching her wildflowers more interested in the dust dancing upon the sunbeams than what was happening around her. She became harshly aware of the inevitable when she heard the words 'I will' repeated loudly, then felt all eyes upon her prompting her response. It took a few moments for her to battle her better judgment and say the words that would cement her fate. Bromme looked proudly over to his parents who were concerned only with having their debts forgotten and banking the generous dowry. Sir Thomas was ill at ease, wheezy and gasping for breath while his lady wife, who was clearly a bitter woman, was eyeing Jane distastefully adding to the general air of discomfort. There was no singing, no celebration such as girls wish for on their wedding day. It was all very matter of factly conducted so that everyone could get on with the really important things they had to do elsewhere. She sighed deeply as her new husband lifted her veil and took her hand to place his band of ownership upon her finger. She looked down at the small and dull ring that signified how her life was to become, small and dull, it took all her strength not to cry. It was all so terribly awkward, Jane searched his empty eyes and felt nothing, nothing but the icy stare of his mother, Lady Ursula, which was boring into her back. As the priest announced them man and wife, Broome began salivating and licking his lips as if his dinner had been laid before him. Jane however was disgusted at the thought of having this clumsy oaf's fat fingers touching her, while Jane's stepfather jumped up from his seat, clasping his hands together, as if he had just sold a horse. He had been restless the entire time, eager to carry on with his Royal duties and was up and out of the church first. Broome took Jane's dainty hand and led her aimlessly down the aisle past the hastily gathered congregation of bored faces. Just as the newly married couple were about to step out into the world as man and wife, there was an almighty thud ! Followed by a shrill scream, followed by further screams. The newly weds turned and cast eyes about as a sense of panic took hold of the chapel. Broome let go of Jane and rushed to his mother who was now in full grief screaming, "he's dead, he's dead, Lord help me."

Jane was stunned into stillness as the whole place erupted around her in alarm. People began rushing over to where Sir Thomas had been as Lady Ursula fainted into her son's arms. In an instant her odd assemble of guests became mourners as everyone began swooning and crowding poor Sir Thomas who had chosen this exact moment to leave his earthly garment ! Suddenly everyone was hysterical, crying and totally distraught. Everyone except Jane's stepfather who was now annoyed at the delay to his plans and Jane, who stood bewildered, abandoned and upstaged on her wedding day by a cadaver ! What sort of omen was this ?

The day could not have been more of a disaster. The wedding carriage swiftly became a funeral cortège with the somber mood saturating everything and everyone. The days that followed were equally sorrowful. Fortunately Jane's grief was mistaken for the loss of a family member rather than her becoming one.

♛

Lady Jane (as she had so swiftly become) wasn't any happier with this new title or her new husband who, in contrast, was greatly enamoured by this new found authority. After the wedding, all time had been taken up with plans to move Sir Thomas firstly from the church and then back to Holton House and he wasn't a small man. Jane's stepfather did the best he could to assist but Broome was rather enjoying making arrangements with people who were keen to help, they were of course Maxwell's men. It wasn't long before everything was hastily packed up and out on the bumpy dusty road that would lead to Oxford. The funeral cortège made its way painfully along the road with Lady Ursula crying and howling, clearly making the most of all the fuss and attention, Broome too was awash with self importance. Jane looked out upon the rolling hills and fields drenched in the autumn sun which although beautiful looked wide, empty and so very far from Westminster and everything she knew. She felt very small and irritated, hopeless and annoyed and unable to voice any of her feelings as all attention was upon the corpse at the back. Fortunately Jane had opted to travel in the middle coach with some lesser known aunts so conversation was polite but minimal. Jane could still hear the wailing of Lady Ursula and thanked her lucky stars she wasn't trapped in there with her or that bumbling husband of hers who now looked every bit as red and puffed up as his father had.

♛

It seemed a very long journey especially for Jane, giving her more than enough time to regret everything, her mind ravaged by the myriad of misfortunes she felt had already been inflicted upon her by this family she was now blessed with. No one smiled or joked, probably due to the impending funeral, but still, Jane had hoped that someone would at least congratulate her, a new bride and all. The startling truth of it was, she wasn't happy for herself so she could hardly expect these strangers to be in the slightest bit concerned for her spirit. Jane sighed heavily looking out across the endless fields while the aunts began to snore loudly in unison. She could see the house from far in the distance, it was intriguing as she had seen nothing other than fields for miles. Jane realised she had never left London before and reprimanded herself for not being more excited, but as she looked over her snoring travel companions she was reminded of how little there was to be enthusiastic about. Holton house was a dreary, cold and grey house that stood at the end of a long driveway giving the impression it was to be impressive but like much of Jane's new life, it fell short. When they finally came to a halt, folk came spilling out of the house and stables to assist in the unpacking and to take care of the horses. Jane soon realised that no one was even slightly concerned about her or these sleeping aunts as they were left till last to be helped. She silently watched the scenes unfolding from the window as Lady Ursula had to be carried from the first coach and Broome was busy directing the men that came to take Sir Thomas to the chapel. Jane thought it best to remain where she was and even found the old ladies snoring quite melodic. There was already enough fuss happening without her stepping into it and she couldn't see where she would fit into it all, besides, Jane was happiest watching theatre and this was certainly a performance.

Like rats, everyone dispersed almost as quickly as they had appeared leaving Jane, her luggage and the forgotten snoring spinsters quite alone. As Jane stepped out to survey her new home, she heard the crunch of her step upon the gravel and was quite taken aback at just how quiet it was. Silence was something Jane was not used to. It was a while before someone came back, they introduced themselves and asked if they could assist in taking her things to her quarters. Jane smiled, nodded in agreement and followed on to see where her new quarters were. The house was just as cold, damp and grey on the inside, no colour or tapestry. Jane's boots clicked upon the bare flagstones and echoed off the bare walls. Her 'quarters' was a large set of rooms up the sweeping staircase and to the left. From the top of the stairs Jane could see down into the sitting rooms which did at least have a roaring fire lit as some sort of welcome. Her rooms were spacious with wonderful views that looked out over well tended gardens, thankfully someone had opened the windows allowing the scent of roses to fill the room. The man whose name she had already forgotten placed her cases down and went back to retrieve the others. Jane was left alone again and sensed this would be a feeling she would have to get used to, she fell into a chair and sighed. The rest of her luggage came promptly with an invitation to dinner which was to be in the 'grand hall'. Jane smiled to herself, for she had been inside many a Grand Hall and wondered if this would actually be one.

There was fresh water so she washed and changed although she didn't unpack, she just took the most comfortable gown that would be acceptable for dinner. Or so she thought. Her mood had lifted slightly so she skipped down the staircase and found her way to the grand hall, which made her laugh as it was anything but. Her laughter, amplified by the bare walls drew sharp stares as all eyes fell upon her with an air of disgust, causing her to abruptly halt by the door. Broome whose face was like thunder cast her a look of such disdain, any lightness she had felt disappeared in an instant.

"And what may I ask, do you find so funny, Madam ? Do I have to remind you, my father is dead. Good God look at you, why have you come for dinner in your nightgown ? Are you mad ? As my wife you will dress properly, how dare you be so disrespectful. Go and change at once. Go."

Jane was startled and had no idea how to react, she had never been spoken to in such a way in her whole life.

"Do I have to tell you again ? Go on, don't just stand there gawping woman, do as I asked, we are waiting to eat."

Jane turned and climbed the stairs to her rooms, shutting the door behind her, unable to stop the flood of tears that fell down her face. Her husband was a monster, she felt so embarrassed and humiliated. Looking out over the rolling hills that led to nowhere, she had never felt more alone. It took all her strength to stop crying as she washed her face and put on her funeral clothes as it felt like she would perpetually be at one, then she descended the stairs every inch a lady, making her way to dinner. She could hardly bring herself to look upon the man she was now wedded to, he snorted and huffed as Jane curtsied and looked for her seat but then she could hardly expect anything less from the pig. Jane could hear his hateful mutterings but chose to ignore them as she took her place at the table.

Dinner was a somber affair, Jane was completely out of sorts and out of her depth with these people. Listening to what idle chatter there was, made her painfully aware that she didn't belong. Broome made no effort to include her and if anything he only propelled her anxiety. As soon as she could Jane made her excuses and left returning to her rooms. Once inside she threw herself onto the bed and cried, again, until her eyes were red raw.

♛

Jane wasn't used to feeling so out of sorts and she'd certainly never cried so much. It took a long while for her to fall asleep with it being so quiet, every single sound was deafening. She was awakened by a knock at her door that was swiftly followed by a turning of the handle. Jane sat up with a start. It was Broome holding a candle in one hand and a bottle of something in the other. He placed the candle down and taking two glasses out of his pockets poured them both a drink.

A feeling of utter dread welled up inside of Jane for she knew what this meant and she knew the inevitable duty she must perform.

"I know you're awake," he slurred, "I have something for you."

Jane took a deep breath then forced herself to answer him.

"Make mine a large one, husband."

Broome laughed as he loosened his collar and began unbuttoning his shirt,

"Ah, don't you worry Mrs Whorwood, I've got a large one for you."

Jane reached out, taking the full glass from him as he removed his breaches. She forced herself to drink it all, then spluttered and coughed as the brandy burned her throat. She handed the glass back to Broome as he climbed into bed next to her. He began drunkenly waffling but for Jane the room was now swimming so she closed her eyes and soon succumbed to sleep.

Totally disoriented and with a banging head, Jane opened her blurry eyes to find her husband lumbering about on top of her. She was stupefied into submission as he gyrated away making her feel nauseous, as if she was at sea and trapped under a whale. He had his way with her before her eyes were fully opened. She could hardly breath, her whole body tensed as he heaved himself into her further then rolled off and collapsed, exhausted. Jane was unimpressed, bewildered and now her legs hurt just as much as her head. She didn't say a word as she looked over at her heap of a husband who almost instantly had fallen back to sleep. She felt a deep sense of shame and disappointment in him, herself, this whole idea of marriage and the wetness between her legs. She tried to sit up but now every part of her body ached, especially her head and she was so very thirsty and needed to wash her mouth and by all accounts the rest of her. She slipped out of the bed and limped to the other room where she could bath herself, shutting the door quietly behind her. Jane couldn't help but cry as she took off her night clothes. Through tear stained eyes she looked out through the windows across the manicured gardens full of roses. It was such a bright and beautiful day, she could see for miles and how she wanted to run across them all, far away from here, from her husband and even herself. How had she allowed this ? She felt so trapped and she'd only been there a day.

Jane returned to the marital room and her bloated husband's snores, she sat next to the window overlooking the gardens, opening it to breathe in the fresh early morning air. She felt stiff and wretched, more so every time she looked at him so she stayed focused on the roses. As the sun rose higher sending great beams of light into the room, Jane became aware he was awake and turned to see him up and dressing himself. He neither looked at her or spoke to her as if he too was ashamed, then briskly he left the room. As he closed the door he said something about joining him for breakfast but Jane wasn't hungry. Turning back to focus on the garden below her, she sighed "so… this is what it's like to be a Lady ?"

♛

Days turned into months as Jane observed the wheels of Holton House turning around her. The funeral had thankfully been uneventful despite Lady Ursula's descent further into bitterness and Broome becoming more stern, authoritative and ultimately more repulsive. The house itself was still dark and depressing, Jane breezed about always on the outside of things, she couldn't find a place for herself, try as she might she just didn't fit in anywhere. She spent most of her time alone in the garden only joining Broome and Lady Ursula for meals which were always an awful obligation. They belittled and humiliated her or they ignored her completely, she felt like a fawn cornered by wolves at every single meal time and she dreaded them.

Jane wasn't used to being treated so badly but she surrendered to the fact that this was now her life, however hopeless. She felt bad and deceitful telling Broome that she was with child, although he was indifferent, just looked her up and down and asked if she was sure. Lady Ursula, who was far smarter than her son, didn't soften upon hearing the news, but continued to view Jane with spite and suspicion. No special arrangements were made she continued to endure the pair of them. However, when it was time to bring the child into the world Jane insisted upon being with her Mother back in Westminster and only because Broome apparently had business in the city did he agree to it but for Jane it felt like an accomplishment.

♛

Jane arrived at her Mother's house so round everyone was convinced she was carrying a girl. Her Mother and sisters were eager to see her and hear stories of her new life but Jane upon seeing all of their beautiful faces burst into tears. Broome unceremoniously handed her over, dumping her bag by her side, then he jumped back in the coach tapping the roof to signal his departure. Jane fell into her Mother's arms and sobbed.

"Now, now don't cry dear, come on, come inside, all is warm and welcoming for you. We're so pleased you're here." Jane's sister heaved her bag inside behind Jane and their Mother, who called over her shoulder to the younger sister to fetch Elizabeth from the laundry which she did. Once inside her former home, Jane was made comfortable with everyone happily fussing over her, only her Mother could see all was not well. She took off her daughter's boots and rubbed her feet which were swollen and almost as puffy as her eyes. Her sisters were all so desperate to talk and tell her their news that they all began talking at once, making Jane cry again for she had missed them all so much. They gathered around her and hugged her tightly, putting her back together and in no time they were all giggles and laughter, each taking turns to share their news or their own version of events. Jane was overjoyed to be home, soon enough the back door swung open and in came Jane's dearest friend in the world, Lizzy, as well as friends and neighbours who all called by to see her for she was so dearly loved in her hometown. They drank and ate and laughed well into the night, with Jane's stepfather coming home only to leave again, overwhelmed by the amount of women all gossiping in the kitchen.

When it was Jane's turn to tell them all of her new life, she fell silent because she couldn't find the words to tell them just how horrible it was and how much she hated every single minute of it. Jane stumbled on her words and her Mother sensing her daughter's misery swiftly changed the subject to the latest tale of scandal and court gossip. As it so happened all was not so well in Westminster either. His Majesty the King was under enormous pressure from his parliament, there had even been talk of civil war, which no one dared to believe but everyone had an opinion as to what was actually occurring, although in truth, no one really knew.

When the fire had died down and everyone had left or gone to bed Jane sat alone with Elizabeth and her Mother. She divulged to them both just how painful living at Holton was and how awful she felt and how she didn't want to go back there, to that house or those people.

"I belong here, with you ?" Jane said looking earnestly at her Mother who, although sympathised with her daughter quickly put that thought out of her mind.

"Dear heart, you can't come here, that would be a step back and nothing in life goes backwards, now does it ?"

"But Mother ?" Jane pleaded.

"No buts, that is your life now and it's up to you what you make of it. They may well be mean, but it says more about them than it does of you. You mustn't let them steal your spirit, don't give in so easily. Show them your strengths not your weaknesses. They may be testing you to see how strong you are and my girl you show them, they are your family now. You might not be able to change them but you can always and I mean this Jane, you can always change the way YOU feel about things, your feelings are always up to you. You don't have to let them bother you, you are stronger than that. This bairn needs you to be strong and I want to see that sparkle back in your eye. The world as we know it is changing Jane, there's been war with the Scot's or was it the Bishops, whoever it is you'd do well to stay far away from London. It's no longer the place you remember, it's become harsh and altogether frightening, no one knows what's about to happen, you see you are not the only one with troubles. His Majesty has the weight of the Kingdom upon him so think yourself lucky."

Jane stared up at her Mother through tear stained eyes and sharply over to her friend who looked equally sorrowful. An eerie silence fell over the kitchen all the way down to the cold flagstones and Jane's feet upon them. She stopped crying and wiped her sniffles away on a handkerchief her Mother passed her.

"Now, you know you'll always be welcome here and the bairn too, when they come, which I dare say won't be long now." Jane's Mother ran her hands gently over her daughter's round tummy and smiled remembering how it felt, kissing her daughter upon her head. "I'm sure it's beautiful out there in the countryside with you, the Lady of the house."

Jane choked, "The countryside is beautiful but I'm not the Lady of the house and I'm only a Lady because my father in law chose to die rather than see me as his daughter or so my husband repeatedly tells me." Jane said sarcastically but it was true she wanted them to know what a beast he was. She wished she could tell them everything, all the horrid little details, the way Broome and his mother had been treating her and how she just couldn't stand it and ...

"MOTHER !"

All of a sudden, there was a pop that brought warm waters running down her legs faster than rain down a drain pipe.

"Mother, what's happening ?"

Jane's Mother looked down at the ever increasing puddle, then looked to Elizabeth whose eyes were wide with surprise.

"Bless my soul, Lizzy, be a dear and fetch Mrs Weathers would you, quickly now." Lizzy turned and left immediately after kissing Jane, who began squirming and recoiling from her own fluids.

"Be peace, breathe with me Jane," whispered her Mother, calmly taking her in her arms. "Your baby is on the way. All is well, I'm right here with you, Elizabeth's gone to get Goodwife Weathers, so I think it's best we make our way to your room, come let me help you my love." She heaved her out of the chair, as Jane felt a twang of the pains that were to come, she was startled and unsure but not afraid for she knew she was in the best place she could be. Jane let out a cry as she hobbled with her Mother's help to the back room where her son would soon be born, a healthy bonny boy with a flash of red hair just like his mother.

♛

Goodwife Weathers had done her very best to make sure mother and baby were safe and with thanks to the Lord, they both were. Elizabeth was overjoyed to have been with her friend and was one of the first to hold the newborn. Everyone was exhausted as the sun came up over the river but ecstatic, it had been a long night so Jane slept peacefully into the day while her best friend cooed over her son.

The days passed quickly after that and the time soon came for Jane to make her way back to Oxford. From the moment her husband wrapped his cane on the door Jane's heart sank. She had prepared herself to be pleasing when he came for her but

Broome was unimpressed, clearly in a hurry and despite leaving them waiting until late into the afternoon made no apology. He wasn't in the slightest bit interested in either of them and wished only to speak to Jane's stepfather as he looked from Jane to the baby then back again telling her to get her things. Her things had been in the hallway since breakfast so were easily and swiftly loaded upon the coach. Jane's sisters took the baby and smothered him in tear soaked kisses as each of them gave him a blessing. Jane stared hard at her Mother who knew exactly what her strong willed daughter was thinking. Broome had clearly come to talk with Jane's stepfather regarding money, exposing his lack of it. He stank of cigars and brandy meaning he'd probably been tucked up in a gambling den or worse, Jane continued to stare at her Mother who moved to hold her daughter tightly and whispered in her ear.

"That is your life now, with your husband and your child, make a family Jane."

Jane began to cry, "but, you are my family."

"And we will always be but right now this wee bairn needs you more than we do, there's nothing here for you Jane."

"Please Mother, please .. don't … I .. you can't …I beg you please don't send me away ?"

"Ah, I'm not sending you away, you're going home…there is no me now lass, now you're we, there's this bonny boy to be thinking of, not what you want and anyways your stepfather would have none of it …your home is with your husband and your baby… in Oxford." She wiped her daughter's face with a delicate cloth and kissed her on the cheek.

"Come now Jane, you are strong, I'm sure you'll be a wonderful mother and maybe …maybe you'll be just as good a wife." Jane's Mother knew this not to be true for she knew her daughter was so fiercely free and Broome so stuffy they were very poorly matched but she wanted to encourage her all the same.

"Now, go, go with my blessing and do all you can to be the best in all you do, remember you are loved …and strong Jane, you are a strong and capable woman."

Jane's Mother had never called her a woman before, with a heavy heart and a trembling lip she took back her son, kissing her Mother and sisters goodbye. She was oblivious to their chattering as she climbed into the coach and waited for her husband, who obviously had some pressing business with Jane's father for he took his time in joining them. He lumbered into the coach taking the forward facing seat opposite. Jane always hated travelling backwards but knew Broome would cause a scene if she didn't and she wanted to avoid one and leave her parents house peacefully. He tapped on the roof giving the driver the signal to move and they were away. All was quiet as they rolled out of Westminster, Jane cradled her son who was well fed and fast asleep, she was too upset to talk, not that she had much to say to the red faced stinking heap sat opposite her. Broome's heavy breathing was interrupted by snorts and coughs which only vexed Jane more.

"All hell is about to break loose you know," said Broome eventually, irritated that Jane hadn't responded to his attention seeking.

"What ? In here ?" Jane turned to him a little surprised.

"No not in here you stupid woman …in London …in England. Damn it.. don't you know anything ? Are you really that stupid? Your father probably doesn't trust you enough ... ah …but then he's not your real father is he ? Your friend, the King... parliament ... it's all about to get frightful …there's talk of war …Jane…war…I tell you and not with France or Spain oh no …our own men fighting each other …civil war ... Can you believe it ?"

Jane couldn't believe he remembered her name but he was clearly ignorant of her situation. She looked from her son to him but she had already opened the door to his rant by responding to him and now he had her attention he spitefully rambled on.

"Do you hear what I'm saying to you ? Are you even listening woman ? Pathetic, you are, of course you've no idea of what's really happening, you've always got your head in the clouds. How in God's name did I get burdened with such a useless draggle, you make me sick ?"

Jane looked at him in utter disbelief, although the feeling was mutual she stayed silent while he launched into his spiteful attack on her, it was sure to be a very long, long journey.

"Well I'll tell you this it certainly wasn't my idea, I deserved better than the likes of you. It was your stepfather's fault, he wanted rid of you, conned my father into taking you and look what that did for him ? You are a witch, that's the truth of it, the country's going to pot and you've nothing to say…Nothing … I thought not … you can't even talk, you stupid good for nothing."

The truth of it was Jane had long given up 'talking' to him, she just patiently waited for his insults to stop.

The sun was low casting a hazy glow upon the waving corn as they rode on the long road to the grey and gloomy Holton house, which was a complete contrast to the flourishing fields. Jane was exhausted when they arrived, completely worn down by her husband's torrent of abuse and verbal assault of everything about her. Broome stepped out first, looking somewhat revived, as if he had sucked the very life out of her. He immediately began acting out his authority, making commands, without offering Jane a hand down from the coach. She felt meek and pathetic as she slowly walked back into the house she hated.

Lady Ursula sat in her wheelchair, with her maid Kathryn, who was every bit as hateful, stood behind her, her beady eye upon Jane or more importantly the bundle she was carrying. Lady Ursula waved her stick in the air which meant she wanted Jane to come to her. Jane felt like a dog, but she dutifully went to present her son. Jane knelt in front of them and gently pulled back the blanket that covered him. Lady Ursula, peered over her eye glass at the tiny baby sleeping peacefully in Jane's arms and in that moment and just for a moment Jane saw a softer side to her. A glow came about her and Jane was sure she even saw a smile upon her withered face as she beckoned them closer and held out her arms implying she wanted to hold him. Jane was quite taken aback at this display of affection and willingly laid her son in her arms. Lady Ursula couldn't take her eyes off him as she wrapped her hands around the tiny creature.

"A little boy," Jane whispered as if preempting Lady Ursula's next thought. No one heard Broome approach so he coughed and snorted in his usual way of gaining everyone's attention and instantly the magic of the moment was broken.

"Let's hope he doesn't take after his mother. Aye ?" He boomed over Jane's shoulder.

"What is his name ? What are we to call him ?" Lady Ursula asked with none of her usual haughtiness. Jane took this to be directed at her, even though she hadn't thought of one and hadn't had a chance to discuss it.

"Why, my name of course, Broome and Thomas for father, God rest his soul. Broome Thomas Whorwood, a strong name don't you think ?" He said as he walked off leaving Lady Ursula feeling proud and Jane speechless. Baby Broome woke up just as Broome stomped importantly into the house giving Jane the perfect excuse to escape. As she gently lifted him up, Lady Ursula held on to her arm and said, "Well done, he's a bonny boy, he'll be glad of the Whorwood name." Jane was soothed but wondered if Lady Ursula had seen that the babe bore no resemblance to her son, for a moment she shuddered with the terror of being exposed. Trying to hide her fear Jane smiled at the old crone as she was wheeled away after her own son by the cold Kathryn who neither smiled nor congratulated her.

♛

It was true what Broome had said to Jane as they made their way home to Holton. England was about to be plunged into turmoil and an air of uncertainty swept the country. Brothers were soon taking arms against each other and every man's loyalty was being questioned. There was a fear that filled men and women alike as everyone became mad with suspicion, no one knew what to think or more realistically what to think in whose company. One false move, word or whisper could have dire consequences. Thankfully Holton house, as grey and depressing as it was, was a world away from the political warfare being fought in Westminster, luckily Jane was so hopelessly in love with her adorable baby boy, she had little time or thought for London.

♛

Broome, Jane's son, grew into a handsome boy, bright, clever and thankfully was just like his mother. Seeing them together only fuelled her husband's envy of her making him more and more insufferable. Poor Jane had to endure his vicious ways and accept it as her lot. His night time visits were rare but she dreaded these the most, she could ignore him at dinner and avoid him throughout the day but when he came to her room, disgustingly drunk, she had no choice but to do her duty allowing him to mount her like a sow. Little did she know these visits were due to Lady Ursula's insistence and demands for more grandchildren.

Just when Jane could no longer stand it, she was blessed with another child, bringing mixed feelings for although she loved her son and would dearly welcome the baby, her life was so miserable. When the time came Jane insisted she went to Westminster to be with her Mother, sisters and the Goodwife that she knew and trusted. Once again she delivered a healthy child, a girl who she quickly named Diana. Broome had not accompanied her this time, much to Jane's delight as it made for a much better visit and a far more pleasant journey. Jane saw for herself the changes that had settled upon London. It was indeed a different place, a darkness had descended. People were ill at ease with each other and there seemed very little joy or celebration, everyone seemed so burdened by their opinions. There was a violence Jane had not felt before and for the first time Jane was glad to be coached out of town. Her Mother was preoccupied by the troubles, her sisters were with their new husbands, Elizabeth busy in the laundries, other than Good woman Weathers, it was not how she remembered her home to be. The ride back to Holton house was blissful. Jane held her daughter close while she looked out over the countryside in peace and when she arrived back at Holton, she felt different. Her daughter had revived her courage and for the first time Jane felt like the Lady of the house. Lady Ursula was as usual, in her chair, like an overstuffed cushion, in the doorway with the uptight Kathryn behind her. Jane smiled at them both and made her way towards them with a confident gait they both noticed. Jane curtsied and presented Lady Ursula with her new grandchild.

"We have a new Lady of the house," whispered Jane and after giving it some thought continued, "and her name is Diana."

Lady Ursula looked at her with some surprise as did Kathryn but then returned to gaze at the beautiful babe in her arms. "Diana .. you say ?" Lady Ursula said eventually.

"Yes, Diana," replied Jane clearly.

"Well… Diana," Lady Ursula said slowly, taken aback by Jane's boldness, "a beautiful name for one as beautiful as you. Welcome to Holton house Diana, this is your home."

Now it was Jane's turn to be surprised, for she had never heard such words from her mother in law, a welcome ? Well fancy that. After she had finished cooing at Diana, Lady Ursula handed her back to Jane, who picked up her daughter and made her way proudly to the nursery to introduce Diana to her brother. It felt like everything was changing.

♛

Indeed it was, Jane could no longer bring herself to look upon her husband, finding everything he did and every word he said, irritating. Thankfully she was able to mostly avoid him, spending all her time with her children, who were oblivious to the side swipes their grandmother and father took at their mother. It took every ounce of Jane's patience and resilience to make it through meal times for they were always the same. The overbearing ticking of the grandfather clock cutting through the deafening silence. Broome's snorting and terrible table manners matched by the icy glare of Lady Ursula who beneath layers the delicate lace was a hard and bitter tight lipped old hag. Jane hadn't spoken at dinner for the best part of the year, other than to thank the serving girls, she hadn't said a word. The children were brought in by their nanny which was always a welcome distraction from the painful event, but they never stayed long for they wouldn't sit still which Jane always found amusing but her husband and Lady Ursula did not.

♛

Jane soon became aware that Kathryn, the hand maid, had started to make more of an obvious appearance at dinner time, making a fuss of Lady Ursula but more overly of Broome. Jane delighted in the observation of the comedy that was being played out before her, having never lost her love of theatre. After dinner it was always the same, like clockwork. Broome would make his excuses as Lady Ursula was wheeled away by the stern Kathryn, whose wandering eye would always be searching for Broome's, this amused Jane for she had no feelings for him whatsoever and if they were being discreet for her benefit they needn't have bothered. Broome would mutter about needing some assistance and Jane would see Kathryn blush in the way lovers do, exposing their affair. Jane would then be left alone with the ticking clock and the abandoned dinner table with plates that were almost as empty as she felt. She would go to the nursery to kiss her children good night before making her way to bed herself, where she would lose herself in the memories of her life before she became a prisoner of marriage. Her wild imagination would always return to the magical masques of Whitehall. Every night her dreams were filled with the fantastic recollection of the wonderment that was. Every morning she would wake disappointed to find herself in her rooms at Holton rather than the elaborate carriages of Inigo Jones or in the arms of James. Those were the dreams she treasured the most.

♛

As the children grew so did Jane's yearning for adventure. The children were kept occupied and busy with nannies and tutors leaving Jane bored and alone. One particularly monotonous morning to elevate the tedium she talked herself into taking out a horse and going for a ride, why not ? After all, it was such a perfect day for it.

Jane returned to her room with a sense of excitement she hadn't felt in years as she changed her attire for one more fitting to ride in. Smiling to herself in the looking glass and pleased with her new found self confidence, she left her room looking for adventure. She had been forbidden to ride whilst bearing the children but now there was no reason for her not to after all they were surrounded by such perfect riding ground.

The stables were empty except for one boy who was mucking out the last of the stalls. He was visibly shocked as he saw Jane walking amongst the steeds.

"Excuse me Ma Lady, can I help you ?"

"Why, yes you can," she answered kindly. "Which horse do you suggest would be the best to ride out ?"

"For yourself ?" He asked surprised.

"Yes for me," laughed Jane, "and then if you wouldn't mind, could you kindly get them ready ?"

"Now Ma Lady ?"

"Yes please, for me, right now."

"Then I'd take that one," said the stable hand, pointing over to a tall and handsome chestnut that already had his nose out. Jane walked over and rubbed him which made him shake his mane in appreciation.

"Yes this one," Jane agreed. It had been a long while since Jane had been in the company of horses but she had never lost her affinity with the magnificent creatures.

"Right you are Ma Lady," said the boy who deftly began saddling up.

"He's steady and safe miss, you'll be alright with him, wait, I just fetch you the block." He looked about him for the step so that Jane might mount him.

"No, no need," said Jane, who had been stroking the great beast's face and whispering to him as he was prepared for their grand adventure. The boy looked surprised, even more so when Jane confidently took the reins and swung herself into the saddle. Thanking the boy, Jane rode out of the yard into the endless fields with an overflowing sense of joy.

♛

Broome was furious, his eyes were bulging with rage. "Madam, I have been made aware that you took a horse out today, is this true ?" He thundered at his wife as dinner was laid out before them. Lady Ursula's eyes fixed upon Jane from the other end of the table in utter disgust.

"Why, yes, yes I did," Jane answered flippantly, not even looking at her husband but she could feel the disapproving stares from both of them. The ticking of the clock took over the silence and filled the void in the room.

"The shame of it, on your own, you went out on your own ... on a horse ...like a common..."

"Oh no, it is not common, Lady Ursula," Jane interrupted, "It was quite rare, for I can't remember the last time I did such a thing," or felt so free Jane thought to herself.

Broome slammed his hands on to the table making Jane jump and drop her soup back into its bowl with the clanking of the spoon echoing off the bare walls. Kathryn looked endearingly over at him and his manly display, Jane however was far from impressed.

"You ...How dare you ? In my house, how dare you have such disregard for our rules. You were, you are forbidden, do you hear me, forbidden to ride and you don't interrupt my mother when she's talking to you, have you no manners ? I will not have my mother spoken to in such a way by you and I'll tell you another thing no wife of mine is to go galavanting around like some, like some harlot come highwayman." Broome was even more red faced than usual and looked to Jane more like a pig than ever before.

"It is never to happen again, you hear me, I am the Lord of this house and I forbid it." He quaffed, stuffing more food into his already overfilled mouth.

Jane sighed, she was not a meek woman but rather one who had graciously accepted her fate and the wishes of her family. She hadn't wanted to marry this man or be trapped inside this house with these people but she had for years now quietly done as was expected of her. She had in her mind fulfilled her role as wife to this red face boar of a man and had provided him with thankfully, at least one beautiful child. She felt she had endured his belittling and mental torture for too long and in that moment Jane had enough of it all. Her day out in the fields had revived her and had sparked her spirit, she could stand him no longer.

Jane took a deep breath and wiped her face, gently placing the napkin down on the table, she got up to leave.

"And where do you think you are going ? Woman, sit down this instant, I said sit down, damn you," commanded the pig.

"No Sir, I cannot," said Jane calmly. "And what is more my Lord, I will not. I apologise to you Lady Ursula, if I spoke to you in an unfamiliar way, but this is my voice, it's just been an age since you last heard it. I will continue to ride for it is the one thing, the only thing that is just for me, not a wife, not a mother, for me. My father, as you know equipped me with a love for horses and my stepfather financed you with the means to keep them, therefore in honour of them both I shall be riding every day from now on or at least when I find the opportunity, which since the children are so well cared for has now become more often. England is changing, Sir as am I. My heart and my mind are…expanding, I feel different, I see clearer and I know that none of this …hypocrisy, yours or mine, is acceptable to me or my conscience any longer. I have no concerns or the slightest interest in how you choose to spend your time so with all due respect to you, I am of sound mind and I feel old enough and wise enough to decide how I shall spend mine. Good night to you." Jane looked over at Kathryn who was open mouthed and as stunned as everyone else. Broome was shocked as he wiped the grease dripping from his fat face, shrinking in disbelief at his wife's new found confidence. Jane nodded at them all, then strode from the room in time with the ticking clock, closing the door behind her.

♛

The days that followed were as painfully eerily as before but now Jane had an escape. Everyday she would take a horse and discover new trails around the beautiful Oxfordshire countryside. Once more her life was filled with colour and wonder as she took renewed pleasure in the beauty that surrounded her. It was late in August, the fields were overflowing, nature was flourishing with an abundance of fruit, fauna, dancing dragonflies and butterflies. Jane returned home from her thrilling ride feeling elated but as she turned into the yard she could see that no one shared her enthusiasm or excitement for life. The stable boy sheepishly greeted her to take her horse and mumbled something of his Lordship, Jane knew better than to enquire any further as the poor boy had quite obviously had been harshly treated by his master. She gave him the reins and thanked him, making her way to the house. She wondered if someone had died given everyone's somber mood and secretly wished it was her husband or his mother or better still both, then chastised herself asking God for forgiveness for thinking such thoughts.

She sighed upon hearing her husband was very much still alive, for she could hear his booming voice as she sprang up the steps into the house. She really was in a buoyant mood and wanted very much to keep it but the dinner bell had rung, giving her just enough time to quickly prepare herself, aware she was already late.

What she wasn't prepared for was the news her husband was about to impart. Jane was surprised to see the whole household had been assembled as she took her place at the dinner table. Lady Ursula, who was also very much alive, was there preened and as puffed up as ever, glaring spitefully at Jane's for her timekeeping, leaving Jane bewildered as to why everyone was gathered so.

"Madam as usual you've kept us all waiting for you, you care only for yourself. It's good of you to join us." Broome didn't mean it of course, he sneered, looking at his wife with utter disdain before tapping the side of his glass, commanding silence.

"You may wonder why I have called you all together. You may have heard whispers, sadly they are true and it is my duty as Lord of this house to inform you that England is officially now at war."

There were various gasps as he went on,

"The King some days ago raised an army and his standard at Nottingham, in a declaration of war upon parliament admittedly due the pressures they placed upon him but in their opinion, effectively waging war upon his own people."

The room fell into a state of disbelief, there had been rumours of the King's troubles with parliament, talk of faraway wars, but this was unthinkable. Most were unaware things were equally as tumultuous outside the house as they were inside.

"Pardon me Sir, but what will this mean for us, Sir ?" Asked one of the men.

"I'm not so sure, the world as we know it is changing and fast, they will come looking for soldiers and all of you able men will be expected to fight."

"Pardon me Sir, but who will we be fighting ?"

"Well lad, it's everyman for himself from here, I have to tell you that we are a Royalist household and therefore our loyalty is to the crown."

"God save the King !"

"God save the King," replied those in the room.

With these words Jane had a small sense of pride in her husband, even though she was shocked by this turn of events. She had heard whispers of trouble with Ireland and Scotland, but the King was of Scottish blood so it seemed ridiculous to Jane that the country's would be at war, now it seemed all the more unbelievable for England to be at war with itself ! Jane was lost in her own thoughts as Broome rambled on before dismissing the men and women who helped them. He had told them what he knew and that they should prepare for the worst. Everyone had left the room in a sad and serious mood for no one knew what to expect or indeed what to prepare for. Once again there was silence as Jane was left with only her husband, Lady Ursula, the ticking clock and Kathryn, who had clearly been crying. She sniffed as she brought in their dinner making Jane almost feel sorry for the poor girl.

"Sir," Kathryn curtsied as she left the room catching Broome's eye with that glint that only lovers share, Jane saw it and smiled to herself knowingly. It was as if they no longer tried to hide their infidelity.

Broome sensing Jane's observations, slurped a large gulp of wine, he really had no manners, "I have another more personal announcement." Jane looked at him with surprise, what could have possibly followed the news that England was at war with itself, it truly was fast turning into some tragic comedy. She lifted her glass to drink, hoping he was about to declare his love for Kathryn, leaving her free to gallop off into the sunset.

"I am leaving for Europe," he said matter of factly.

"What ?" Jane coughed on her wine as Lady Ursula dropped her glass, causing Kathryn to swiftly return and clean everything away, whatever else she was, she was a good maid.

"Yes," Broome added nonchalantly, "I sail for France in the morning."

"What ?" Echoed Lady Ursula.

"Mother, I said ..." He began sheepishly.

"You fool, I heard what you said but, but I just can't believe it, have you lost your mind ? You've just told us that we are at war." Lady Ursula suddenly roused with more life in her than Jane had seen in weeks, her tired beady old eyes now on fire and searing into him.

"Mother, the King has raised his standard, this will be a terrible war, not one far away like the troubles in Ireland or Scotland, which I remind you I only just managed to avoid, it will be fought here, right here on English soil. I cannot be pulled between them. I have loyalty to both parliament and of course to His Majesty, it would be foolish of me to choose between them. No, I must take my leave, whilst this works itself out, I assure I am not alone in this way of thinking." Broome sat back in his chair looking boyish and somewhat pleased with himself as he drank his wine and continued, "to me it seems the most obvious and certainly the most agreeable course of action."

"Action ?" Interrupted Jane who by now was wildly indignant. "Your idea of action is to flee ? You would abandon us, your mother, the children ? The King ? Is that your idea of action ?" Jane was in total shock, as were her husband and his mother when she spoke, they both turned their attention upon her.

"No one asked for your opinion," spat Lady Ursula with her usual spite although she was just as taken aback as Jane.

Broome slammed his fist down on the table sending all the plates tinkling.

"How dare you madam ?" He snarled, "you dare to question me, you infuriating woman. You have no idea, no idea the pressures this puts upon me ... as a gentleman, the pressure to choose sides, you've no idea what's at stake…you stupid woman, whining away, do you think all this… just happens for you ?"

As a matter of fact she did believe everything happened for her, except this marriage, which she had never been able to see the benefit of. All this, Jane thought to herself, it was her stepfather's money that enabled him to keep his father's seat, money he made because of his loyalty to the King and to the crown. Broome continued to bellow at her, while Jane sat dumbfounded that he, this man who she had the misfortune to have married, was making excuses for himself and his forthcoming absence. Jane had to admit it wouldn't all together be a bad thing, but still, he was revealing himself to be just as she had always known, a useless coward.

Lady Ursula's beady little eyes were almost popping out of her head as she and Broome argued over his intentions, Jane observed them silently although she was seething, to her it was inconceivable to flee, it was apparently also abhorrent to Lady Ursula, at last thought Jane, we agree on something.

"Kathryn, Kathryn ? I cannot sit here a moment longer. I have lost my appetite and heard quite enough …Kathryn ?" screeched Lady Ursula, " Kathryn !"

Kathryn dutifully appeared and wheeled Lady Ursula away, the pair of them as stony faced as each other.

Broome finished his food, it would take more than a civil war to stop him filling his guts, he really was repulsive. He looked over at Jane's and as usual mistook her silence for respect rather than resignation.

"Look what you've done now you've upset my mother, you did that. At least I will no longer have to suffer you, your rudeness or your stupidity, you disgust me. I shall take my leave in the morning, I expect the house to still be standing when I return."

"When will that be ?" Jane asked as he got up out of his chair.

"When all this is over of course, one way or another."

As he hurried out of the room, no doubt after Kathryn, Jane realised she was glad to see the back of him and she knew, deep to her very soul, that she never wanted to set eyes on him again. Alone with the ticking of the clock she raised her glass and whispered, "God save the King."

♛

Holton House carried on much as it always had, blissfully ignorant to the war raging around the British Isles and its Lordships absence. Jane, who was largely ignored by everyone anyway, sought solace in her riding and stayed as far away from the people and the house as possible. Her only obligation was to take Sunday meals with Lady Ursula and the children. It was always a joy to be with her children but she felt painfully aware they were being pulled further and further away from her. Not much else had changed at all, there were less men and maids darting about the house with less visitors and deliveries but all in all days passed much as they always had, slowly. News of the King's triumphs or alas, his tragedies were reported to Lady Ursula via the local priest who took great pleasure in relaying the gossip and draining the remaining wine store. Jane would loiter outside of the drawing room stretching her ears overhearing what she could of the events outside the walls of Holton House. She was after all adept at tiptoeing around unnoticed and found some joy in slipping about, although the things she heard were not always joyful.

♛

Late in the autumn when the light was low and the trees had lost most of their leaves, the priest rode in with the latest news. Jane had watched him galloping up the driveway, he either bears grave news or he is very thirsty she thought. Jane watched as he gave his horse to the boy and made his way hastily into the house, she quietly went to greet him, but as usual he had been sequestered away by Lady Ursula and Kathryn to the drawing room and Jane could already hear the clink of glasses as she slipped into the shadows to listen.

"I bring terrible news, Lady Ursula …most terrible," said the priest as he held out his glass to Kathryn, as if the worse the news the fuller it should be. He took a large gulp before holding it out again,"truly awful." Lady Ursula nodded to Kathryn who duly filed his glass to almost overflowing, then following the waft of Lady Ursula's withered hand, she curtsied and left.

"Lady Ursula you are so fortunate to be far from the madness that is erupting in every part of England, there seems to be violent conflict everywhere, I tell you, dreadful news comes from every corner and I fear the King has not fared well. He moves about the north, with very few men or arms, he has called upon his nephew Prince Rupert, who has by all accounts fought well and boosted morale but parliament's response has been fierce with a great many men following the Earl of Essex, to meet His Majesty in battle."

"The Earl of Essex you say ? Wasn't he the one whose wife went off with King James favourite ? He didn't take that at all well, especially when King James wouldn't support him, he's harboured those grievances for a long time hasn't he ? Making the King pay for the sins of his father."

"Yes that's the one, but to be honest Lady Ursula, some if not all of this puritan parliament hold grudges and resentments towards the old King. His Majesty is certainly up against it. I heard news of a most brutal battle, south of Warwickshire, at Edge Hill, a bloody and useless one, great loss of life and nothing, absolutely nothing was determined but death for a great many innocent men, who have no idea what they are fighting for. With all their godliness, it's hard to imagine how or indeed why those puritans are all so filled with spite and vengeance, it's dreadful what's become of this land, so it pains me to tell you that the war rages on. The King is said to be making his way to Oxford for the winter, all talks have invariably broken down so the prospect of further fighting is inevitable but no one is winning Lady Ursula, the Lord only knows what will become of us all."

Jane's stomach dropped and her heart raced as she listened to the woeful tales of war but her eyes grew wide when she heard that the King was coming to Oxford ! If the King comes, that means the King's court and possibly her dear friend Elizabeth would be there. The image of James flashed into her mind as the fire crackled making her jump, nearly knocking over a vase and exposing her hiding place. Would James be there too ? She felt a rush of excitement as she carefully placed the vase back and deftly made her way back to her rooms, her mind a whirl of what if's.

♛

Sure enough it was just as the old priest had said, the King returned to Oxford, bringing his court and a great deal of soldiers with him. Jane was overjoyed to see them all make their way to the city and she hoped her newly married and dearest friend was with them and the very thought of James being there too had kept her giddy for weeks. Even though the reasons and conditions for the King's return to Oxford were treacherous, Jane was heartily pleased to see the progress of colour moving past the Holton Estate, making its way to town and filling up the fields over the Wheatley Bridge. She could hardly contain herself, forgetting instantly her miseries of being confined at Holton House. Seeing the familiar wagons pass by filled her heart with gladness, knowing her children were safe with Lady Ursula, who much preferred to be alone with them anyway, Jane was only too happy to oblige, taking a cap and shawl she ran out of the house to follow them. She was breathless by the time she had caught up with them.

"Ah, well I never, Ms Ryder," said a soldier doffing his hat as he sailed past, much to Jane's delight.

The procession wound its way to the Palace stopping at the Royal quarters with everyone assuming their position and part in the unpacking, it was busy and Jane loved it. Every one of the lavenders were pleased to see her but it was Elizabeth that held her the closest.

"Oh my dearest Gin, thank God and all that is good, I am so happy to see you."

At once baskets were handed to her and the gossip began with everything and everyone finding their place, boys on errands weaving between the women, men and horses going about their business.

♛

In no time at all Jane was a welcomed guest at Oxford, being the Black Rod's daughter had its advantages, she was easily granted passage allowing her to spend every day she could amongst the folk she once knew well. Jane hadn't felt so comfortable or at ease in ages, she loved the bustle of city and court life.

The King soon became aware of her presence there too, he had noticed her from his windows having remembered her and her family fondly. He called to his trusted Officer of Arms, Elias Ashmole, Solicitor, mathematician, alchemist and above all staunch Royalist and between them they hatched a plan. With great patience and perfect timing Elias made it his business to become acquainted with Jane and went out of his way to cross her path or be in her company. What she thought to be polite conversation was actually a test of her character.

Elias was sat at the chess table in the courtyard when he saw Jane and waved her over, she joyfully accepted for she was as much at ease with gentlemen as she was amongst the common folk of kitchens and laundries. Elias, who found Jane to be charming, trustworthy and above all enjoyable company had already relayed to the King his confidence in her loyalty. Jane was equally charmed by Elias, fascinated by his knowledge of curious things.

"Ah, Miss Ryder, what an absolute pleasure to be seeing you today, auspicious also as the moon is new and here you are beaming like a bright new pin, you shine much like the sun does, caressing the senses with your rays of joy, tell me how do you do it ? How do you stay so untouched by the horrors of war ?"

Jane curtsied, "I have been fortunate enough to be far from it Sir and I was already living the horrors of a married life, well before this war began."

Elias wryly smiled, "Your husband, he's gone abroad hasn't he ? Has he ever told you how agreeable you are to the eyes as well as the soul ?"

Jane blushed.

"I thought not, not everyone appreciates beauty madam, neither do they seek it many won't dare to even notice it. Much like these mad puritans, who are so afraid of it they wish to stamp out all expressions of it. Beauty is the bedfellow of love and we all know that love is the conqueror. Have confidence, for you are a rare creature, it is seldom seen, a lady such as yourself, blessed with happiness and beauty the way you are and may I add it suits you."

"Why thank you Sir, you speak rare words also, for I have seldom heard compliments regarding my nature," Jane smiled back at him then looked at the chess board that was set for a game.

"Do you play ?" He asked.

"Not well."

"We all seek to play a better game, do we not ?"

"I suppose we do."

"Please," he gestured for her to sit and play, " indulge me."

"I will amuse you Sir," smiled Jane, taking a seat.

"My good woman, you delight me."

They set about playing, Jane concentrating fully on the board, Elias focused fully upon Jane.

"I like the way you play Miss Ryder, the way you protect your King."

Jane looked at him bemused for she wasn't aware that a great deal is revealed when playing the game of Kings.

Elias smiled as he swiftly took the game to checkmate leaving Jane mystified.

"Well played Sir," she said, raising her hand to shake his.

"And you accept defeat graciously, wonderful Miss Ryder, truly wonderful."

Jane was confused, "Sir, you are mocking me ?"

"Not at all, anything but my dear, I admire your spirit, you rose to a challenge, knowing you were out matched."

Elias reset the table as the low sun cast dancing rays flickering through the leaves of a nearby tree. After a few moments of silence, he continued, "although I feel I must apologise, for you find me distracted."

Knowing Lord Ashmole would not have mentioned this unless he was open to her enquiries, Jane happily obliged.

"Would it be appropriate for me to ask why that is my Lord ?"

He looked at her warmly, glad she had asked.

"May I speak frankly ?" He asked.

"Yes Sir, you may speak with confidence, you have my word, nothing you say will go any further than this table." Jane looked into his eyes allowing Elias to continue.

"Thank you my Lady. It is of course what pains and ails the King. Our cause, you see, is in need of money and as luck would have it we have many gracious and generous supporters who are fully on our side and are willing to loan us large amounts of it as well as send us a good deal of gold."

"How fortunate."

"Yes indeed it is, unfortunately though this generosity currently lives in London and as you are aware, things are slightly, shall we say, trifling ? Parliament controls the traffic, it's hard enough for us to send messages so I can't see them taking too kindly to us receiving such generous support or worse I wouldn't want them taking it from us, so here you find me rather perplexed as I consider our next move."

"Soap," Jane said nonchalantly.

"I beg your pardon ?"

"Forgive my intrusion into your thoughts Sir, but I said Soap. The soap barrels would, in my mind, be the easiest way to transport your ... goods."

"Well I never, may I ask how you think that would be possible?"

"The soap comes in huge barrels and the laundresses are never checked, they have relatively free access to and from London, it wouldn't be at all suspicious. Oxford regularly receives many barrels of the finest soap for His Majesty's laundry."

"Soap, now why didn't I think of that ?"

"Why would you ?"

"Ha ! Why would I ? Tell me Ms Ryder do you believe that such a thing would be possible?"

"Yes I really do, by all means make your own observations, but it seems to me the easiest and most obvious idea. I believe you could easily move as much as you like this way. With the help of the lavenders of course. It would mean you'd have less soap but I assume you would be far happier with the barrels filled with gold ?"

Elias was taken aback by this revelation.

"Soap, now there's a thing. What an ingenious, brilliant idea. Thank you, well seeing as you had this momentous ...shall we say inspiration, would you be willing to facilitate such a daring plan ? Would you help us ? I believe His Majesty would be extremely grateful to you if you were to assist us in such a way, I know I certainly would. It would be a thankless task of course, no one would ever know and should, God forbid you be discovered, you would be cast adrift, unknown to us."

"Like a spy ?"

"Not at all, nothing so undignified... more like ... an agent, someone trusted, trusted to move about unseen, trusted to use one's own initiative and judgment. Sadly nothing is what it seems out there Miss Ryder, unfortunately there are a great deal of scoundrels sniffing about, even here at Oxford, so I must be direct and discreet. Would you ? Could you even consider such a proposal ? To help us ? To be unknown, unseen ?"

Without a moment's hesitation she replied,

"Absolutely Yes ! Sir, nothing would make me feel more alive, it would be an absolute honour. I move easily through parliamentary controls, they rarely check me and I could use my married name, for she is already unknown as well as unseen, even within my own house."

"You see, that's why I like you, Mistress ?"

"Whorwood," Jane interjected.

"Madame Whorwood, wit as well as guile."

Smiling, Jane leaned forward to whisper.

"I am at your service Sir."

"Ah," said Elias, sitting back with a satisfied smile upon his face, "I was hoping you would say that."

Jane's life began anew that day, at first she began by relaying small messages, gaining trust which she did effortlessly and effectively, moving freely between Oxford and London. As she became entrusted with greater intelligence she met with the financiers, merchants and wealthy supporters whom she vaguely knew through her stepfather but she met them now as an agent of the King. Esteemed men of the East India Trading Company were able to funnel money to His Majesty via Jane and her network, especially a certain Mr Pinder, who lavished the cause with thousands of pounds. Jane facilitated it all with stealth as she moved silently around the streets of London she knew so well, proving herself to be a most trustworthy servant. She even helped the lavenders bring the King's crown out of London and with the help of her dear friend Elizabeth was able to smuggle a great deal of gold into Oxford too, all hidden in barrels of soap, right under the army's nose, which amused the girls no end. She was instrumental in bringing much needed funds and morale back to the King's cause. So buoyed by this abundant boost to the coffers and spirit, life at the Royal court of Oxford returned to far more favourable and peaceful conditions. With this bounty of gold, jewels and free flowing money, the King was able to restore a sense of regality, soldiers were paid and life for the cavaliers regained a certain flourish. The Queen rejoined the King at Oxford and although the war continued with words, life inside the Royal court regained its composure with the people there, once again living in joyful celebration and nothing could have irritated the puritans more.

Glastonbury 1644

A far cry from its pilgrimage hay days, Glastonbury, nestled in the Mendip Hills, was now a sleepy little town, a mere stop on the Bath to Exeter road. The memories of its grander past had long disappeared into the dust and were largely forgotten.

Good wife Gollop, a cheery plump woman with a kindly smile and bright eyes that sparkled forth from her bonnet and scarves, was busy. There was an expectant air that blew in that day setting her senses on edge. Something was afoot ! Ma Gollop came from a long line of unmarried mothers and was a mystic of sorts, one of Glastonbury's finest. She knew every inch of the land, the brush, the marsh, the levels and the hills and spoke freely with the birds and the beasts, she had a great knowledge of the natural laws and a great deal more of human nature. Her family, as far back as anyone could remember, had always run The Bluebell Inn, halfway up the High street, where you could be sure of a warm welcome. Somehow those Gollop women always managed to be hospitable even in the harshest of times, it was said that the old Abbot had blessed them many years ago and if anyone knew the whereabouts of the Abbey's great treasure, it was sure to be them.

Like all Gollop's before her, Ma was wise to all the herbs and roots that healed and put herself at the service of healing mankind and the earth itself. Usually she was a beacon of calm, but today there was an apprehension in the air that ruffled her skirts and her nose, in a good way for it was a good feeling rather than a dark one. Ma Gollop busily set the girls to work at the Bluebell as if she was expecting visitors, even setting fresh flowers into the window.

"Oh Ar ? What's got into you then ? What's on with all your fancy ?" Laughed old Joseph," folk will be wondering what you're up to putting flowers up like that."

"Ha ! Wouldn't they be disappointed on finding me behind them ?" Replied Ma Gollop.

They caught each other's eye and laughed as she poured him a cider and set it upon the counter.

"Today is a good day Joseph."

"Bah ! There's been no good days since this senseless war," he shook his head.

"But, today I am hopeful Joseph, the old apple tree was full of tits and finches this morning. They were lively I tell you, all chirping and singing, telling me to be ready, ready for something, it's filled me with hope, so it has."

"You and them birds, well then I'll be glad, for that's what we all need right now is some hope, God save the King." He raised his mug to drink.

Joseph was an old friend she was happy to confide in, he had farmed the Abbey orchards for years and always bought Ma Gollop the best apples for her cider press, she was quite particular about what she gave to customers but then she could afford to be. Having no money worries meant that she was freer than most and was generous with it too, especially kind to the poor women and children about town. Everyone knew they could count on the Goodwife's kindness and hospitality, not that there were many left in the town or even came past these days.

It had been many years since the Tudor King ordered the ruin of the Abbey and of the Abbot, God bless his soul. Abbot Whiting was a kind, good and decent man, embedded within the very landscape of Glastonbury. He was well aware of what was to befall him, his town and his beloved Abbey but he had not one grain of malice about him, he gracefully accepted his fate as if it were his destiny. The Abbot bore no grievances as he prepared the town and all the good people within it, generously handing out coins and gold to make sure no one would suffer when and if their livelihoods should be torn from them. He gave many families the means to start anew, elsewhere. Ma Gollop's ancestors had benefited greatly from his kindness their whole lives but especially towards the end of his. He confided in the towns folk that great change was upon them all and beseeched them not to let fear in any form take hold of their hearts. He encouraged the town to meditate and align with the perpetual prayers and chants that now rang out from the Abbey more fervently, more devotedly. The Abbot then told everyone to be free of any guilt or shame for there was nothing anyone could do to stop what was about to happen. He reassured them that he was anticipating leaving his earthly body by his own means of prayer and fasting and was preparing to become one with the supreme being, with God. He also warned them that the King's men may commit heinous crimes against his body, which indeed they did but he encouraged them to look away and trust that he would have already left his mortal garment long before and his soul would be safe in the arms of the Heavenly Father.

Many of those that chose to stay continued the practice of meditation that he taught, the way of the single eye and control of the breath which allowed them to do and see all manner of wonderful things. Holding the vital energy of Glastonbury maintaining its Elysian tradition.

Abbot Whiting had given the keys to the Bluebell Inn and the money to keep it open to Ma Gollop's grandmothers ensuring there would always be a warm welcome in Glastonbury. Many guest houses and Inns were forced to close or the proprietors fled when there was no Abbey to protect them and no steady stream of pilgrims to fund them. Even fewer people came now that the war had displaced and affected everyone. In some ways the locals enjoyed the peace and quiet, especially when news reached them of the madness, suspicion and plots that had gripped the rest of the country. Agitating, unsettled and most unnatural thought Ma Gollop.

"You mark my words Joseph, there be hope coming for us, a newness, new life, a new visitor, new child, renewed hope I tell thee."

Joseph drank all but the dregs of his cider, as usual he left just enough to hang about for he liked to be in Ma Gollop's company.

"Now I know you be off with the fairies," he laughed, "there's no woman with child this side of the Mendips, you know that as well as I do, besides there's no man able."

"Ah but I feel it Joseph, I sense it, it's upon the breeze and you know us Gollop's have a nose for such things."

"Aye, you be nosey alright."

Ma Gollop joined him in his good nature laughter, for she shared a long and warm friendship with him.

The day passed slowly as it does when one is awaiting. No one else but Joseph had seen the cleanliness of the Bluebell or had noticed the flowers in the window. It turned into a beautiful spring evening, all blossoms and birdsong, Ma Gollop had whiled away the hours silently watching, waiting and anticipating. The church bells of St John rang out calling everyone back from the fields although these days there were only a few who answered the call of the chimes. It also marked the time when Ma would attend the Abbey, an old family tradition she upheld, even though these days it was more of a quarry, having been ransacked these past hundred years. She often shook her head at the Abbey's sad fate. Once the burial place of Kings and Queens, sacred spirituality manifested in stone, now mostly dismantled and shamelessly sold for rubble and roads, it was but a ruin of its once majestic past. Ma made her way around the great church as if the walls were still standing because in Ma Gollop's eyes she could see them, shimmering and glistening with the heavenly glow that exists between time and space. Every so often when she was very still and deep in her meditation she would see the old monks moving about their business as they did for the thousand years that the Abbey stood in this world of men. Ma Gollop made her prayers for the Abbot, the Abbey, the townsfolk and these days for King Charles. Tonight she sat longer than usual on the plinth of stones that had at one time been part of the choir, the sense of expectation hadn't left her but now with night falling she wondered if she had been fanciful as Joseph had said. The day had passed by as slowly and as quietly as any other, had she misread the signs ?

It was almost dark when she left the ghosts of the Abbey although she never felt afraid there, only comforted by whatever spirits lingered within its broken walls. She chose to leave by the west gate, which she didn't usually do, the north gate being closer to her home but tonight she felt guided to walk and take in the town she loved. There were some children playing by the water trough at the market cross, "Evening Ma Gollop." they chimed. She stopped and smiled broadly at the mischievous little cherubs and waved to them before she carried on walking up the High street. Suddenly, she could hear the sound of a coach coming from Bath in the distance. It seemed to her that the horses were galloping and thundering down the road in a hurry, so she quickened her pace homeward.

Having so diligently cleaned the Inn from top to bottom there was not much for her to do but restart the fire and set a fresh pot upon it. Satisfied her senses hadn't misled her and that Joseph was far from right, she settled on her chair breathing rhythmically for she now felt the enormity of something and needed to stay calm. "Trust…New life," she whispered as she drifted off to the sound of the fire. She hadn't been in her settled state for long when she felt a tug at her skirts. "Excuse me Ma, Ma Gollop ?"

She opened her eyes and looked down at the scruffy little fellow at her feet.

"Ah, my dear sweet boy," she knew him and his big brown eyes well enough and he was indeed one of the sweetest.

"Patrick the coachman has sent for you Ma, he's just pulled up at the George said I was to come for you straight away, he has a lady in the back heavy with child and she's moaning and crying out and he told me to come for you and fast for he fears the baby will come in his coach and that won't fair well for the trip to Exeter." He beamed, proud to have been the messenger.

"Oh my they're here," Ma Gollop jumped up excitedly looking about her to remind herself everything was just so. She poured a handful of nuts in the boy's tiny hands, his fingers wrapping tightly around them.

"Now run along, tell Patrick I am coming, that I'm right behind you."

The boy knelt in thanks and for a blessing.

"We've no time for that dear heart, you know I bless and pray for you everyday, now go quick or I shall be there before thee," and like lightning he was gone.

♛

When Ma Gollop arrived at the back of the George, the coaches always stopped there for they alone had the room for horses, she found Patrick pacing and useless beside his wagon with the doors wide open.

Ma Gollop laughed, "I take it the child isn't yours then Patrick ?"

"Ah, thank God you've come, Goodwife. I knew I shouldn't have taken them when they approached me at Bath, I could see the little lady was just as wide as tall and all restless, fidgety."

"They ?" Ma Gollop interrupted

"Aye, they, there's the woman with child, a mute, has a maid with her she's recovering she said, probably from the pox or something so she's all wrapped up but I could tell, you know, see the way she waddled, I wouldn't have bought them but they begged and begged me."

"Paid you well, you mean ?"

"Well yes, that too, but I did it out of goodness, they're trying to get to the woman's husband and well, I couldn't just leave them there the two of them like that, still we've made good time and you know how these hills are I wouldn't be surprised if the journey hadn't bought it on for her, they paid extra for a faster ride I swear it."

"Don't worry Patrick, bless you, I know you have a good heart, thank you for bringing them to me."

Ma Gollop looked into the darkness of the coach and saw two sets of wild and wet eyes, clearly frightened, the rounder one under a heap of fine blankets.

"Hello my loves, welcome, everyone knows me as Ma, I'm the Goodwife of this town. Your driver Patrick here has sent for me because he feels I may be able to help you. So I invite you to come with me my dears, you've nothing to fear, I have a warm place all ready for you, come I'll take good care of you, you have my word." She held out her hands as she sent her soothing words into the coach. The passengers were startled but reassured by her soft voice they began making moves towards her. The maid hopped out helping her mistress emerge from the heap of blankets revealing her fair and delicate face, covered in sweat and clearly preoccupied.

"Oh my goodness it's you. Come, come with me, I've been expecting you, are you able to walk ? Silly question, sometimes my head has no idea what comes out of my mouth." Ma Gollop quickly took control of the situation, taking the lady's dainty hand as she swayed into her arms.

"Patrick, Patrick I need you to carry this lady, most careful mind, up to the Bluebell and fast, forgive me… your… Miss, but it is the only way."

Patrick, who was a good strong man with a wife and family of his own, knew well the risks of child bearing. He immediately did the Goodwife's bidding and swiftly lifted up the tiny bird in blankets that was all bone and baby. Ma Gollop turned to the maid who was amazed at her daring and her efficiency.

"Don't worry my dear, the young lads here will bring your bags, won't you boys ? They are all known to me and are trustworthy, now you come with me."

They all scuttled off towards the Bluebell in a hurry. Ma Gollop held the maids hand and a lantern leading the way along the road and round the corners, eventually through the Bluebells door, up the stairs and into the best room in the house. Patrick carefully laid the precious cargo upon the bed then briskly left the room without saying a word but nodding to the ladies relieved he didn't have to scrub out his coach. Ma Gollop waited for him to leave then fell on her knees before the delicate lady that was perched upon the bed.

"Your Highness, I am truly honoured, you are most welcome here in my humble home. I ask only for you to trust me and I promise you I will do all I can for you and your baby. May I ?"

In between breaths and the sharp twinges of pain the lady nodded in agreement. Ma Gollop moved her hand above the writhing blankets and smiled, "ah, it's a Bonny lass for you and your family and an impatient one too, we'll be seeing you with your baby well before the morrow."

Neither of Ma Gollop's guests uttered a word, they only marvelled at her competency and exchanged knowing glances that they would trust this good woman.

Turning to the maid in the doorway Ma Gollop gave her instruction. "I'll need you to make yourself useful my sweet, go downstairs you'll find fresh towels, hot water and there's bread, cider and cheese on the bar, bring everything. Oh and would you be a love and shut the front doors." The maid promptly curtsied and left the room to find all things she had been asked to bring. Ma Gollop went to her store of herbs, salves and poultices and made her way back to the ladies side before the maid returned.

"Bless you Lass, well done for finding it all, set those things down over there, now will you kindly reassure the mistress in her own language." The poor girl's eyes grew wide. "Don't worry, I know dear, I know her Highness is fine versed in English, but at times like these it is a comfort to hear your native tongue." She smiled while mixing up a tonic, "and know this my loves, you are welcome to pray how you please here, I mind not how you worship the Lord, old ways, new ways, to me it is the same God who looks over us, so have no fear to call upon the Lord as you wish."

♛

The baby came quickly as Ma Gollop knew she would and she placed the babe straight to her mothers breast. This was an unknown experience for the Queen and a slightly uncomfortable feeling at first. This soon subsided as the new mother suckled her tiny baby and felt closer to her new child because of it, bringing tears of joy that flowed down her cheeks. The mother was soon in the full swell of pride, looking down at her beautiful daughter sleeping soundly in her arms. Barely taking her eyes from her, she watched the princess's eyelashes unfurl and her perfect rosebud lips turn pink.

Ma Gollop was relieved and well pleased as she began packing her things away. She looked about the room, thankful they had done such a good job tidying, everything was thankfully clean and neat. She didn't have so many guests these days and with the door shut, locals, which meant Joseph, would know she was at 'work'. Although this was hardly work, welcoming new life into this world. was an honour, a privilege and the greatest service she could be, besides Ma Gollop had the easy time of it. Everyone was thankful that all had been smooth, other than the carriage ride. When Ma came back to the room with hot and fresh camomile, she smiled at the perfect picture of the mother fast asleep with her baby still at her breast and her maid praying at their feet holding her rosary. Startled, the young maid lowered her hands as Ma Gollop smiled at her. "Be peace, dear heart. You are quite safe here," she set down the tray and stoked up the fire. "There is nothing so beautiful as a mother and child."

She poured out some camomile for them both and passed some to the maid causing her to relax a little. They drank together in silence, listening to the babe whose adorable contented snores had sent her mother to sleep.

"How can we ever thank you Goodwife ?" Whispered the maid.

"Ah, to see them both blissful like that is thanks enough for me dear heart, what a blessing." They smiled at each other and returned to the silence they were now comfortable in.

"Tell me, do you bring news as well as a baby from Oxford ?" Ma Gollop asked humorously.

The maid was a little surprised but she cleared her throat and began to speak quietly, with respect for her sleeping Queen and out of habit for fear of being overheard.

"There is no good news coming from Oxford, not now. The parliamentary siege became unbearable and far from safe for us, it's all treachery and misery if you ask me, forgive me Goodwife but I fear it's only getting worse. It's as if the minds of men have been taken away, it's ferocious out there, everyone blaming each other and changing sides. It's madness, one is never sure who to trust. I thank God we were brought here to you."

"I too give thanks that you came to me," nodded Ma Gollop, encouraging her to go on.

"God willing, we make our way to Exeter, not knowing if we shall be received there, for no one knows, other than yourself, that we are on the road, with no escort and no protection other than God's Grace. We hope to find refuge with the Earl of Bedford but in all honesty who knows ? We do not know if the Earl still lives or if he will welcome us as the King trusts he will." The poor girl was visibly frightened as she held back the tears that were building up behind her eyes, "who knows what's to become of us Goodwife, what's to become of us all."

♛

Ma Gollop was up with the sky larks and just as joyful for she was blessed with a happiness that was infectious and unquellable. She cheerfully prepared a tray of fresh flowers, bread, jams and honey, until she heard movement, then she climbed the stairs, eager to see her guests in the morning light.

"Good Day, joyful rising and a joy to see you all," Ma Gollop bowed and curtsied as she set the tray on the side where their night time candle had long since burnt down.

"Tell me how you are feeling today, Your Majesty ? You and the little one ?"

"With thanks and praise to God and to you Goodwife, we are safe, well and alive."

Ma Gollop opened up the shutters letting the sunlight and spring breeze into the room. Now Ma could have a proper look at them all, especially the newborn who the maid was gleefully holding, while the mother moved about the room with the elegance and grace of the Queen she was.

"Does the Princess have a name ? If I may be so bold to ask, Your Majesty ?"

The Queen of England gently laughed and with her beautiful soft French accent she replied.

"I am already quite fond of your boldness, never have I fed a child myself as I am sure you will understand, this is my 9th child and it has taken me until now, to see the richness in it. There was a closeness, a love between us that I have never felt before, now I know I never had this feeling with my other children, much to my regret. Ah ! Mon dieu, we have no time for regrets, such is the way of my life. In answer to your question, the princess is to have my name, we will call her Henriette and Anne, in honour of my dear husband's mother." The Queen tried in vain to hold back her tears.

"Henriette Anne, that's a beautiful name for a princess." Smiled Ma.

Elizabeth and Jane had spent most of the afternoon lazing by the riverside before their peace was interrupted, "Lizzy, there you are, have you been here the whole time ? I've been looking everywhere for you."

Elizabeth looked up to the man she loved, a good and loyal guard to the King.

"Yes, Will, you found me, and yes we've been here the whole time, you didn't think I'd run off with those roundheads did you ?"

Jane and Elizabeth laughed but William looked at them both seriously.

"That's not funny Lizzy, you've been gone for hours, I've turned the whole place looking for you. Good to see you again Miss Ryder."

"This is why you have my heart," Elizabeth giggled as Willian tipped his hat.

"And what is it you are wanting me so desperately for my dearest ?"

"You're needed back at the kitchens, right away."

"Yes and I, I too must be getting back," said Jane, looking over her shoulder to the road that led out of town.

"Oh no you don't," laughed Elizabeth getting to her feet. "You're going nowhere Jane, you stay with me. I can still work and listen you know and besides I'm starting to feel hungry so you must be too, come with me to the kitchens, I'll raise some sup for us both."

Jane had to agree she hadn't anything to race back to Holton for and she hadn't enjoyed herself so much in years, she also knew she wouldn't be missed so she reached for Elizabeth's arm.

"Why not, yes please Mrs Wheeler, if it's ok with you Mr Wheeler ? I would love to come with you." The three of them linked arms and walked through the lanes that led back to town.

"Excuse me Miss, Miss Ryder .. is that you ?" Asked a soft and familiar voice. Jane turned around to see none other than the King himself, the girls broke arms to curtsy and William took off his hat and bowed.

"Your Majesty," said Jane, still facing the floor.

"Ah, splendid, I thought it was you. I'd recognise that flaming Scots hair anywhere. I am so deeply touched and much as I appreciate your etiquette ladies, I am afraid we are well past that, do rise and come, come Miss Ryder, would you join me ? It is so very pleasing to see you."

"It would be an honour, Sire," said Jane in a heartbeat.

"Would you be so kind as to bring something for us Mrs Wheeler ?"

"Yes, of course," curtsied Elizabeth who slipped into service mode instantly as she and William continued their stride to the kitchens.

Jane followed the King, his chamberlain and his dogs across the courtyard and up the steps that led to his quarters. Elizabeth swiftly arrived with a large jug of wine for them both, pouring it perfectly into delicate little glasses then, smiling to Jane, she left the room the way she had come in along with the chamberlain and the dogs. It was such a beautiful room with its ornately carved high ceilings, every wall was covered in some form of beauty. In fact every corner was filled with art or sculpture, different expressions of wonderful were everywhere. Huge books filled one wall all neatly packed together and upon a large table was a map and different figures much like a giant game of sorts. She looked up amazed at the grand arched window and the magical ways the light came in, a world away from the plainness of Holton.

"Please, Miss Ryder," the King motioned for her to help herself, having been brought up in and around the court of King Charles she was well at ease in his company.

"I have much to thank you for Miss Ryder, I wanted you to know that, I am aware of your service, your success, how much you have risked and how much you accomplished for us." He raised his glass to her.

"It was my pleasure and you are too kind, Your Majesty. I am honoured that you trusted me. I must say, I enjoyed every moment, it was an adventure and it brought me back to life, so it is I who am thankful to you."

The King smiled while twisting his moustache as he was so fond of doing.

"May I ask one further request of you ?" said the King with his slight and soft Scottish accent.

"Yes of course Your Majesty, anything," Jane answered eagerly.

Jane put down her glass and listened intently as the King laid bare his fears and woes. He mentioned names and grievances, pains and perjury. Jane was lost for words, she could see how weary and forlorn the King was, having remembered him from happier times he honestly looked half the man.

"I see," replied Jane, although she didn't.

"You may be wondering what part you will play in this ? It is this, I have something that I wish to be kept safe, hidden and I hoped I could ask you to take care of that something."

"You honour me, I swear to you as God is my witness that whatever you ask of me, I will do." Jane looked up and impulsively crossed herself.

"My dear child, bless you. I am sadly surrounded by snakes and my faith in men has been crushed. I wish to entrust you with something very precious to me, something I wouldn't want Fairfax or Cromwell's men to get their hands on or anyone else for that matter, it would only be until such a time when I can retrieve it from you."

"Sire, you have my word, I will take the utmost care of …whatever it is and guard it with my life."

"It is this Miss Ryder, this rather pitifully holds everything I now have of material value." The King passed a little wooden cabinet over the table to her, it was small, polished and well made.

"Your Majesty, I shall hold it safely and protect it until you say otherwise."

Jane and the King then relaxed, recalling happier times and remembering the wonderful masques that although a distant memory still dazzled their minds. Then there came a heavy knock at the door that brought them back to present day Oxford. A courtier had arrived with important news which signalled an exit for Jane who with perfect poise bowed to the King simultaneously whisking the small cabinet up and under her cloak.

"Miss Ryder," called the King after her.

"Yes, Your Majesty ? " Jane said as she swirled around.

"Thank you."

"The pleasure is all mine," Jane bowed again as the courtier traded places with her and raised an eye in suspicion but quickly refocused on the business he had come for, closing the door behind her.

Jane wandered down to the kitchens and the laundries, hoping to say goodbye to Elizabeth but she was nowhere to be seen. Jane didn't want to linger with the King's effects so she made her way back across the fields to Holton, under a brilliant blue sky.

♛

The puritans attacked Oxford mercilessly, it suffered terribly under the siege and was soon emptied. The King and his court had thankfully escaped in disguise and long since ridden North but all was soon lost for the cause at The Battle of Naseby where the Royalist force were shattered. The King then rode further north in the vain hope of some or any assistance but to no avail. It seemed as if all was truly lost. It was high summer and usually the fields would be filled with folk but these days the fields were, much like Oxford, barren and empty. Jane missed everyone terribly and had since given into melancholy, her only escape from Holton now was to take long walks alone along the riverside. One such day when she was returning heavy heartedly to Holton House, she was startled by what looked like a whole herd of horses out the front with grooms busily attending to them. They were not in the habit of accepting visitors at Holton so Jane at once became alert and wary. The grooms were busy taking care of the horses allowing Jane to make her way discreetly and nimbly into the house, up the wide staircase and to her rooms. She could hear many voices coming from down stairs that stirred her curiosity. Removing her cloak, she checked her hair and appearance in the mirror before sweeping downstairs to see what was happening. Jane was in no way prepared for the sight that greeted her, around the large oak table was Lady Ursula, clearly in her element surrounded by parliament men. Two men sat either side of Jane's mother in law and they seemed to be concocting something, behind one of them stood another man who was listening intently and had the appearance of a weasel, sharp eyed with a pointy nose which he no doubt used to pry into the business of others. It was he that noticed her tentatively standing in the doorway, he nudged the man in front who in turn focused his eyes upon Jane and within a moment all eyes were on her.

"Ah there you are, at last, this gentleman is my son's wife, Jane," Lady Ursula waved, beckoning her to join them.

"Madam," said the men together, standing in welcome.

"We are very honoured to have such esteemed guests with us tonight Jane, Lord Fairfax and this is General Cromwell," said Lady Ursula indicating with her hands who was who. Jane smiled at them both and curtsied. She was astonished for these were the very men the King had spoken of, they had also crushed His Majesty's forces only days earlier.

"Please Mistress Whorwood, won't you join us, your gracious mother here is being most generous and has welcomed us into your home and we have put forth intentions that I hope you will be in agreement with." General Cromwell growled.

Jane sat while one of the maids poured her tea, it was then she became aware of three twittering ladies sitting back from the table, by the window.

"May I introduce my daughter, Bridgette… Bridgette," The plumpest girl stood up. Jane nodded in greeting as did Bridgette.

"God willing, there will be a fine wedding, right here, with the thanks to the Lord and to you Lady Ursula, of my daughter Bridgette and Lord Ireton and we couldn't be happier." Cromwell was clearly proud but Jane had the feeling that this Ireton fellow was more seeking to be his husband than hers. Jane was also surprised that they would even consider any type of celebration given that they had insisted the rest of the country go without any. Jane's curiosity was aroused as she sat back to observe the unfolding drama.

It soon occurred to Jane that the busty Bridgette was a handful, after the niceties, Bridgette became more and more demanding, like a spoiled child. She was whiny, lusting and practically pawing at Ireton which drove her father to distraction. Ireton it seemed only had eyes for Cromwell while Fairfax, on the other hand, was more of a gentleman and cut from a very different cloth. Jane, with her appreciation for character unfoldment thought this to be a most unlikely cast of players, who amazingly had England and the King in their grip. Lord Fairfax was slightly removed and aloof to the plans being put forth by Cromwell, who so desperately had to do something with his insatiable daughter who was relentless in her wants and wantonness. She continued being overly seductive, surprising for a girl with such a puritan stalwart of a father. Ireton gave her little attention which only made her more demanding of his and her fathers. Jane found the whole thing amusing but like everyone else, dared not show that she had noticed Bridgette's libido bursting out of her seams. She did however notice Cromwell's mounting fury and frustration and Fairfax's disinterest and Ireton's attempts to wheedle into every thought, word and deed of the General's. It was a performance of epic proportions. Cromwell was somehow oblivious to the weasels cunning and blind to his daughter's voluptuousness and licentious behaviour. Lady Ursula was simply thrilled to be entertaining and of the honour of having her house as a venue for such a prestigious event. Jane silently observed the King's enemies planning to stage some sort of celebrations despite making sure that countrywide everyone else was to do without such luxuries and all the while the King's effects were safely just a few feet above them all. She drank to their health and wished them every success in married life for she felt they would certainly need it !

♛

The day for the wedding was set for the following week, Lady Ursula was soon busy directing, demanding and preparing, it seemed quite pointless as there was to be no decorations and no flowers. This puritan wedding was to be a somber affair, which saddened Jane as it was such a waste of the beautiful summer roses that would have brightened the austerity of Holton but perhaps that's why they chose it, for its dark and foreboding nature. Even Jane's own pantomime of a wedding had flowers, she knew she had very little in common with these people.

Jane had to play the part of subservient daughter spending most of the time at Lady Ursula's side, in Broome's absence she was the only other family representative. Thankfully the children were being kept busy and out of sight by their nanny, not that they missed anything. Jane had been to better funerals, she had initially felt sorry for Bridgette who seemed indifferent and disinterested, unaffected by the day's events but it soon became apparent that she was blatantly only interested in giving up all her virtues and being as sinful as possible, as quickly as possible. This lewdness was ignored and avoided for although Cromwell was driven to distraction and clearly irritated, if he was ignoring the obvious it meant that everyone else had to too. Jane assumed a puritan such as he, would be mad having a daughter so overly seductive for she would make a natural nymph upon the stage ! Ireton seemed for all intents and purposes to be doing Cromwell a service by taking this daughter to be his wife and therefore now his problem. What was laughable was how everyone was clearly pretending they were having a wonderful time. They praised God a lot and slapped each other on the back more times than Jane could count but no one seems to actually be enjoying themselves. It was so very strange, the bride being so consumed with lust as to make even her husband feel uncomfortable, the groom seeing this purely as a career move, while the father and mother of the bride were beyond vexed, stressed and irritated, constantly seeking further assistance from the Lord. Jane stayed as far back as politeness would allow. After all she had been neither invited nor involved, if anything it was bewildering to her that a wedding of such prominence would take place here, no disrespect to Lady Ursula, but Holton was almost in ruins. It was in such a state of disrepair that Jane had half expected the General to give orders to tear the whole place down rather than use it to host a wedding, but then these puritans probably loved the dourness. Jane nodded, agreeing with herself as Holton practically oozed that. After the nuptials or whatever they did, having banned so much of everything that people knew to resemble a wedding, there were only more and more farcical escapades, worthy of any London stage. The weasel faced groom, who not only looked as one but also acted more so, was constantly scampering after General Cromwell for fear that anything that might escape his ears. It seemed to Jane that his ears were pointing in every direction about the room so as not to miss a whisper. Cromwell, who was clearly a proud father, was also visibly harassed, not just by the weasel but by his far from blushing bride of a daughter. She was on hot on the tail of the weasel making grabs for him in a desperate attempt to gain his attention and affection. Lord Fairfax was becoming more and more uneasy, he began to distance himself from the whole carousel of catastrophe, rightfully so Jane thought but she couldn't help herself in wondering how this would play out ? Either the plump bride would keel over from sheer exhaustion or would she eventually pounce up on the weasel and devour him for her wedding breakfast. The energy was mounting, Cromwell was distracted and despairing, while Bridgette, the bride was almost falling over herself in her craving for her new husband to deflower her. Jane noticed the weasel hadn't even looked at her lovingly, his eyes were fixed only upon Cromwell, who didn't know where to look. He was clearly uncomfortable in such surroundings, a far cry from the battlefield. He finally snapped finding something trivial to raise his voice over and assert his authority. Poor Bridgette burst into tears and had to be comforted by her maids or her sisters perhaps ? The weasel smiled, actually more of a sneer, in complete satisfaction as if he had triggered the outburst or in some way benefited from it. Cromwell had finally blown his top, red with rage he began throwing his arms up and flailing about in such a way everyone shuddered, save the weasel who was still sneering by his side. Jane saw Lord Fairfax, who probably had had his fill of theatrics, walk out of the front, round to where the horses were and in no time at all he passed by the windows on his mount, followed by two other men who clearly also thought that the party was over. Cromwell finished spitting his fury and as if to justify his actions and maintain his Godliness, he gathered those that remained round in a prayer of sorts but nothing that Jane could hear or even understand. Lady Ursula was in her element, it was probably as much as a bitter woman such as herself could bring herself to enjoy. Jane was sure she saw a smile on those dry pursed lips of hers, even though there was no love lost between them Jane was heartened to see the old girl chattering away, at least someone was enjoying themselves. What an unfunny, funny lot, Jane thought to herself as she slipped away unnoticed and quietly retired to her rooms.

It didn't take long for the house at Holton to recover from the wedding. Lady Ursula, being a stickler for such things, had a wonderful time bringing all the staff to the task, shouting commands as she was wheeled about by Kathryn. The only part of Lady Ursula that was visible through all the lace was her piercing eyes that didn't miss a speck of dust and of course her mouth, through which she screamed instructions. She held a cane in her withered hand which she used to direct the course of her chariot. Jane was never more thankful to Kathryn, for not only had she taken her oaf of a husband off her hands but she had taken her mother in law also. Jane thought this to be a tremendous stroke of good luck, while the smug Kathryn thought she had somehow out done her, Jane was more than happy to let her continue to think so, as long as she continued pushing. Jane curtsied as they cruised past and wandered out into the gardens where the children were at play with their nanny. Jane's children were bright, strong and very clever but they had already been twisted to the ideals of the Whorwood family name and heritage. Her marriage being the sham that it was, Jane had been coerced and obliged to hand them over to Lady Ursula and her way of doing things but this had given her the freedom to come and go as she pleased and allowed her to fulfill her duties to the crown. Thankfully the children thrived, they were well cared for and educated so Jane was happy for them. With the whole country in turmoil, she was happy knowing that her children were far removed from the madness outside the walls. Young Broome and Diana came over with their nanny who wasn't a bad woman, just a harsh one and she encouraged them to greet their mother formally. How Jane wanted to squeeze them, to tear off their stiff tight clothes and let them run bare foot to feel the grass beneath their feet or ride the many horses that were stabled there but alas, these pastimes were considered unsuitable for Lady Ursula's grandchildren. Jane smiled and told them how beautiful they were but the wedge between them had been encouraged since they were born. The maid bowed to Jane and hurried the children back inside for some lessons deemed far more proper and worthwhile than being with their mother and her leanings toward freedom. Jane felt so useless and idle, roaming the garden, a hue of red, green and gold while the fragrance of honeysuckle filled the air. She inevitably made her way to the stables and on finding the stable hand asked that her favourite be saddled up for her as she wished to make the most of the sun set. Taking the reins and full command she kicked her horse into step and galloped full speed into the setting sun with tears streaming down her face. She had no intention of becoming a stuffed pillow wheeled around by mean maids or a frightened figurehead for her children. She cried because she had no place in this world, everything felt so uncomfortable, she didn't fit into the life that had grown up around her, the one she had been assigned. She felt so trapped by it all, when Holton was far behind her and the prying eyes out of sight, she pulled her blouse open with such angst, that the buttons went flying into the air and fell somewhere on the ground behind them. She pulled down her hair, letting the wind catch it like the tail of a kite as she screamed, screamed with utter release, letting out all of her fears and frustrations, holding tighter into the reins, she rode her horse faster and fearlessly into the distance far, far away from the constraints and controls of Holton house, wishing she could leave it behind forever. With no particular plan or course she rode on and on until finding the river where she let her horse rest. It was a perfect picture of paradise, wildflowers and long leaved willow trees with the hazy sparkle of evening sunlight dappling on the flowing stream. Hot and bothered, she impulsively began to take off all her dusty clothes, eager to be in the cool water. She wanted to wash away the day. It felt so good, she leant down into the sparkling river as she lifted handfuls of cool fresh water to her face while the horse drank next to her, as she looked over at him she slipped and fell in, head over heels. Gasping at the initial shock but then laughing to herself as she laid down to let the cool water rush over her, with every ripple she felt all her woes drift away. She felt so relaxed and experienced the sublime feeling of total liberation as the water skipped and sparkled over her beaming face with the sunlight bouncing and dancing about her like sprites. Jane gave up everything to the stream, it was this act of surrender that changed everything. It was as if her whole body was tingling with life as she laid there like Ophelia but she knew she wanted to live, really live. Her melancholy left her and drifted downstream along with all her other cares. Sitting up in the ebbing sunlight she wound her hair squeezing all the water out, thankfully the barmy summer warmth meant it was easy for her to be naked. She looked about her for her horse who was happily munching nearby. It was a peaceful moment, feeling in tune and at one with nature. She loved the light and the warmth of summer, the flowers, the birds, the trees and the feeling of the soft moss under her feet. Jane absorbed it all, her surroundings felt a part of her and she a part of it. She felt transformed somehow, everything felt and looked so different, more alive, more vibrant. Jane dressed herself slowly as she sat and watched the river flow past until the sky turned the greenish blue of dusk then she climbed upon her horse and rode back on the path to Holton.

♛

With all the angst and desperation had gone, the way home was more of an amble as she slowly plodded back in the evening twilight. The stars were just peeking out and twinkling, everything felt so right in the world.

But, as the road became more familiar and Holton got closer, the air shifted and Jane became aware of a heaviness in her being and all around her, even the trees lost their lustre and the birds had stopped singing. She suddenly felt apprehensive and anxious as if pulled into a completely different reality and she was descending into something dark, had it always felt like this ? She observed the feelings swirling around her in direct contrast to the wonderful feelings she had beside the river.

The sun had long set when Jane finally rode into the yard under the beautiful turquoise and purples of a summer evening, her hair was still damp unlike her spirit. She handed over her horse then bounded up the steps, uncomfortably aware of the coldness and harshness of the place. The house was mostly in darkness with a few candles burning giving just enough light for Jane to find her way when she heard the familiar creak coming from Lady Ursula's drawing room and the shrill sharp tone of her voice.

"Who's there ? Is that you Jane ?"

"Yes it is," said Jane, stopping her step and swirling around to address the direction of Lady Ursula's voice.

"So you've come back have you ? What time do you call this ? We've been half mad with worry, young Simon said you'd taken a horse out by yourself, all day ... again ! You know what I think of that...where are you ? Come in here."

Jane sighed and retraced her steps, pushing open the door to see the old maid puffed up and propped up in her wheelchair by the fire. Covered in her nightcap and blanket, she was, Jane remembered, far too wicked to sleep.

"Here I am Lady Ursula."

"Yes... Well, I'm just glad the children didn't see you going off like that ... on your own ...on horseback ... giving them wild ideas ... completely irresponsible...and dangerous... What if you'd fallen ? Would have taken us days to find you or probably weeks. Simon knew nothing of which way you'd gone, Kathryn laid your place for dinner and the children were disappointed not to see you, we had to make excuses for you. Disgraceful."

Jane felt a twinge of guilt for she loved her children, she was also secretly glad to hear they missed her, for she often thought they had forgotten her altogether.

"Forgive me Lady Ursula."

"Forgive you ? Forgive you ? No, I will never forgive you, this is just one more unnecessary and unfortunate encounter with you ...Jane Ryder. I have had to suffer in silence for years, years. I've watched you running amok, coming and going as you please. If it wasn't for my foolish husband running up debts, you would have never come here. You have never loved my son, nor shown any kind of gratitude for the home and life he gave you, especially as you came here carrying another man's child ! Oh, Yes, we knew, did you think you were fooling me ? I knew that boy was not of my blood from the moment I set eyes on him, I've always known. For the sake of my son I've had to live with your ... despicable secret, clearly it has pained me more than you. I've had to bite my tongue for years, years ! Otherwise you would have only brought further shame and ruin to our family. So no, no I will never forgive you, never !"

Jane flushed with humiliation, she had been discovered and what's more the old hag had known all this time, Jane wanted to say something but she thought better of it, Lady Ursula was on the rampage and there was no point in upsetting her any further.

Jane stood scolded like a child as she listened to the one sided flood of Lady Ursula's well thought out attack, which Jane had to admit was her own fault for giving her so much time in which to think up her viciously well placed words.

Jane saw the fire flickering in her eyes or perhaps it was the fire of rage and hatred she felt towards her daughter in law but this time Jane saw something else, she understood the jealousy underneath. It suddenly all became clear to her how Lady Ursula envied her spirit and wished she'd had an ounce of it herself, she had wasted her entire youth trapped, much like Jane, in a cruel and loveless marriage. Jane now understood that actually they were similar in many ways and for the first time Jane felt a fondness for the old crank, she smiled, really smiled at Lady Ursula, then in one swift move, without saying a word, Jane fell to her knees and kissed the hands of her mother in law. She sat for a moment just looking up at her imagining the young woman she once was and the one she might have been. Lady Ursula who was quite unaccustomed to displays of affection, let alone an act of devotion such as Jane had just given her the grace of, was moved to tears that came straight from the melting of her frozen heart. Together they sat silently holding hands in the firelight.

"Thank you," whispered Jane eventually. "Thank you for loving my son, I never meant to hurt anyone."

For the first time, Lady Ursula looked surprised as if sensing that Jane had seen the parallels between their lives and that Jane clearly held no hatred towards her despite her best efforts to antagonise her.

Slowly, without taking her hands from her, Lady Ursula whispered, "in truth, you saved us in many ways, young Broome is one of them. I have always loved him."

Summer ended abruptly but the change in season was a welcomed one, the summer had been so very hot this year, everyone appreciated the crisper, cooler air and the vibrant red and gold colours of autumn that draped the landscape. The mood at Holton had changed significantly too, Lady Ursula certainly seemed more cordial towards Jane and even made efforts to speak to her and showed genuine interest in her replies. Dinner times became a more pleasant, relaxed affair which everyone enjoyed for the better, especially the children. Lady Ursula was less insistent that they be marched off allowing Jane more time with them, their days still being regimental. All in all there were small but significant changes within the house that Jane was thankful for.

With winter the weather turned harsh much like the puritan regime, icy winds wrapped themselves around the towns, villages and the hearts of men. It seemed to Jane that most people were sick of the war, tired of the senseless fighting, there didn't seem to be any real victors, depending on who was talking of course, for each championed their own side. Jane along with Lady Ursula and the children were largely spared from the awfulness that was ransacking the rest of the country, the walls at Holton being so thick as well as Lady Ursula's cunning. It hadn't occurred to Jane at the time that Lady Ursula was seeking anything other than the prestige of hosting the General's wedding party but since the day she galloped off with the setting sun she was a changed woman with a changed perspective. Lady Ursula, had rather cleverly, unbeknownst to Jane, encouraged Lord Fairfax to suggest her home as a wedding venue, therefore saving it from ruin. Her loyalty had been firmly with the King but this was an opportunity to appease the puritans and save them all, even if they did have the pleasure of footing the bill. This cunning move was missed by Jane but she now saw events very differently. Lady Ursula too had changed and warmed to her daughter in law and the months up to Christmas were pleasant for them all. Jane made more effort with her and there were days before the frost when the two of them would sit silently watching the children play among the last of the roses in the well kept gardens. Yes, it had been astute of Lady Ursula to host that wedding here, rather than disloyal. Sometimes the silence between them brought other images and replayed other events in Jane's mind, when she had believed Lady Ursula to have been unfair or unkind which now showed themselves to be otherwise. Jane always appreciated these revelations as bitterness is such a heavy burden and she was glad to be free of it. She even found herself wheeling Lady Ursula into the house when the rain came much to Kathryn's displeasure as she saw it as strictly her role and up until that day it always had been. Jane did so without even thinking and as they rolled into the house there was an enormous rainbow positively glowing against the dark grey sky.

"Well I never, look," Lady Ursula muttered through her lace bonnet and countless blankets, stretching out her bony finger towards it.

Jane instinctively spun the chair around and in awe, amazed at the colours pulsating across the sky. The children who were behind them with their nanny shrieked in absolute joy at seeing such a miracle. There they stayed in unspoken agreement, that they would all treasure this spectacle until the very last glimmer had gone and the grey clouds had devoured the last rays of sunlight. They were getting soaked through, all except Lady Ursula of course who was well protected from any element. No one seemed to mind getting wet and if anything it only made the day more magical and certainly more memorable. When all the colour had gone and the rain really came in, Kathryn came to whisk Lady Ursula away, she couldn't stand it a moment longer and saw it as her duty to shield Lady Ursula from everything.

"Must you fuss Kathryn, wait …I wish to thank my daughter in law .. leave me."

"But, Lady Ursula you'll catch .."

"There is no danger of me catching anything, I can't even get up !" Lady Ursula cut in before Kathryn could finish, Kathryn instantly let go of the chair, returned her hands to her side and stood silently looking at the floor.

"Jane, I wish to thank you. I haven't said it and it's probably time I did. Thank you, for these wonderful children of yours, my grandchildren, whom as you know I cherish." She looked over adoringly at the children as they were being dried and scuttled away, smiling at them as they passed by giving Jane their towels to dry herself.

"Thank you for staying here with me even though I've never made it easy for you."

Jane was about to say something but Lady Ursula raised her finger.

"And …thank you for being a good wife to my son, he wasn't ready for marriage and well…" She cast her eyes round without focusing on Kathryn who was blushing, her eyes fixed firmly to the floor.

"Well, it's true he didn't deserve you. You are a fine woman Jane, well educated, smart and beautiful, which only drives him mad with envy. I should know for I was jealous too. I envied your spirit, your freedom and yes if I'm honest your beauty but none of that has been wasted Jane you still have a life ahead of you. A life outside these walls, no doubt a great and good one. With every beat of my heart I ask your forgiveness, for I see now, we treated you most unfairly. I do love that son of mine, but alas he's too much like his own father, a drinking, gambling, fool, more's the pity. His father, God rest his soul, was a terrible man, near on gambled away the entire estate which only made him violently angry. Poor Broome suffered and didn't stand a chance with him as his father, he was a cruel man. We were ruined and despairing at what would become of us, when your stepfather came to our aid, in more ways than one. We have so many reasons to be thankful to you but we were ashamed that's the truth of it. I am sorry. I wished things would have been, could have been different for you, for both of you, as you weren't really meant for each other." Kathryn tucked in her chin to hide her smile but then no one was looking at her.

"But I hope with all my heart that you both find the one that is, as my mother used to say, every pot has a lid !"

At that very moment the image of James jumped into Jane's mind as clear as day, it had been so long since she dared to think of him.

Lady Ursula tapped the floor with her cane signalling to Kathryn. "Now come on, quickly now, I'm hungry and ready for dinner." Kathryn promptly jumped into service and in one swift move had turned the wheels of her chair in the direction of Lady Ursula's dressing rooms.

Jane was astounded and quite taken aback by her kind words that had etched themselves forever in her heart, that rainbow really was a miracle.

At dinner everyone was relaxed and in a joyful mood. In Jane's mind it was the best evening she had spent at Holton and every mouthful of the meal tasted more delicious because of it. Jane didn't mention Lady Ursula's earlier speech but then neither did she, it was as if everything she had ever needed to say was said and that was that.

♛

Whether the rain had got through her blankets that day or whether she had just naturally given into the inevitable, it was to be Lady Ursula's last day outside. She rarely made dinner after that and took her meals in her room where she refused visits even from the grandchildren, soon everyone was aware of her frailty and expected the worst, they didn't have to wait long.

Lady Ursula departed this life at the beginning of February 1647 and insisted on a private burial at Holton chancel, according to the ancient common prayer of the old ways, which endeared her further to Jane. She was so very glad they had had some kind of reconciliation and was thankful for the day they shared a rainbow. Her departure sparked Jane's spirit, encouraging her to be more daring. She was glad Lady Ursula would now be as free as she wished to be but her leaving inevitably meant the return of Jane's husband, which filled her with absolute dread.

♛

Jane read the letter then slumped into a chair much like the plumped up bag of feathers that Lady Ursula had become and the thought of that being her future terrified her. Broome was returning. Her children were being encouraged to be happy but Jane on the other hand was feeling sick to her stomach at the thought of seeing her husband, who at the first sniff of war was off like a Jack rabbit, disappearing to the relative safety of Europe. Why couldn't he have just stayed there ? As she reread the letter, she already knew the answer to this. He crept into her dreams, occasionally, but she couldn't do anything about that, other than feel dismayed in the morning to recall strange interactions with the man she wanted to forget. The dreams of James were of a different nature altogether. They had a magic about them, a fantasy of light and colour but as soon as she got close enough to touch him, or hold him she would wake up. Jane looked out through the windows across the gardens and into the distance, she loved absorbing the whole of the horizon and the curves of the landscape. She decided she would take a horse to clear her head, it was after all a fine day. She left the letter on the side as no doubt everyone had already seen it or at least been warned, then strode out to the yard to find a horse.

She was greeted rather timidly by the young man whom she liked and looked after the horses wonderfully but she soon sensed that all was not right.

"Good Morning Simon, I'd like to take .."

Before she could finish she saw him shaking his head and stopped,

"Is everything alright ?" She enquired.

"I'm sorry Miss, not today."

Jane was taken back.

"The horses are all to be rested and groomed Miss, the master is returning and …well he likes everything just so... I've had strict instructions Miss, forgive me ... I'm sorry." He hung his head to the floor embarrassed and certainly uncomfortable at telling the mistress of the house this news.

"But ... that's not for days yet," Jane said kindly, for he was a good lad and she didn't want to make trouble for him.

"Strict instructions Miss, I'm sorry."

"Can I ask who gave you these instructions Simon ? For they certainly have not come from me."

"Kathryn, Miss, she's doing everything to make sure the master has a right welcome on his return. She has his authority."

"Does she ?" said Jane, who was now livid she spun around again taking another deep breath to calm herself. "Very well, it looks like it might rain anyway, not to worry…Good day Simon."

"Good day Miss," he said sheepishly and out of sight.

Jane didn't hear him, more determined than before she took great strides back to the house. She began to feel the constraints of her husband tightening around her, how she hated this feeling of restriction. This simply wouldn't do, who in the hell did she think she is ? Clearly Kathryn was preparing herself to be the lady of the house, no doubt her and Broome would be very happy. Jane stopped herself in her tracks, catching a glimpse of herself in the mirror. 'Who do you think you are ?' She asked herself. 'What have I become ? Well I'm certainly not this, I'm not bitter, why should I care what they do ? I'm not in love with that man and this is not my home.' Jane said out loud to herself.

"Are you alright Miss ?" Came the smug sound of Kathryn, "only I heard you talking and I was …well I was wondering if the master might be home, half hoping he had come early for we are so looking forward to seeing him again."

Jane couldn't believe the gall of the girl.

"I'm sure you are Kathryn," Jane saw her in the mirror and spoke to her through it, without turning round she continued.

"I can see how pleased you are and how busy you've been making the place ready for him. I'm sure he will be delighted. I would like you to send for a coach, I have urgent business in London so I must leave immediately, I will inform the children and I shall pack myself." Jane stood statue still as she watched Kathryn's reaction in the mirror. She looked confused and concerned.

"Of course Madam, I shall call one straight away, does that mean ... if I may be so bold to ask…"

"Oh don't worry Kathryn, I'm sure his lordship will be here at the agreed time and will be all the gladder for my not being here."

Kathryn couldn't hide her joy or the smile of one who enjoyed the business of betrayal. Jane saw it and pitied her, saying under her breath, "You are so welcome to him."

"I'm sorry Miss ?"

"Don't be. My coach if you please Kathryn."

"And when shall I tell the master you will be rejoining us ?" This was too much for Jane the 'us' had tripped and triggered her to the point she knew there was no coming back from.

"Actually, as you are so obviously interested, I'm not sure I will be rejoining you, so you will have absolutely no worries or reason to discuss me, my actions or my whereabouts whatsoever. I'm sure you will have little inclination to do so anyway. I simply don't belong here or in any way to him, I never have. That's why I am so very grateful to you." Jane turned slowly round to face her. Kathryn was now scarlet and fidgeting with her fingers, clearly uncomfortable but at the same time excited by this turn of events.

"I have much to thank you for Kathryn. Firstly for the excellent care you gave Lady Ursula, especially in these last months …you really were very … patient and secondly for keeping and running the house so," Jane looked about her searching for the words that wouldn't expose her venom for the woman. "Efficiently…and lastly but by no means least, I thank you for the attention you give my husband, you really have liberated me, thank God, my spirit and my heart were never really his. I'm thankful for my children of course but other than that I have absolutely no reason, need or want to be incarcerated here a moment longer. I wish you both the very best of luck and pray that you never need it …now, my coach if you please." Jane spoke clearly and sharply and felt so much better for finally speaking the truth and facing up to it.

Kathryn was trembling as if some awful secret had been exposed but she knew as well as Jane that the whole house was fully aware of their extra marital exploits.

"Yes Miss …right away," stuttered Kathryn, without taking her eyes from the floor, feeling as if her head might explode with shame, she curtsied and left Jane to return to herself in the mirror. This time Jane saw a different reflection, she no longer looked contorted or fretful, she saw an air of confidence in herself that she hadn't seen in a long while and it looked good, a sense of satisfaction washed over her as she said aloud. 'Well, I'd better go and pack then.'

♛

With flow and ease Jane bought her effects together. She chose her sturdiest boots and her warmest cloak, she looked through her extensive wardrobe and realised she hated everything anyway. Those stuffy and starched dresses always made her feel uncomfortable so she took the items she felt most relaxed in and left everything else. She looked about her room there really was nothing to be sentimental about, all the gifts from her parents had been swallowed up in the costly running of the estate and had as Jane knew, had been the saviour of it. She then went to the hiding place of the King's cabinet which had remained hidden and untouched since the King placed it in her care. She held it close, remembering that day and how proud she felt to have been entrusted with it and how daring it felt to have had it hidden practically an inch away from the enemy. Packing it in her bag, she took one last look around, sure she was making the right decision, she left her room with a determination never to return to it, closing the door behind her. She could hear the rattle of a coach and horses coming up the drive, Kathryn had wasted no time in sending for one making Jane smile again, all in all this was turning out to be a very uplifting experience. She knocked gently upon the nursery door and matter of factly informed the nanny that she would be leaving and wished to spend a moment alone with her children. Although the nanny was surprised she agreed to Jane's request and brought the children, who had been playing at the other end of the room, then left to busy herself elsewhere.

"Mother," the children bounded over gleefully, then seeing she was dressed for travel her son asked, "Where are you going ?"

"Come here my darlings, let me hold you" Jane crouched to their level and wrapped her arms around them both.

"I'm going to London, to see my friend Elizabeth." She kissed both their heads.

"I am so very bored here, there's nothing for me to do. I may be gone some time, so I want you to be good and keep at your studies and take good care of each other, you'll do that won't you ?"

"Yes Mother," they said together in a confused way.

"When will you be back ?"

"Well, I'm not entirely sure but I don't want you to worry about me, I'll come back soon to squeeze you I promise." Jane held them both tightly.

"All is well my darlings, be kind to nanny and remember me in your prayers, I'll be back before you know it, be brave, be fearless and most of all, have as much fun as you possibly can." Jane looked them both in the eyes and smiled right into their hearts, kissing them both goodbye.

"I love you both very much with all of my heart and I am so very proud of you both."

She whispered her own prayer over their heads, blessing and kissing them again, "now run along my darlings. I love you."

"Yes Mother," they chimed, they were quite used to Jane's absence but were nonetheless slightly bewildered returning to their games at the other end of the room. Her son blew her a kiss and waved as she left which brought tears to her eyes although she didn't let him see, she caught his kiss and blew one back before closing the door. Jane stopped for a moment to compose herself outside the nursery, holding her bag in both hands, she tested her resolve. Taking a deep breath reminding herself that if she didn't want to stay, this was the only course of action open to her. On hearing the children happily back in their games, she confidently took steps towards the staircase that would lead to the front door, her coach and the road out of there. Kathryn was waiting by the outer door, attempting to be out of sight.

"Thank you Kathryn," Jane called loudly letting her know that she had seen her in her hiding place, Kathryn, slightly embarrassed, stepped forward.

"As you instructed Miss, will you be ... alright ?"

"Yes Kathryn, I believe I will, Good bye."

As Jane walked out of the house the clouds parted with the sun pushing everything out of its way in order to shine upon her. Jane felt the warmth upon her skin confirming to her that this was indeed the way. As her Father used to say,, 'the sun always shines when angels travel.'

The coachman jumped down and opened the door offering to take Jane's bag which she declined, insisting it stayed with her. Jane turned and looked up at the nursery half hoping to see her children looking out for her but was glad they were undisturbed by her leaving, she nodded to Kathryn and climbed onboard taking her seat with the coachman closing the door behind her.

"London Miss ?" He enquired.

"Yes please, driver, Westminster."

♛

After being in the back water of Holton for so long, it felt good being back in her childhood home. She loved the busyness of the city and immediately felt the rush of life there. Thanking the coachman was on account so she had nothing to pay but Jane tipped him all the same. He dipped his hat to her as he rolled on to an Inn further up the road. With a smile as wide as the river she made her way to Elizabeth's house, she knew the way and loved the feel of the cobbled stones beneath her feet. She took a sharp turn and a short detour to where her parents used to live, stopping to run her fingers across the old wall where she spent so many happy hours idly watching the world go by. Her parents had long since moved to a far grander house and estate, her stepfather fortunately being still so wealthy. Stopping outside Elizabeth's house she felt unsure as to whether to call round the back or knock on the front door as she wasn't expected. She decided on the latter and firmly tapped the door knocker. She didn't have to wait long, smiling to herself as she heard the unmistakable sound of her friend singing whilst moving the locks and latches aside.

"Well bless my soul and thank the Lord. Oh my goodness, it's you, Jane. Come in, come in" Elizabeth overjoyed at seeing her friend threw her arms around her as Jane burst into tears. Without asking the why or wherefore, Elizabeth bundled her friend into the house and shut the door behind her.

"Oh Lizzy," Jane sniffed.

"Oh, hush dear heart, you can explain later, I just want to look upon your beautiful face. How very, very wonderful to see you, come sit by the fire." Elizabeth's eyes shone a love at her friend that had been missing from Jane's life for so very long. Jane wiped her nose and dried her eyes feeling the relief of being relaxed and welcomed, Elizabeth motioned for her to take the seat next to the fire while she sat opposite still smiling, so very happy to be seeing her friend. It felt like so long since they had been together in Oxford and so much had changed. Elizabeth hadn't much in the way of work these days, she had followed the King as far as she dared, then returned to London and her home. William had thankfully returned after the battle of Nasby and they had lived quietly together since.

"Honestly Jane I could pinch myself, to be sure this isn't a dream, I was thinking of you only yesterday and I'll tell you why. I can hardly believe I've got the chance to tell you myself and in person like this, it's as if God wills it. Oh wait… you're not with child are you ?" Elizabeth stopped herself, remembering Jane's last visit to London was when she was heavily pregnant.

Jane laughed, "No, absolutely not, no man has been near to me."

"Good, in that case I can talk freely as I'm sure you'd like to know."

"Know what ?"

"Well, you'll never believe it but yesterday I was running errands up by the Strand and guess who I happened upon ?"

"I've no idea ?"

"Oh come on I bet you have ?" Elizabeth smiled.

"There can't be anyone here that remembers me."

"But isn't there someone that you remember, a young man ?" Her smile grew wilder as she gently rocked herself, about to burst with the news.

Jane's thoughts escaped her, her mind blank.

"I really don't know," she was thinking of children that might remember her but then the war had stripped so much of the community she knew, especially surrounding the palace.

"Oh come on you can't have forgotten, …handsome ... has a way with words and …with you ?" She laughed.

A flash ripped across Jane's mind and eyes as she sat bolt upright, instantly forgetting her tiredness.

"Did you see... James ?"

"Why yes I did," gushed Elizabeth.

Jane's mind at once transported her back to the night of the rehearsal.

"Really ? Is he ok ? Was he ...I mean ..." Jane couldn't speak, luckily Elizabeth couldn't wait to spill everything she'd been so desperate to share.

"Yes, by all accounts, yes, he's in fine shape, still very handsome and alive, I'm happy to say. I'm sure he must be staying with the rest of those actors, they're all still together but much out of sight and out of work, due to, you know the troubles. He looked dandy though and sharp and he has his hair long now. For a moment, I thought it to be the King himself, they being so similar, have you ever thought that Jane ?" Without giving her time to answer, Elizabeth drew a breath.

"Well, he was with that Inigo Jones, you know the gruff looking chap who did all the buildings for the King and Queen, God bless them, at least, I took it to be him," she thought for a moment then continued.

"They were making their way across the road all animated and that, all theatrical, the pair of them, looked engrossed in something, I dare say they've still got business, anyways both dipped their hats, proper towards me and I knew straight away it was him, no mistake and it made me think of you and I imagined just how happy you'd be to see him and then here you are. What are the chances Jane ? Isn't it good to know he's not taking any part in that crazy madness that's going on out there ? And he's not dead ! In fact Jane, I'm happy to say he looked a picture of health. I remember when you were all wild over him." Elizabeth's eyes sparkled as she saw she had rekindled the memories locked in Jane's heart.

"Yes, I was pretty wild about him, wasn't I ?" She sighed.

"I'd say, you'd talk of nothing else, actually thinking of it Jane, you did nothing else other than follow him round, remember ? Always at the masques you were or sneaking round the rehearsals, remember ? I do, I used to love how you brought it to life for me when I was up to my ears in soap in the laundry, remember ?" Jane smiled as the long forgotten memories and images rushed forward, putting all other thoughts out of her mind and bringing such a feeling of joy with them.

"Yes Lizzy, of course I remember," she giggled. They were soon lost in their childhood memories forgetting the reason why Jane had come or what for, just happy to be in others' company, sharing happier times in the glow of the fire. Elizabeth then made up a bed for them to share and the pair of them climbed in, falling sound asleep, happy and thankful.

Elizabeth had already been up and attended to her morning chores by the time Jane's eyes saw the world or heard it. She awoke blissfully, having slept so well and so comfortably even the bustle of Westminster couldn't wake her. She had the most wonderful dream about James, she was so used to seeing him in her world of sleep. She had walked alongside the river with him and he had said the word, 'US,' and as she had looked into those eyes of his that she remembered so well, she had said it back to him, US !

"Aha ! Good morning to you," sang Elizabeth when Jane finally did join her and her husband at the kitchen table.

"Good Morning, dear heart and to you dear William."

Jane nodded to Elizabeth's husband who was sitting at the top of the table.

He was slightly unsettled at having no explanation as to why Jane was here and sleeping in his house but then Elizabeth herself hadn't asked for one so she couldn't very well offer one to him.

"Madam," he said seriously, Elizabeth picked up on his tone immediately.

"Oh William, no, no, no that won't do, you know very well Jane is my best friend in this world and more like a sister to me so our home is her home. Now …who's for pancakes ?" She smiled at her hungry husband who loved her dearly, he softened and smiled back, letting her know that he was more than ready for breakfast having waited all this time.

Jane smiled a knowing smile at them both and knew intuitively that she ought to explain herself.

"Forgive me Will, I owe you an explanation. I've left, I've left Holton .. the house and the life and I can't go back there Lizzy .. ever." Elizabeth turned round slowly, her eyes wide, her ears even more so.

"Go on Jane, what happened ?"

"He's coming back," Jane saw William's puzzled look and offered further, " Broome, my until now absent husband only he's not coming back for me, thank God, he's taken the maid as his mistress and she's already running the place ... and I just couldn't stand it there a moment longer."

"What of Lady Ursula ?" Enquired Elizabeth, who knew something of the Holton Household.

"She died, that's the only reason he's coming back, no doubt to Lord it up, honestly the very thought of him fills me with dread. When the King needed him, he turned tail and ran, but now ... now his mother is dead and our dear King is in misery, he's returning like some prodigal son to claim what's his and it turns my stomach, it really does but then he always has."

"What of your children Jane ?"

"They are beautiful, happy and well cared for, they won't miss me. They've been kept busy and away from me for years now." Jane sighed.

"For fear they'd catch your wildness ?" winked Elizabeth dishing pancakes into Williams held out plate.

"More than likely, but I'm thankful they're content. Kathryn, who was the maid but is now seen as the mistress of the house has become just as unbearable as him. Honestly they're so suited to each other, like a pot with a lid." She smiled to herself remembering Lady Ursula's words.

"Do you know what she did ?"

"Tell me," said Elizabeth, not a bit concerned or worried for her friend but quite caught up in the drama.

"Kathryn, with Broomes authority apparently, instructed the groom not to let me take a horse out, can you believe it ? I was furious, something inside me snapped. I knew that if I didn't free myself right then and there it would only be a matter of time before I was shackled or confined to some attic space or...or ..."

"Thrown in the river," they both said at once, the girls catching each other's eyes and heartily laughing. Oblivious, William sat back in his chair satisfied, he was a simple creature with simple pleasures, his wife's pancakes was one of them.

"So here I am."

"Thank God, I'm glad to see you and I'm so glad you came here, you are a free spirit Jane, you know you are welcome to stay here as long as you like, this is your home …isn't it William ?"

William, nodded to her in agreement.

"Yours was the first place I could think of to go in such a hurry, I'm so very grateful for this welcome, thank you both so much."

"No need to thank us, your happiness is thanks enough, anyways I've never liked that husband of yours, I'm glad you'll finally be rid of him."

"I can't say I liked him that much either. I hope they'll be very happy together. I expect there'll be some repercussions, he'll be mad that I've robbed him of the chance for him to belittle me with his lord and master act."

"Furious, I'd wager," laughed Elizabeth. "Anyways, this day isn't about him it's about you and you're here, in your home town and I've got the rest of this day to do anything with you, anything you'd like so, what my dear shall we do ?"

Jane's eyes lit up because she knew already what she wanted to do, what she yearned to do and Elizabeth saw it in her straight way.

"Well ..."

"Yes Jane ?"

"I'd quite like to, perhaps look around the palace ?"

At this William sat forward, "No ladies, you'd really not want to be going anywhere near the palace." Jane and Elizabeth swung round and looked straight at him, they could instantly feel the energy drop .

"I dare say it's not the place you once knew Jane, not anymore, not since the army has taken hold of everything. I warn you London, it's a frightful place now, it's edgy and rough. The soldiers of the new model army as they call themselves are not the gentleman you remember walking these streets. These are rough rouges with God, well certainly Cromwell, on their side. It's harsh out there, the friendliness has gone, now all is fearful, terrible business, you dare not speak or be seen even. Best to keep your nose clean, head down and mind your own, they are a law to themselves. I plead with you and especially you Mrs Wheeler, to stay far away from the Palace and anywhere else parliament men might be."

Elizabeth looked at William, feeling his fear for her.

"My dear, sweet husband, I love you so much and I am yours, if that is your wish then that is mine also, you have nothing to fear, we will stay far away from the palace. I don't even think we can rightfully call it that anymore anyways, not since our dear King has left it."

"Ah yes, the King and where might he be these days ? I trust my stepfather is still with him ?"

"Yes, as far as I know Maxwell is still there, thank God and may he have mercy on us all, for things are not looking so good for us, our King or our liberties."

"What do you mean ? How could things have possibly gotten any worse ?"

"Well I'm sorry to say Jane but the King surrendered so we heard, to the Scots, only they were fearful, presumably they thought they were no match for the new model army so they took him prisoner and sold him back to parliament !"

William shook his head in dismay as Jane looked wildly between them not knowing what to think, she'd had no real news since they were together in Oxford, having been so caught up with Lady Ursula and Holton house, it was a total shock to hear such things.

"Sold him ? They sold the King ? I can't believe it ? Don't tell me it was for 30 pieces of silver, as Judas did ?"

"Who knows, but yes I'm sorry to say, they sold him, sold the King to parliament . I'm guessing in the hope that it would bring an end to things, one way or another, everyone's so very tired of it all. I'm just not sure what they expected to happen after that. I'm sure they've had second thoughts about it now, mind you."

"But …What does this mean for His Majesty ?" Jane asked, surprised. "He can't be a prisoner of his own government that makes no sense. What's happening ? We must do something ?"

"What can we do ? It's all been done, half the country is dead, the other half mad with fear, it's a crying shame that it's come to this," said Will, not taking his eyes from the fire.

"Maybe Jane," said Elizabeth slowly, in a rather knowing tone. "You being so well known and connected and now evidently so free, why don't you offer your assistance to the King ? Much like you did in Oxford ? You have such brilliant ideas, you worked everything out, right under their noses, it was all down to you. His Majesty would never have been able to fight as long as he did without your help and that's the truth, why don't you offer some help to him now ? Honestly, Jane you'd be the perfect, wouldn't she William ? You could help His Majesty in this misery."

"You think so ? But how …How could I help ?"

"Well, for starters Jane you already have, you've already proved yourself to be trustworthy and His Majesty, might just need someone he knows he can trust and he knows he can trust you. You're so spirited, you got yourself here without any bother or trouble at all, not a care in the world, it's almost like you're unseen, besides, what were your plans ? Wouldn't you rather be putting your brilliance to better use ? I'm sure His Majesty would be glad of a true and loyal friend right now."

Jane thought carefully for a moment, "but, how ? What could I do ?"

William leaned forward, "Anything and everything, who knows ? If I were you, I'd send a letter to the Queen. Offer her your service, your loyalty ? Seek the Queen's counsel first if you ask me and if you're willing, that is, most of all Jane, if you're sure ? For the country is still at war, remember, you've been mostly shielded from this awful business, so think hard upon the world you'd be throwing yourself into."

"Will," Elizabeth looked at her husband lovingly. "Sometimes, dear husband of mine, you remind me why I married you."

Jane's mind was racing, it felt exciting and seemed like the most obvious and logical next step.

"Yes, William, yes, what a capital idea, I shall write to her."

William nodded then got up to tend the fire.

Jane started to compose the letter in her head.

"Yes, I shall write to her at once, that is a brilliant idea. Nothing would make me feel more worthy right now, than to be of service to our kind and gentle King in his hour of need, nothing." She looked about her for pen and paper, while Elizabeth, having already read her thoughts, was fetching the items from the other room.

Jane rose early the next morning with her mind set upon this new and daring course of action. Elizabeth was right, there could be no one in the whole of London so well connected as her. She had an intricate knowledge of the workings within the palace, from the laundries to the messengers and knew a great many, Lords, Ladies, business men, importers and money lenders. Jane's network extended to guards and a great many defectors, who although now men of parliament, were still kindly towards her enabling her to move deftly throughout the streets of London and beyond. Jane knew exactly where to send and receive messages and knew how to reach the Queen's ear quickly and unnoticed. She had great faith in all those she chose to engage with and place her trust in, handing over the letter to a laundress called Nell, she felt a flurry of excitement. For in that decisive moment, she had changed the course of her life forever and she knew it. She felt so thankful and eager to be of service to the King, the Queen and her beloved England.

Jane spent the days in Westminster with her friends and was happy to be there, far happier than she had ever been at Holton. She would often think of her children and blow them kisses knowing deep down they probably hadn't given her a thought at all, which she had to admit, given the life she was now about to embark upon, was probably for the best. William and Elizabeth, made sure she was comfortable and had everything she could need. They enjoyed meals together and even danced in the kitchen because they could and especially because there had recently been a proclamation banning such activities !

"I ask you, how can anyone ban dancing ?" Sang Elizabeth twirling through her friends arms.

"Moreover, the question is how can the people be going along with such madness ?"

"They've been driven mad Jane, everything they held dear has gone, the people that are left have been frightened for their very lives, they'll go along with anything so long as they are left alone."

"But without any joy or celebration, what's left of their lives ?"

"Work and prayer Jane, work and prayer."

♕

There was a sense of change in the air when Jane awoke, the birds were singing brightly and chirping louder than of late, encouraging Jane to seize the day. She felt sure they were saying a message had come so she dressed quickly and left the house to see if any news had come from France. It was early so the streets were quiet and just coming to life as she stepped across the cobblestones to the place she hoped would have a letter for her. She was wrapped up in her woollen green cloak as there was an early morning chill in the air, the sun not yet quite high enough in the sky to warm her but the crispness of the air gave a spring to her step. She hadn't expected to see anyone, least of all have heard her name.

"Miss Ryder ?" A soft gentle voice called, stopping her in her tracks but as she looked about her she saw no one. She was so sure she had heard it she looked about her more eagerly, still there was no one there, no one at all, she shrugged and carried on her path. A few streets further, upon turning a corner she bumped full force into a man coming the opposite way, sending the papers he was carrying flying into the air around them.

"Forgive me madam," said the man trying to catch the papers cascading around them.

"No, forgive me," said Jane, falling to her knees to help.

Gathering up the fallen notes she stood up and held out the papers she had recovered to the gentleman who was still grasping and collecting them.

"Are you hurt ?" he said, not looking at her or her outstretched hand as he picked up the remaining few falling sheets.

"Good Lord, no," said Jane, "I...I just wasn't looking, I mean … I wasn't expecting to see anyone, it being so early."

"Ah, likewise," said the man putting his papers together and reaching for the ones she held out, there was something so familiar about him.

"Thank you," he said as he looked into her eyes and she recognised him instantly as the man who had filled her thoughts, dreams and heart for all of her life. She gasped, as he smiled at her, "Don't I know you ?"

Jane could feel the blood rushing to her cheeks and was glad her hood covered most of her face for she felt sure it was on fire. She couldn't take her eyes from him or let go of the papers. He was trying to find her eyes under the hood of her cloak as they stood holding on to the papers but he made no effort to take them from her either. After what felt like an eternity Jane relinquished them and placed her hand back under her cloak, unable to take her eyes from him, dumbfounded, she muttered, "Forgive me."

James looked deep into her eyes, unaware he was reaching into her very soul and said joyfully, "My lady, I'm sure I said it first, it is I who seeks your forgiveness… Miss ? …Tell me, have we met ? Haven't I seen you somewhere before ?"

Did he remember her ? Jane quivered all over as if fireworks were rushing through her veins and she felt unsteady in her boots.

His searching eyes suddenly sparked with recognition as he remembered the wild red haired and big eyed girl who was there for every performance, every rehearsal, every masquerade.

"Ah ! Yes, now I remember you, isn't it …Ginny ?" He whispered, half to himself, "that's it little Ginny…Jane Ryder that you isn't it ? I remember you, you were always there, back when days were filled with wonder and charm, I trust that you remember me ?"

"How could I forget you Sir ?" She whimpered, laughing nervously while looking into the eyes that matched her sons.

"My dear lady, you flatter me, I am then, most pleased nay, I am delighted that it was to you I revealed my latest offering, for no one else in this world has seen it," he shuffled his papers and bowed low before her.

"Hot from the press, I hope you enjoyed it ?"

"Every word," smiled Jane, instantly enthralled by him.

"My lady, you are too kind."

Jane was beside herself with glee at his display of chivalry and theatrics, she pulled back her hood revealing her face full of joy. How she wanted to tell him, it had been her, that night of the last rehearsal.

James looked about them as he came in closer to whisper.

"This here is everything I have felt these past years and everything I aspire too. It is called the Triumph of Beauty, for I believe, nay, I know it to be true, that only beauty can save us now. Only beauty can conquer this ugliness that has so contaminated the minds of men and triumph. Therefore I am placing all of my faith in beauty and of course love, for as I am sure you know, they are the purest and strongest of all the forces known to us." There was a certain amount of electricity between them as he looked at Jane, taking her hand to kiss it.

"May I ? Enchanté," he whispered, without taking his eyes from her.

Jane smiled back, unable to speak, for her heart was pounding in her mouth and every part of her was fluttering at his touch.

"It has been so very long, I can't tell you how reaffirming and comforting it is to see one such as yourself who, who remembers," he winked. "And, as luck should have it, we, I mean myself and the company that I keep, will be reading this …this theatrical feast," he said modestly whilst he waved the papers in the air, "Tonight ! And, furthermore I am confident in my thinking that they, as well as I, would be most encouraged and thrilled if you would grace us with your presence and dare I say it with your enthusiasm ?" He searched her eyes, "That is, if such a thing would be pleasing to you ?"

Without hesitation Jane blurted, "yes…it really would .. it would be most pleasing to see you and hear your words, for I do remember, I remember you write so beautifully Mr Shirley."

James was instantly impressed she remembered his name and his work.

"Well then you would do me a great honour, please, please do join us, come to the house of our dear friend Ben, come alone as," he looked about them. "As I am sure you will appreciate, one can't be too careful these days but nonetheless it would be a pleasure to receive you there and you will be welcomed. It's just off the strand, the tall house with the brown beams, go through the iron gates, you can't miss it, we shall, God willing, be starting at… let's say six, there may or may not be supper, but the welcome you can be sure of," he smiled.

Jane could hardly believe her ears or her good fortune.

"Now I must ask you to forgive me further, for I am in great haste but I shall very much look forward to seeing you there, when the clock strikes six … tonight."

"At six o'clock," Jane repeated.

"Perfect, until then, I wish a good day to you, Miss Ryder." He smiled and with a flourishing bow he swanned off swiftly in the direction from which Jane had so recently come, she watched him with such intensity that she almost forgot to breathe.

"Good day," she said after him but mostly to herself as he was too far away to hear. Jane stood in utter amazement at what had just occurred and held on to the hand he had so recently kissed. As if seeing the man of her dreams were not enough, he had recognised her and he had kissed her ! Jane was in such an elevated state it was as if she were floating in the air. What perfect timing, it was nothing short of magical, as if all of life had conspired to bring her this wonderful moment, she felt she might burst with sheer happiness. Jane wrapped her cloak around her unbounded joy, saying over and over to herself the words she had heard from his lips that were just for her. 'Enchantè.' She could hardly control her excitement, how he spoke, how he looked, nothing else filled her mind.

♛

Jane eventually stopped and noticed she had walked far past the way she had intended to go, so she had to turn back. She was immersed in thoughts of James and the moments they had just shared, her dream had come true ! She kept recalling every detail to keep every bit of their meeting at the forefront of her mind, she didn't want to forget a thing ! Every crease of his skin, every line on his lips, it was true she had spent a great deal of her life transfixed upon this man's mouth and there it was moving right in front of her eyes and what's more directing every word from it to her, no one else ! It had been a private performance and she revelled in it, in him, the lashes of his eyes, the way the breeze caught his hair, the way his hand held hers, the fact that she had been between his hand and lips again and once more under his spell. She was elated because this time he was fully aware it was her who he had kissed. Jane had to keep stopping to compose herself and bring herself back to the moment and the task at hand, which she reminded herself was to see if there was a response from the Queen. Try as she might, she couldn't shake James from her mind. Every attempt Jane made to ground herself was useless, she was euphoric, upon a cloud. It took a great deal of determination to reach her destination and even when there she could hardly command her thoughts to anything other than the man who had so recently stepped out of her dreams and kissed her hand.

"Good day Miss. Miss ? ...Jane ?"

As if waking her from a dream, she turned to see the familiar face of the man she sought.

"Oh I'm so sorry, I've a habit of bumping into people today, forgive me Sir."

The man laughed at her flushed and dreamy state.

"Why, goodness me what's happened to you, lass ? You look like Cupid's arrow has struck your heart, got in your eyes and muddled your mind." As indeed she did, so filled with amour it poured from her like liquid sunshine.

"Oh my, forgive me," she repeated in a fluster for she couldn't focus or slow her raging pulse.

"No need for forgiveness, you've done nothing wrong here Miss, now you run along to Nelly, she has news for you, I believe." He nodded and signalled for her to go along the passage which ran alongside a bank of houses facing the river not far from Charing's cross.

"Right, yes thank you." Jittered Jane, taking deep breaths to settle herself and her heart.

Nelly was washerwoman to a great many nobles, mostly parliament men now, although she was a staunch Royalist she kept her views to herself, besides she was never asked for them. This prime position allowed her freedom to move and converse with a great many others in service and her network was huge, far and wide and most of all trusted. She was a round woman, short and stout with a rosy face and wise eyes behind tiny eye glasses with a bonnet pulled tight around her head. She was pleased to see Jane, for she had known both her mother and father well.

"Bless my soul, you have perfect timing dear, news has come not more than an hour ago, here," she bustled about her skirts and pulled out a small neat package with the unmistakable seal of the Queen of England.

"Thank you Nell." Jane bowed, taking the letter from her friend and held it under her cloak while she made small talk. Nell was full of gossip regarding folk Jane didn't know or care for so it made not listening all the easier. Jane smiled and nodded at the appropriate times giving the impression she was attentive but Nell knew she wasn't and cared not, for as is so often the case when airing gossip or problems we listen only to our own voice and tend to work things out for ourselves, which she duly did. Then making her excuses to get back with her work she squeezed Jane and blessed her for she remembered the bonny child she was and had loved her a long time. Jane responded warmly and thanked her heartily for she greatly appreciated everything Nell had achieved so swiftly and easily. With the letter in her hand and her head still very much in the clouds she drifted back to Westminster and her friends.

♛

Jane sat excitedly awaiting Elizabeth and William to come home, it wasn't yet midday and yet so much had happened. When they finally returned Jane thought she might burst so eager was she to share the events of her morning. Elizabeth could see the shine in her eyes and the sparkle about her knowing at once that something magical had happened that day. All ears, she motioned for her husband to join them and she pulled up a chair next to Jane giving her her full and undivided attention.

"Tell me, tell us everything."

"Well…" smiled Jane, as she began to recount every moment of her day with such detail and enthusiasm that Elizabeth and her husband were spellbound.

"And then ?"

"And then, …he invited me to his performance…tonight !"

"Tonight ?" Elizabeth shrieked with delight.

"Yes, this very night at six o'clock."

William, who was not quite as excited as the girls, said quietly, "and what news comes from the Queen ?"

Instantly Jane and Elizabeth snapped out of their excitement. "Oh yes, forgive me Will. I have it here but I wanted to wait for you both before opening it," Jane's eyes darted from Elizabeth to her husband, then to the letter which she picked up and opened by cracking the seal, reading it aloud.

'Dear one, It is as if our prayers have been answered, I am delighted to hear from you. Our friend is on his way from Holland but I pray you will get to your father quicker for his good health and spirits. Mon dieu, there is not a moment to lose !

I know only this,

all's so hushed but unfortunate rumours negate harmony although maybe …

I trust that peace will prevail.

Godspeed.'

Jane looked up into the faces of Elizabeth and her husband.

"What do you think that means , Negate harmony ? Get to your father ?"

"Well I think it means that the Queen trusts you and that you have business in the North," Elizabeth beamed proudly at her friend. "I said so, didn't I ? If anyone can aid the King, I'd have every confidence in you Jane, in fact I'd trust no one else, well apart from you Will, I'd trust you." Jane passed the letter to him, overwhelmed with pride, purpose and the faith that had been placed upon her. "In that case I shall leave in the morning."

"Aye, just as well as you have a rather engaging invitation tonight don't you ?" Said Will as he re-read the Queen's letter.

Jane blushed, "I suppose you could call it that."

"And what would you be calling it then ?" Elizabeth laughed as she made her way to the kitchen to prepare food for them all.

The rest of the day passed quickly as they discussed the best way for Jane to find the King. She decided that in order to travel as light as possible she would leave the King's effects with them. She hid the cabinet in her room deep under the stairs, letting her friends know that she had placed something of value there for safe keeping. Jane was pleased that so much of the day was devoted to her leaving, for it meant she had little time to fret over her evening plans. William suggested she call upon Sir Lewis Dyve, whose name Jane remembered from her childhood. A staunch and proud Royalist who, as of late, was in residence within the Tower, given Jane's family connections, William felt sure of Jane's ability to gain access to him and in all likelihood he would be better informed of the world Jane was about to ride into. Feeling this an opportune time to inform herself and while away some hours, Jane set out for the Tower taking the river path she knew so well.

Jane loved the walk along the riverside, with its tidal waters and noisy seagulls bobbing about on its surface, the River Thames was the gateway to all England. She loved the way the wind whipped up the water sending the sunlight dancing and sparkling across the spring tide. She could clearly see the folk going about the business on the other side and it seemed as far away from a war torn town as one could imagine. It took Jane no time at all to make her way to Tower Hill and the imposing castle that stood before her. Having known her way around since a child, she easily gained access and was politely granted an audience with Sir Lewis. Although he was a prisoner he was treated respectfully and her being the Black Rod's daughter, she was treated similarly. Sir Lewis was a huge mad looking fellow with wild hair and even wilder eyes covered with unruly eyebrows. He had a loud and deep voice, full of confidence and self assurance. His giant hands clasped Jane's as he greeted her like a long lost relative.

"Miss Ryder," he bellowed. "Well I'll be damned," he laughed with such frivolity, one could almost forget he was imprisoned.

"Sir Lewis," Jane offered politely.

Sir Lewis waved away the guard as if he was quite at home and the guard more his servant than attendant."You can go, be gone boy, I have conversations of a personal and family nature that are no concern of yours … away with you."

"Welcome, welcome Miss Ryder, to my rather grand but temporary abode. How delightful to see you. To what do I owe the pleasure of your company ?"

"My Lord, I am saddened to see you confined so."

"Ha," he boomed, "don't be, had I not been in here you would have had a damn sight more trouble in finding me," he laughed, making Jane feel no pity whatsoever.

"Have no fear Madam, I am well tended and cared for and dare I say it ... FED," he shouted over his shoulder to the guard who was still within ear shot.

"I am on my way north to see the King," whispered Jane.

"Are you indeed," said Sir Lewis stroking his unruly beard.

"Yes, I wrote to the Queen, who suggested it. I hope to be of some service to Him, but, I am unsure Sir, as to what I might find and how I can best help ? I was hoping, actually I was told to seek your counsel so this is the main reason this led me to you but may I add, that now that I am here before you, it is thrilling to see you so full of life and vigour whilst …" she looked about her, "Well, while you're in here." She smiled apologetically.

Sir Lewis beamed, "my dear lady, I suffer nothing more than what the King himself endures." He took a deep indignant breath, "damn scoundrels and treachery, that's what you'll find my dear. It pains me to say it but you'll find nothing but damn disloyalty. Keep your wits, for nothing and no one and I mean this, NO ONE is who they seem. These are dark times indeed, this fear that's saturated us all, where did it come from ? Someone is perpetuating this rubbish and benefits from it too, you mark my words. It's poisoned the hearts and minds of men, trust no one .. no one .. not even me," he laughed. "The King has never had an easy time of it, many of the men that took up arms against him bore some grudge because of his father, King James and his quest for peace. Not much money in peacetime, although many were already wealthy men. A great many of them had been in the service of the late Prince and they weren't happy being dismissed and then overlooked like that. They were greedy men who grew resentful and bitter, only too happy to help bring about the downfall of the Stuarts and so they have. In the most barbaric and dishonourable way, not a gentleman amongst them. Now they've been whipped up into a frenzy of revenge and remonstrance, forcing their grievances upon the people under a banner of Godliness ! Godliness, my arse ! They've wiped out everything England was and stood for. There's more to this than meets the eye, I'll tell you that for nothing. They want us to forget ourselves, our Englishness, our celebrations, our joy, the minds of men have been driven mad with bitterness. That Cromwell is a beast and as for that shadow he keeps, that Ireton he has a heart as black as soot and a soul far darker. This 'army' they've gathered wishes nothing but ill upon our dear King and all he stands for. They've cultivated a deep hatred and resentment that stems from nothing more than jealousies and envies. All the while dividing and stirring up the people, aggravating, they won't be happy till they've dragged us all to the gates of hell," he shook his head. "Cromwell is vengeful and that Ireton he stirs and stokes the flames of his fury, forever at his ear."

Jane listened intently, she knew he spoke the truth, thinking back to their wedding, when Ireton was chasing Cromwell about whilst his wanton wife chased after him. She had to stop herself from laughing at the memories as she didn't want to distract Sir Lewis from his divulgence.

"Free born John, " he continued, "John Lilburne, himself a guest within these walls, now he's no Royalist but even he has said to be watchful of those men. He has warned a great many others of the 'Cromwell Ireton consulate' as he calls it, most of parliament supports them only under duress. So fearful are folk, that even those who wanted change, now fear the instability of parliament as this army of Cromwell's challenges even them. It's Tyranny ! Like the very one they say they are saving us from ! Bah ! They're nothing but tyrants and beasts the lot of them, they've bribed or bought those you'd think unshakable, I'm sorry to say. I've seen strong men crumble to the fanatical fear mongering, so be mindful. They use guilt and shame to undermine, it'll turn your stomach and chill your heart but.." Taking her hands and looking deep into her eyes he said, "But, if you feel to go and help the King, then go, he would welcome a friend for he is surrounded by vipers, even those closest to him, I'm ashamed to tell you ... betray him. If, and that is a big IF, if there's any chance of liberating His Majesty from the clutches of those fools, take it, take it and run. Get him as far away from that seditious and deceitful rabble. By any means possible, it is the only way to help him, mark my words there is now no stopping this, this puritanical nonsense that has taken us over. Its momentum is far too strong, this army is a force, a force that will wipe out all in its way and dear heart that's the whole point, to wipe the minds of men so they forget their liberties, shocking but true. Much like the Roman army wouldn't you say, disguised as something else, under another name, another banner, essentially the same brutal force wiping out everything in its path. If you want my advice and I take it you do, it's this, get out of its way ! Get well away and let it grind to a halt itself, for any resistance to it will only bring more force and force they have. So let them have their day as dreary and as dull and as damn ugly as it is, liberate the King and get him well away. Then you can prepare yourself, His Majesty and his children for the swing of the pendulum. Our day will come, our day will come my dear, when this darkness has devoured itself."

Jane sighed sadly, "So what should I do ?"

Sir Lewis smiled, "Have confidence my dear, it seems to me that the Queen already has a certain amount of faith in you. I suggest you do as she instructed and you go to him. You asked her advice did you not ? Then you already have your answer, you need not have come to ask me when you already knew exactly what you must do... could do, besides you'll have no problem with it, I'm sure. After all, have you not just breezed into the Tower of London with absolute ease ? And may I add with a great deal of much needed elegance and grace," he said loudly for the guards benefit but mostly for Janes. "You need to have faith in yourself my lady, you already know the answers you seek, trust in yourself and the beauty you've been blessed with. For that's one thing these puritans can't stand beauty, beauty or joy. Go to him, you'll soon discover who betrays him. In my experience women have an eye for such things and if you can, spirit the King away, it's our only chance, our only chance at holding on to our liberties and dare I say, it might just save his life. We are not of ...this..." Sir Lewis leaned his head towards the guard and boomed over at him, "I said we are not of your world ! ...Just look at them, all their life has been shamed and sucked out of them. May God save the King and keep him safe from all harm, he is so far removed from all the grievances they placed before him. If they are so willing to take down the King of all England, then no man, I tell thee, no man in this land will be safe from them. You must be daring, dare to live ! Dare to believe in your own power ! Dare to be honest and trust in yourself and your God given beauty my dear." He winked.

Jane took a deep breath feeling the enormity of his words and her intentions.

"Thank you Sir."

Sir Lewis smiled broadly as he stood up, taking Jane delicate shoulders in his great big hands.

"Never doubt. My lady I am your servant and from this moment forth your friend," he kissed both her cheeks as the sound of the guards' lacklustre dragging of feet came ever closer to summon Sir Lewis back to his quarters.

"Aha! Cheer up my good fellow," joked Sir Lewis, "you can't be with me all the time. I take it, my dinner is prepared and awaiting my presence below ?"

Jane smiled and said, "may I come again ?"

"I very much hope you do," called Sir Lewis as he was led away, " if I'm still here that is," his bellowing laughter echoed around the walls as he was led down the stairs.

Jane couldn't help but laugh to herself at the spirit of the man who had just held her so tightly. She was positively invigorated by him and their brief conversation and was now more determined than ever to help the King. She politely nodded to the guard that came to escort her out of the Tower and back to the banks of the Thames.

♛

Jane breathed in the invigorating salty spring sea air that came on the waves of the Thames, how she loved London, even the Tower with its long and dark history. Lost in her thoughts and the words of Sir Lewis, Jane looked out over the water and saw fishermen returning home, pulling up their boats and nets, people hauling, shouts from men leaping about the quay side, like the town, every part of the river was teeming with life. She sat down to soak up the view and to gather her thoughts. Was she really about to jump into this world of skullduggery ? She smiled to herself, knowing full well that she was. Deep down she was excited, Jane knew she was about to embark on an adventure and felt sure she would be able to assist the King in some way. Occasional moments of doubt crept in but the respect and loyalty she had for the Royal family never wavered, it was in her bones. Quietly watching the river roll past with all the life upon it, Jane was quite lost in her thoughts and memories and of course her intentions. The most vibrant colours blazed across the evening sky, purples, oranges and red contrasting against the brilliant blue, clouds of dark grey with gold and silver linings rolled by so wonderfully, Jane felt incredibly lucky as if the sun had made this perfect picture show just for her, it was beautiful. 'Beautiful…. Beauty !' As she spoke she reminded herself at once of where she was meant to be. Jane jumped up, confused as to which way to go and all a fluster, James… the invitation…6 o'clock .. and of course the triumph of beauty ! She took a long look up at the sky as the last of the colours drained over the horizon and skipped off in the direction of the Strand.

♛

She deftly danced over the well worn streets, finding the house James had told her of easily, his introductions being so clear. Jane tapped gently upon the door, nothing ? Her heart sank, she had half hoped he would be waiting, desperate to see her. Slightly disappointed she tapped again, nothing, she leaned and nosed about hoping to see or hear someone, taking a step back making sure she had the right place, she suddenly heard footsteps right behind her. She swung around to see a small man in glasses, carrying a whole heap of papers. Jane expected him to come her way so she hid her disappointment.

"Hello ?" She said as he came closer, "I wonder if you'd be so kind, I'm looking for .."

"Waste of time knocking, no one will answer, they'll be in full swing by now .. round the back, this way Miss." Without waiting to see if she was following he took a sharp right down the narrow passage that separated the houses and led Jane round to the back. As they approached Jane could hear voices and imagined there to be a good number of people inside other than just the one man she'd hoped to see. The little man in glasses disappeared under a heavy curtain towards riotous noise and Jane followed with trepidation. She was taken back by the glowing warmth of the place that was busy with people moving in every direction. Jane was overwhelmed at the sight of so many in such good spirits. There was drinking, singing, dancing and a great deal of joy and humour being shared freely and easily with merrymaking of every kind, in every corner. It was as if she had slipped through time and entered another world, all brightly lit and sparkling. It reminded her so much of the masques, the theatre, the productions, that fateful rehearsal and everything that made her heart leap. Her eyes flitted about this feast for the soul and senses she felt very much at home and at ease. She slowly undid her cloak, taking it off as she took daring steps into this other world, a scantily clad beauty with long loose hair swayed past and handed her a drink and a kiss in welcome before swirling off again. Jane was so very happy to be in the company of actors and musicians, it was like a dream or rather the world outside was the dream and it took her no time to forget it. There then came the clinking, tinkling sound of glass being tapped for attention as the Master of Ceremonies who was shamelessly drunk, jovially called for Order. All eyes were soon upon him as the room fell silent.

"My Lords...My Lords, ladies, gentlemen and dare I say it .. puritan ?" He cast a finger about the room as it filled with boos and hisses. "Of course not .. they would have shrivelled up and died at the door, .. but oh ! What a wonderful way to die !" The whole place erupted and roared with laughter.

"Order, order. My Lords, ladies, gentlemen. Tonight I welcome you, the Queens men welcome you, one and all to my most humble abode, where you will be dazzled and delighted and not one bit a frighted .. as we begin a tale of old, brought before you with some daring .. for as you know .. those putrids out there, care not for joy or laughter sharing .., but come with us now, laugh with us and know deep, deep, deep within your heart, for all that is true, all that is really, really real .. and all that we desire, desire most truly .. is the Triumph of peace ... and the Triumph ... of ...Beauty !"

He took a low bow, wobbling and nearly falling from the stool he was perched upon as the whole place erupted with whistles, shouts and calls. Jane couldn't help but join in, caught up in the joyous good feeling swelling all around her. Suddenly all candles were blown out as the troupe appeared above them all to wild applause and made their way round and down a rickety iron staircase that led to a makeshift stage. They took their places and a hush fell about the audience as everyone held their breath in delicious anticipation of what they were about to witness and be part of, all eyes were focused upon them and there at the front, was the man Jane had come to see. Jane could see nothing else, no one else and nor did she want to, every cell of her being was locked upon the vague outline of the man who had invited her. She wanted to get closer but there were far too many people squashed together equally vying for his attention. There really was a magnetic presence around him, even the dim lights seemed to enhance his outline and his physique, so perfectly honed in his slightly opened pink shirt, which only enticed Jane more. He began moving things and adjusting himself, unhurried by the baying crowd, settling himself into his performance. He ran one hand through his hair whilst the other waved his hat, directing players about the stage so that they were all where they were supposed to be. Jane was thankful for the glass of warm beer because her mouth was so dry and her throat was more so, she was so hot and flustered by the sight of him in his element that she thought she might faint. Finally he began, as his words flew about the room, every part of her tingled with the sound of his voice, she hung on his every word, captivated, enchanted and bewitched by him. Hours passed by, it was spectacular, far exceeding anything Jane had ever seen or felt in her whole entire life. It had none of the flashy, expensive and elaborate extravagance that were so much a part of the masques she remembered but this had something else. Something raw, something daring and courageous that reminded Jane of everything she loved about life and of living. The finale was a rapturous euphoric spectacle that wrapped everyone in bliss, hope and beauty. The whole place was bubbling over with joy and enthusiasm. James disappeared under a wave of supporters, well wishers and lovers that wanted to congratulate him, deservedly so, thought Jane. She hoped he had seen her, hoped he knew that she came, hoped he knew how much it meant to her. She was suddenly overcome with guilt as the memory of the last rehearsal took over her mind. Not wanting to embarrass herself or appear desperate she decided to leave the revellers to their revelling, leaving quietly by the same door she came in, drunk upon the events of the evening she smiled and danced herself back all the way back to Westminster.

♛

The next morning Jane was woken early by the sound of birds singing sweetly outside her window. After recollecting all the wonderful events of the night before, she rose beaming and overflowing with sheer bliss. She also had a clear sense of purpose, today was the day she would embark on her journey north to offer her loyalty and service to the King. She heard the clatter and movement from the kitchens below signalling that Elizabeth was awake and there would be someone to tell the tales of her evening too. She bounded down the stairs with such enthusiasm, eager to share all her tales of the evening before.

Elizabeth was equally pleased to see her friend.

"Good Morning," she smiled, as Jane breezed in full excitement.

"Yes it is, isn't it ? What a very good morning and what an amazing night ! Oh Lizzy…I can hardly speak of the wonders that I saw or the sounds that I heard so delightful, so incredible, it was…" with a sigh she dropped herself into the comfortable chair Lizzy had ready for her to fall into, knowing her friend so well she had half expected her to be in a state such as this.

"Tell me all …and don't you leave a thing out, I want to hear everything, I want to know everything… Did you see him ?"

"Of course."

"Did he see you ?"

"Oh Lizzy I hope so, I didn't take my eyes from him …I couldn't. I was transfixed, he spoke such perfect poetry …"

"How was he dressed ?"

"Desirably," Jane laughed. "Everything, everything was a world away from what people are living with out there and a great deal better for it. I saw so many smiling faces and heard so much laughter. It was joyful from beginning to end and I never wanted it to end, I never want it to end. I could listen and gaze upon that man until the end of my days Lizzy. I have never known such feelings as the ones he stirs in me ... still."

Elizabeth sighed for she too wanted to be stirred, awakened like her friend.

Jane delivered a blow by blow account of the evening's entertainment with such enthusiasm that Elizabeth half believed she was there too ! Jane just finished as William joined them.

"Good Morning ladies."

Elizabeth kissed her husband and asked,

"Did we wake you dear ?"

"Why, the shrieks coming from this kitchen would have woken the dead madam," he smiled at them both. "I take it you had an enjoyable evening Jane, it certainly sounded like it, but don't go giving my wife any wild ideas now, I'd be lost without her."

Jane laughed, as Elizabeth smiled at him lovingly.

"And what of your visit to Sir Lewis and the Tower ?" William enquired with a more serious tone.

"I am so very pleased I went to see him, thank you Will. He was in good spirits and sound mind, gave me good advice and you know I really like him, he told me to be careful, which I will, but he supports me and has offered to continue to do so, wherever he may be," she smiled.

"He's a wild one, no wonder you like him Jane, wouldn't surprise me if he hadn't escaped already. And so ?"

"And so, I leave today, this very hour. I have my things, I only wanted to see you to thank you and receive your blessings, then I shall take my leave and be on my way."

"After you've filled my wife's head with fancy I see, no doubt she'll be full of this for weeks."

"As will I," laughed Jane.

"You have our blessing and our love, may God go with you Jane and may you happily return, for we shall keep your room exactly as you've left it, be careful."

"I have nothing to fear," said Jane, "with your love and your blessing and the evening I've just had, I feel I could conquer the world."

With much hugging and tear wiping Jane eventually left her friends and the warmth of their kitchen to step out onto the cold grey streets of Westminster once more. The clouds were heavy with rain and a forceful wind had whipped up as if blowing Jane on her way so she hurried to meet the coach. She made good time and climbed aboard with a polite 'Hello' to the two others who would be travelling alongside her. In no time at all, London was behind her and who knows what would lie ahead. As they rolled along Jane smiled to herself, her thoughts full of the man from her dreams who she had seen so clearly and vividly the night before.

♛

It wasn't long after Jane left that Elizabeth went out to run some errands. Crossing the road she saw a familiar man looking up and down the street, he appeared to be looking for something.

"Aha, my good woman," the man called over to her, catching up with her.

Elizabeth did a double take as she saw his face, instantly recognising him as the man her friend had described to her so perfectly for all these years.

"Yes Sir, how may I help you ?" She answered coyly, unable to take her eyes off him.

"I certainly hope you can," he smiled.

"I was wondering if you could tell me where I might find your friend, Miss Ryder ? Jane, with the red hair ?" He asked hopefully.

Elizabeth smiled and her heart skipped a beat. She was so excited for Jane but then instantly it sank knowing that she was on the coach already.

"Oh no, goodness me, I'm so sorry Sir, you've just missed her."

"Missed her ? How can I have missed her ? I saw her just last night," he nervously laughed as he looked up and down the streets around them.

"Forgive me Sir, but my friend, Jane, she left town this morning, on the coach, not more than an hour ago, she has gone to visit her father… in the north."

"The north !" He exclaimed, " But …"

It was obvious that his heart sank too, he coughed and quickly composed himself.

"May I ask when she will return ? I mean she is coming back isn't she ?"

"Oh yes, yes she is Sir, only I'm not sure when but she most certainly will be returning and when she does she will be staying with me and my husband, over there," she pointed her house out to him so he could see.

"Oh," he sighed. " I had hoped to, oh never mind, thank you." He smiled. "Sir, if we ran, perhaps we could catch up with them ?"

"No, please, don't trouble yourself madam. It was just not meant to be. Maybe another time. Good day to you." He hid his disappointment behind his smile and walked slowly away.

"Who should I tell her came calling Sir ?"

He stopped and turned, "Oh, I wouldn't worry about it, just let her know, that someone was looking for her. Be seeing you." He waved up his hand and was gone.

Elizabeth dared not move as she wanted to remember this moment and relay it to her friend exactly and precisely and she didn't want to forget a thing. James was looking for her and he most definitely had seen her that night ! She could hardly believe the excitement she felt, much to the delight of her husband, Elizabeth would spend every hour of Jane's absence imagining her response to this truly most wonderful news.

Meanwhile, Jane who was oblivious to this turn in events, was sitting watching the world roll by the window recalling all the happenings that had led to her being in this position, which was now uncomfortable. The coach was overstuffed except for the seats which were hard. Jane decided this would be the last time she would travel in such a way and would much rather take a horse herself. It did however give her plenty of time to contemplate her feelings, especially towards James. He was so desirable. When he was surrounded by those people baying for a pound of his flesh Jane was thankful she was at the back of the room, for had she been at the front she would have, no doubt taken hers first and made a fool of herself. He was charming, elegant, well mannered and he spoke beautifully, poetically. As she remembered his mischievous smile, it made her feel quite reckless. But then the further they rattled up the road the more Jane convinced herself that she was stupid, that her wild imaginings were nothing but pure fantasy. Jane then decided the best way to spend the rest of this uncomfortable journey was to batter herself further with unkind thoughts and self pity. She made herself so miserable that even the heavens cried, opening up and causing such a downpour that they all had to seek refuge from it. It amused Jane to think the weather was influenced by her feelings, making a note to think more bright and beautiful thoughts in future, especially when travelling. The Inn was welcoming with a giant roaring fire in one corner and many more tables than there were people, portraying a much grander time in its history. The Innkeeper was a kindly man with a fine moustache and whiskers. Jane took a seat by the fire hoping to burn all her depressive thoughts away. She said James's name into the fire and vowed not to think of him again. "God save the King," she whispered, staring into the flames. She began formulating a plan. She trusted her stepfather's judgment so would seek his counsel first, she would then seek this messenger from the Queen. If it had not been so very serious Jane would have revelled in the drama of it all, as her life had suddenly become very exciting, not only when in the company of actors, damn it ! There was no way in this world she could keep that man from her mind.

The weather soon cleared and the clouds parted much like Jane's thoughts, she was just about to rejoin the coach but stopped herself before she resigned to the uncomfortable seats for the league's ahead. She paid the coachman for the journey thus far and went back to the Inn to ask for a posthorse. Having procured a fine and able mount, she swung her leg up and over him with all the skill of a guardsman, taking the reins firmly, she dug in her heels and spurred him on, soon overtaking the coach and leaving it far behind.

Jane made good passage to Northampton upon calling into another Inn on her way, she discovered that the King and what was left of his court were under parliaments guard and nearby at Althrop or Holdenby, accounts differed. What she was soon certain of was that they were a lot closer than she first thought and thankfully her father was still in the King's company. She thanked the locals for their news and their concerns, for not one of them thought it was a proper place for an unaccompanied lady to be. Her horse, having been well rested and ready, she threw herself upon him and set off in the directions she was given.

Jane approached Holdenby house with trepidation, having ridden so confidently she now was overcome with a mix of nerves and anxiety. She was met by guards at the gatehouse who upon hearing she was the Earl of Dirleton's daughter, her stepfather having been so recently bestowed the honour, she was granted entry easily, without hesitation. Jane's stepfather was delighted, if a little surprised to see her and took her in his arms. Not being under guard but rather in service, James Maxwell had no limitations imposed on him so was at liberty to walk and talk freely with his daughter, although still under the watchful eye of the Parliament men. She told him of her letter from the Queen and he brought her up to speed with the recent twists and turns of fate that had led them to be prisoners. It was a sad tale indeed and James Maxwell had resigned himself to the failure, defeat and collapse of the life he had known. He now wanted nothing more than to be with Jane's mother to live out the rest of their years quietly, in peace.

"I am so very sick and tired of this war and so full of pity for the King, who I fear will be killed before this year is out. Mistrust and betrayal have taken over every aspect of life, everyone, not just the King, is careful, anxious and damn frightened, it is no way to live, no way for a gentleman to live, let alone die. The King's life is under a constant threat, daily there comes some other intrigue or fear mongering, it is shameful that His Majesty should be treated so cruelly, it's unforgivable, truly unforgivable to see him reduced to such an existence." Her stepfather, now seemed an old man, weary, worn and so very tired.

"Father you should go, go and be with Mother, enjoy being an Earl. You've earned it."

He looked at her through his aged and Misty eyes.

"What of your family Jane ? What about Broome ? And the children ?"

Jane sighed. "The children are well, their father provides for them but we all know it is with your money that he does so. I have no place there, I was hoping there to be some way I could be of use here ? Is the King not also our family ? Are we not truly children of the Stuarts ? Having lived so well with them our whole lives, I feel there must be something I could do, you and Mother have devoted your life to them, now I wish to."

"Bless your sweet heart. Darling girl that is so very brave of you, The King I am sure will be charmed, but …You know all is lost Jane ? It is…You must know that, we have no army …we have no …ah lass, we have nothing left. The King bravely barters for his life. I'd fear you would be going to your end."

"If that be the case, know that I shall run towards it, for I have no fear. I believe that everything will work out in favour of the King. However dire it may look to us now."

"That is courageous talk Jane but I don't want you to be naive, you know nothing of this war of the horrors we have seen, I fear for him and now I shall fear for you."

"Your fear will not help us father but with your blessing I would like to stay and do whatever I can to be a good and loyal friend to His Majesty."

"Well, my dear girl that is what he needs the most, he misses his wife and his children terribly, he trusts no one and I don't blame him either for so many of our men have been easily bought. They're selling their very souls now, so ravaged are their minds and hearts, have your wits about you, be as the King and trust no one, no one. I'll take you with me for supper and we shall share our thoughts with His Majesty. If he is in agreement I shall find you a room. Watch your words and pay extra attention to how things are, get a feel for the place. I know you to be a sharp and smart woman, just like your Mother." He smiled.

"The Queen in her reply to me suggests a friend comes from The Hague ? Do you know who this may be ?"

"Aye, he's not here yet, when and if he comes I shall introduce you, there are many agents and servants of the Queen in and around the house, I'm not sure what good they do but they're here all the same."

A bell rang signalling supper.

"Come let us eat, then we shall ask the King who I'm sure will be most pleased to see you, as you know he loves beautiful things and welcomes friends, come now." Maxwell hugged his stepdaughter then led her gracefully across the lawn, to the great glass doors that led through to the dining hall. Holdenby, having so many huge windows, had such a wonderful light airy feel about it. Jane's stepfather continued talking in a hushed tone as they walked.

"There are 120 members of the King's household Jane, acquaint yourself with them all. A great deal of them will already be known to you but some one here among us, betrays the King. Perhaps with your fresh eyes it may be possible to ascertain who." He looked to the floor in disgust. "I trust in your judgement Jane, perhaps you can help us to wheedle them out !" He whispered with the accent of his homeland, checking his attire he opened up the doors to a writing room where the King sat composing letters.

"Maxwell !" The King stood up to welcome them both.

"Ah and how wonderful, you've brought me a visitor. A joy to see you Miss Ryder, please," he invited them to sit.

The King was visibly weary, his hair was turning grey and he appeared slightly nervous, but then that was to be expected. Jane took a seat and at once there was a friendly air, she shared her scant news of London and quietly of her correspondence with the Queen. After a thoughtful silence, Jane playfully offered her services.

"Why of course Miss Ryder, you'd be most welcome here within, my, what are we calling this Maxwell ? Incarceration ? Restriction ? Misery ? It's a far cry from the world we once knew my dear but knowing you loved and remember those finer times, lifts my spirits."

"Oh yes I remember them well, Your Majesty," smiled Jane, once again thinking of James.

They spoke of London and Oxford and laughed a little but Jane could see in her stepfather's eyes great pity for the King and she couldn't help but feel it too, he was so clearly defeated in every way. The King told how he amused himself with bowls, chess and brisk walks in the beautiful gardens but he admitted, without his family by his side he felt dejected and fallen.

♛

With His Majesty's full blessing Jane immersed herself into his household. From the footmen to the laundresses Jane made it her business to befriend them all and they in turn welcomed her. Jane's stepfather filled her in with all the gossip as they took long walks sharing news and views, he valued her fresh perspective and she was keen to know the workings of the place. It was on one of these walks that her stepfather suggested she write to her husband, having not mentioned him before and him being so far from her thoughts, it took her quite by surprise, followed by a flood of guilt for abandoning her children, her stepfather could see this.

"Now, now, Jane, it's not the time to be berating yourself. You are in service to His Majesty, and as such you too will be under observation and no doubt…Suspicions, that's why you should write to him. The letter upon leaving here will most definitely be opened and read, giving you a prime opportunity to direct their thoughts about you."

"Write to Broome ? What will I say ? I mean…he would be furious that I even dared to think of writing to him. He would never answer it."

"Exactly, we wouldn't need him too. It is purely to distract the parliamentarian spies. You could say whatever you want, why not ask him for money ?" He smiled, knowing Broome well.

Jane burst out laughing, "That would make him positively mad."

"In that case why not ask him to send you one hundred pounds ?"

"I just as well ask for three. He would never entertain it anyhow."

"But just think how much fun it will be for you."

"Fun ? It makes me shudder just thinking of him, let alone asking him for anything."

"The spies that open your letter will form their opinions of you by what you write, perhaps tell him you've come to assist me, me being so old, make up some kind of story to throw them off the scent as to why you're really here."

♛

The King for all intents and purposes continued to behave as the ordained King he was. Some saw this as arrogance but it was his sheer determination not to give any authority to the puritan army. He continued as much as he could within their confines as he would have done had he been at Whitehall or Hampton Court. As such his house arrest was cordial with as much joy and celebration as the King could muster, much to his captives annoyance but then he was the King, which no one could deny. There was gossip that the army were unsure as to what they ought to do with their prisoner, allowing the King an advantage in making sure he had every comfort available to him. Jane's father alone knew the sadness that was in his heart for he was still the closest to him. Having observed the whole household for almost five weeks Jane had yet to find any incriminating evidence against anyone. Finally the news that she had waited for came.

♛

There were whispers that the Queen's messenger, William Bosvile, would be arriving from The Hague but Jane was still unaware who he was and had no clear instructions as to how to meet him. The King, having his own intelligence, commanded a carriage ride out to Althrop, a pleasant ride he was used to taking so it raised no suspicions. Jane however felt there was just something odd about this day, an apprehension that she couldn't ignore. Feeling restless, she slipped out to the stables and daringly took a horse that was saddled, setting out to follow the King's carriage. She easily caught up with it but stayed back a comfortable distance so as not to draw attention.

It was a wonderful day for a ride and Jane enjoyed the thrill of being in the saddle. The lanes were a fine example of spring in all her fullness, bursting with life and teeming with birds and butterflies. There seemed nothing a miss so Jane relaxed, taking in more of her surroundings while gently plodding after the carriage, no doubt the King was feeling refreshed and replenished by his ride in the country too. It was only when the carriage approached the little bridge that crossed the river that things changed. Up until then it had been a quaint little jaunt with no one on the road. Now, in the middle of nowhere a man had appeared by the river side. Jane from her position had a clear view of both sides of the river and the King's carriage. The guards who were usually relaxed and affable, were now alert and expectant, Jane having lived amongst them these past weeks, instinctively knew something wasn't quite right. She dismounted, tied up her horse and crept closer, luckily there was a good amount of cover. She couldn't quite hear what was being said but she could tell from the way they were talking that something was wrong, the guards were expecting something, something about the man in the river. Watching from afar Jane could see that a situation was about to unfold way before the carriage even came to a halt. The horses slowed and stopped before the man in the river even acknowledged them. Jane looked on nervously, was this an ambush ? Was the King about to be assassinated ? Something wasn't right, her breath became staggered as she crept as close as she dared, her eyes darting about watching the events unfold. Even checking behind as a paranoia swept over her, she tried to calm herself, to sharpen her focus. There didn't seem to be anyone other than this fisherman who was now upon his feet and talking to the coachman. Jane couldn't hear what was being said but she could feel a foreboding sense of fear. The guards were getting ready for something confirming to Jane that this was an expected event. The fisherman still speaking with the coachman with his hands in the air made steps towards the carriage where the King had clearly asked for the door to be opened as a footman jumped down and opened the door out of which the King then appeared. The King with cane in hand stepped down from the carriage and greeted the fisherman who fell to the floor. Jane was transfixed, how she wished she could hear. The King and the fisherman, whose face was still on the floor, were feet apart but clearly in conversation. The guards began to dismount and surrounded His Majesty, who was clearly unafraid as he held out his hand. The fisherman lifted his head, rising slowly with his eyes fixed upon the King. Whilst still on his knees he reached for the King's hand but was then quite suddenly pounced upon ! Two of the guards pressed him back down to the floor while the King recoiled in disgust. They swiftly bundled the poor fellow whose screams of unhand me, Jane could hear. He certainly didn't seem like an assassin, but it was still unclear just what was happening, the fisherman was fiercely apprehended, and thrown on the back of the carriage while the King was briskly forced into it. In what seemed like no time at all the carriage was turned around and now at a much faster pace made its way back whence it came. Jane was stunned, had she just witnessed an attempt upon the King's life ? Jane's eyes were still fixed upon the bridge and the river bank, she waited a moment to see if any others would reveal themselves but no one came. Once the rattle of carriage and the pounding of hooves had dissolved into the distance, all was still and as peaceful as it had been before. Jane was bewildered, she crept back through the brush and cover of trees to where her horse was tethered, unsure what she had witnessed. It made no sense, she replayed the whole scenario in her mind again and again as she climbed her mount, taking the reins she patted his head and turned him back the way they had come. Kicking him into life they took great strides and easily overtook the King's carriage. Jane arrived back in plenty of time to stable the horse and make her way back to the kitchen where she was meant to be that day. She put on an apron and made herself busy picking things up and moving around in such a way that no one noticed her absence. The familiar sound of the carriage and horses were overpowered by the shouts of the guard which sent everyone into a state of alarm. All at once there was an uproar of utter confusion. Jane along with two other girls from the kitchens made their way up the stairs to see what all the fuss was about. Jane, being taller than the other two, stood behind them seeing just as well. The King was escorted from the carriage in a rather hasty way, clearly not one of concern Jane thought. The poor unfortunate fisherman was afforded even less respect and was heavily handed and pushed into one of the rooms being used as an office.

It didn't take long for the gossip and whispers to reach them, apparently he was a spy who was caught passing letters to the King. Jane who had witnessed the event knew this to be untrue, he hadn't passed the King anything, he hadn't gotten that close, yet if that had indeed been his intention, how did they know ? There was no mention of any threat or assassin attempts or any concern for the King's person. Jane was suspicious.

♛

A hush fell over the house as the air settled, messengers were quickly sent to London and elsewhere, to Cromwell and Ireton certainly. The guard was ramped up and quite suddenly everything changed. The relaxed atmosphere was extinguished and one of bewilderment and paranoia, much as Jane had felt earlier, fell upon them all. The kitchen was a hive of suspicion, opinion and discussion. It soon became apparent that the fisherman was none other than the Queen's messenger Major Bosvile, who did indeed intend to pass a message to His Majesty from the Queen but was caught red handed ! Jane saw that he was expected by all parties and apprehended well before the King had a chance to accept, let alone read this letter from his wife. Jane was crestfallen when she heard this news and discovered who he was. How heartbreaking that once again the King's private correspondence with his wife had been trifled with. She could only imagine how devastated the King himself must have felt. Thankfully the contents of the letter were never divulged, certainly not to people of the house because the last time the King's letters were intercepted, they were exposed in a most shameful manner.

♛

No one saw the King for days after this, he took his meals in the study and no longer ventured outside. Jane pondered these events a lot. It was clearly a set up, the King had been betrayed. Jane's stepfather was right on all counts, someone close to the King was the culprit, but who ? Very few people knew who the Queen's messenger was, let alone when he would arrive or where he would be. It occurred to Jane that only a very few of the King's more intimate household could have known, which narrowed the net. For one thing was certain to Jane, having viewed the whole scenario, she knew the guards were expecting him. The idea that someone that close to the King could have betrayed him upset her greatly and she became more determined to coax this rat out. Jane's mind whirled in many circles of intrigue. The King was put under a closer guard and the whole house became somewhat shifty and nervous. Jane saw very little of His Majesty but when she did he was fretful and jumpy, lost in his thoughts and clearly very alone. Jane wanted to discuss these events with someone but trusting no one at Holdenby, she made excuses to visit London and early the next day Jane made her way to the stables, finding a horse to take her back to Westminster.

Elizabeth, who was not expecting her friend, was delighted to see her, flinging her arms around her. "Jane, thank God, how wonderful to be seeing you come in and tell me everything." Jane was only too happy to oblige.

Jane fell into the comfortable chair in Elizabeth's kitchen. "I bring no good news, it's true the King is again betrayed. I needed to think, to get away and most of all to talk with you and Will as I don't know what to do. It's all so strange, to see His Majesty this way, kept like a prisoner. The Queen's messenger came, eventually, but he was quickly arrested. Someone close to the King must have known who and where this messenger was. I saw it all, it was a set up. As usual they've put their spin on it saying he was caught red handed, but I saw it all Lizzy and that's not what happened at all. Someone obviously wished to intervene, to stop the King getting this message from his wife. Heart breaking isn't it ? And there's not a soul I can discuss this with, my step father retired weeks ago. I fear I'm not being as much help as I'd hoped."

Jane slumped further back into the chair and sighed, she tried hard not to give in to the sense of helplessness that was all pervasive as it didn't align with her true nature.

"Hmmm," pondered Elizabeth, returning to her business in the kitchen. "You suspect someone very close to the King ?" She called over her shoulder.

"Well, yes and no, I mean it must have been someone telling the guards as they were so prepared, but who is anyone's guess, everyone is so …friendly, but then I suppose that's the nature of betrayal."

"And that's why you are there, to get another perspective, to look in from without, a wider view. I've always found the best way to catch a rat is to trap it." Elizabeth winked at her friend.

"I knew you would know what to do," Jane smiled, taking the hot bowl of soup Elizabeth gave her.

"Together we will, but for now be easy, feast and sleep and we shall reconvene on the morrow, for I find all the best solutions come to me whilst I sleep, don't you Jane ? Besides you look like you need a good rest, all that riding and running about must be so very tiring but no doubt very exciting ?" She smiled for they were both born with a sense of fun and adventure that thankfully neither of them had lost.

The comfort of the soup, the fire and her good friend lulled Jane into a state of peace and for the first time in a long time she felt relaxed. Knowing her friend spoke wisely, she heaved herself out of the chair. Her body now felt stiff and tired as she made her way to her room which was just as she had left it. It made her smile as she closed the door, undressing in silence before she fell onto the bed and into a deep sleep.

♛

Elizabeth's kitchen was cosy and centred around the fire. The large table dominated the room, leaving just enough space to squeeze around. There was an old feathered, horse haired chair that was set next to the fire which was Jane's favourite as well as Elizabeth's husband's, but when Jane visited it was always left empty for her. Jane awoke to the familiar sound of Elizabeth clanking round the kitchen which put a huge smile on her face and not just because this meant breakfast. She jumped up still yawning and made her way downstairs.

"Aha ! Good Morning dearest, have a seat, William and I have been up since first light, haven't we Will ?"

"With what ?" Jane yawned, looking between Elizabeth and her husband who sat as he did when Jane was there, at the head of the table.

"You're not ill are you ?" She asked, taking a seat to his right facing Elizabeth who never sat, preferring to bustle about.

"Heavens no we both are well, more well than we've ever been, isn't that right Will ? And before you ask, no I'm not with child." she smiled. "Tell her Will."

"We've been thinking about this betrayal business that bothers you and whilst it's nothing new for His Majesty, it's none the less beastly when you experience it first hand like you have. From what Lizzy told me, it seems to me .."

"Him being a man," Elizabeth interrupted,

"Wife, will you let me finish ?"

"Yes of course dear heart, forgive me." Elizabeth breezed past, kissing her husband as she went.

"We were thinking Jane that you ought to lay a cunning trap to catch the snake," William continued.

"Snake ? I thought a rat, but that's exactly what I said, wasn't it Jane ? A trap.."

William gave his wife a hard stare, "There we agree my dear."

Elizabeth playfully put her finger to her lips signalling to her husband that she would interrupt no further.

William sat up straighter, adjusted himself and continued,

"Lizzy tells me that you feel the business with Queen's messenger was a set up ? Then what could the letter have revealed, so obviously coming from the Queen, what would be so important she would send her advisor in disguise like that ? What did she want the King to know? Or perhaps she was fully aware that one of his camp betrayed him or was about to ? Perhaps she knows who this someone is ? Strange how nothing more has been said about the letter when last time they took great pleasure in printing them ! Has any of the household spent any time with the Queen of late ? Pull the net in tighter and focus only on those who are in the King's immediate company."

Jane sat up as a scurry of cats ran under the table and weaved their way between her bare feet and the flagstone floors as William continued.

"So here's an idea, find someone loyal, someone you could trust ?" All three of them sighed. "I know, I know they may be few and far between but ... there must be someone, but not of the household, who would be willing to act as a decoy of sorts ? You must know of someone Jane ? Then set them with a blank letter, tell only the ones whom you suspect that this person has news they wish to pass to the King. Tell no one else. Ask this trusted soul, to act as if they would attempt to pass the King this blank paper. They will undoubtedly be caught but the paper being blank means they will be in no terrible danger but the traitor will have revealed themselves."

There was a moment of absolute silence around the three of them in that cosy kitchen. Each of them deep in their own thoughts, William let out a sigh and rose to his feet, "it's just an idea but it is an idea at least." Picking up his hat he bowed to Jane and gave his wife a kiss before making his way out the door.

Elizabeth poured out two bowls of hot oats and cut some bread as she sat with Jane at the table.

"It pains me to say it, but what then ? You may well discover who betrayed the King this week but what then ? What difference will it make ? Just another traitor. They seem to be coming thick and fast these scoundrels. I have to tell you, there's talk Jane. God awful whispers that Cromwell plans to kill the King, that he wants the crown for himself, he's already taken up residence in the palace, you know."

"That's treason !" Jane said with a start.

"Aye it is, but that's the gossip round here, supposedly that's what that Cromwell and that rat he keeps about him are plotting."

"Ireton ?" Jane offered.

"Aye, some snivelling fellow, has a demented look about him, always at Cromwell's ear, you ought to see them, parading around here. It's like they wish to clear our minds of all happiness, would you believe it now they want to cancel Easter and Christmas ? Cancel Christmas ! I ask you. They've already stopped the dancing and the merrymaking, what more do they want to take away ? It's no wonder that Cromwells so mad and miserable, him trying to be all pure and pious while them girls of his are all wild and lusty, it's hilarious ! Of course he's got no eyes to see what's going on in his own house, under his nose, and that boy of his is nothing but a wastrel, we've all been shortchanged I'll tell you, with new restrictions and new taxes ! It's a sad thing to see, all the while our King is a prisoner, worse he's their prisoner, while Cromwell sleeps in the King's bed ! May God have mercy upon us, the world has gone mad and I can't see this ending well, however much I pray for him."

"Then dear heart, we must double our efforts and change that ending," smiled Jane.

Elizabeth smiled at her friend who always managed to make even the worst of situations seem exciting, her eyes perked up.

"Yes," Jane went on, "I should return to Holdenby and try or at least suggest this plan you've thought up. It might just work, besides we don't have any other ideas and at least it would be doing something. Yes, I should go back." Jane got up dusting off the crumbs of her bread from her skirts.

"I trust you will find them and I hope it brings you all some comfort at least. You'll all be able to sleep better knowing you've one less scoundrel about you I'm sure. Well Godspeed dear heart …Oh but wait, Jane oh my goodness me, how could I forget. I have news that far eclipses all this nonsense, something wonderful happened when you left," Elizabeth smiled. "You might want to sit yourself back down. The day you left, well, someone came looking for you."

"Looking for me ? Who ?"

"A man, a handsome one, all theatrical and dandy."

Jane's eyes and smile were brimming over, "Really ? James ? What did he say ? What did he want ? Tell me... tell me everything."

"Well obviously he wanted to see you silly. He asked if I knew you and I said yes but that you'd just left not more than an hour before, I said I'd run after you and I would have done but in truth I'd have never have caught you up. He was so upset you weren't here, said he'd seen you the night before so how could this be ? Then, he just asked me to tell you that 'someone came looking for you' those were his exact words. Someone came looking for you, then he wandered off, in a dream, if you ask me he looked mighty disappointed at having missed you."

"No ! Did he really ? Oh I can't believe it, James was here, looking for me ? But, oh Lizzy now I shall be in a dream. It feels as if my heart might burst. I wonder why he was looking for me ?" Jane dissolved into bliss as she blushed and fawned like a child.

"Well you can believe it because I saw him with my own eyes and heard him with my own ears. He most certainly was looking for you and it was most definitely him. I knew it to be him straight away, you described him so well, I would be able to spot him a mile off. I can see now what you see in him, he was charming, a real gentleman but I could also tell that he has a wildness, an untamed beauty about him."

"I think that's what beguiles me so," giggled Jane.

"Probably a philanderer too mind you, probably a string of women behind him."

"Oh Lizzy."

"Well with looks like that and all that flair, he's bound to break hearts isn't he ? Just trying to keep your feet on the ground Jane, I wouldn't want him to toy with your heart, with your feelings... again."

"Oh but Lizzy, he sets my heart on fire, he makes me want to be toyed with."

"Jane !" Elizabeth shrieked as they both fell about in girlish giggles.

"I'm not surprised in the slightest, you were right about how handsome he is. I'm just saying, he's sure to have toyed and broken the hearts of many other star struck women and girls, I mean you can be sure of it. Only got to look at him," Elizabeth raised her eyebrows, "probably has a string of children behind him too."

Jane's thoughts immediately sprang to her own children. "Oh ... yes children." She replied sadly.

"Oh I'm sorry Jane, I didn't mean to, I should think before I speak." Elizabeth could see how she had directed the thoughts of her friend and taken all the excitement out of the air. She hadn't intended to cause her any upset.

"I meant him not you, not your children, ah there's no way out of this there, I'm so sorry I mentioned children."

"It's alright Lizzy, it's more my guilty thinking than yours. I should make efforts to call on them en route to Holdenby, I got so caught up in the King's misery I forgot my own. It's not like I really forgot, but as I know them to be safe and well. I .. well I ..." she hung her head as tears welled in her eyes, Elizabeth crossed the kitchen to wrap her arms around her friend.

"Sweetheart those dear children are best out of all this and are thankfully safe and far from it all because of you. It's a brave and daring thing that you do and no one else could do it, no one else would do it. One day they will be very proud of you and all you've done for the King," she whispered. "And that man, the one you've loved your whole life, he knows full well who you are and he hasn't forgotten about you." Elizabeth wiped away her tears.

"I'm so glad you spoke with him, charming isn't he ?" Jane sniffed. "I'm so happy ... and surprised that James was actually looking for me ? Ah ! Why are these joyful feelings so scary ? I will go now because I won't be able to sit still and you'll get no sense out of me. Pray for your plan to work in the King's favour. I pray that I will be seeing you very soon and please let us pray that James comes back. Thank you my love, thank you, for everything." Kissing her friend's cheek and taking one last look at her, Jane smiled and turned out of the door onto the streets of Westminster as they chimed "God save the King".

Jane made her way out to the stables where she had rested her horse. She strode unseen through the people and streets she knew so well, past the old wall where she would sit and wait for her father, instinctively running her hand across it as if reaching out for those memories. She turned down to Scots yard, making her way past to the laundries which were just before the stables. She loved the convenience of her father and stepfather still being so highly respected and remembered, especially when she needed horses or stables. She thanked the boys before swinging her legs around her mount, there was nothing she enjoyed more than having her hands on the reins and her seat in the saddle, turning her horse out towards the Oxford road she kicked him into step. Jane was excited to be seeing her children but she was beyond thrilled to know that James had been looking for her, she couldn't help but smile and laugh to herself all the way back to her former home, Holton House.

Time is so peculiar and Jane's perceptions of it were in complete disarray. Even when she and her horse rested, time passed like a dream for all of her thoughts were focused fully upon James. She imagined all the things she might say to him and all the ways she would look at him. So many scenarios circled around her mind, she was near dizzy. Without really realising how she'd got there Jane had arrived at the large gloomy and imposing gates of Holton House, her marital home. She had no recollection of how she came to be here so swiftly and looked back down the lane to see the long and winding road she had missed. Shaking herself into the moment Jane resolved to be more vigilant. Tying her horse out of sight of the main gates, she made her way along the servants path which was by far the prettiest. It ran along the riverside which was brimming with butterflies and birds dipping in and out of the water and branches. The mighty willows that lined the path were swaying in the breeze and everything was bursting with beauty and life. As she approached the back entrance to the house gardens, Jane could hear voices, children's voices, the shrieking and crying out in delight. Her heart lifted as she picked up her pace to gain sight of them. She peered through the hedge and saw her two beautiful children running and skipping. It was such a perfect picture, the summer sun was shining upon them and the pair of them were happily playing, beaming with joy. Jane smiled in contentment, for seeing her children brought a swell of such wonderful feelings, until the thunderous booming voice of her husband jolted her out of her whimsical observations and made the children stop and stand to attention like little soldiers. It broke Jane's heart and her peace as she shuddered at the sight of him. There he was, the master of the house, striding across the lawns shouting and belittling some poor boy and right behind him like a little puppy dog, was Kathryn. Jane shrunk back, there was no sense in her exposing herself as this was certainly not the moment to do so. Broome wild with rage repeatedly struck the poor fellow while shouting furiously, Kathryn thankfully took the children and led them away. It definitely was not the time to breeze back into their lives. The poor fellow apologising over and over, limped away as Broome, all puffed up and red faced went back to the house. Silence, in an instant everything had changed, no laughter, no joy, no life. All returned to exactly as she remembered it, depressing, dark and dismal. Jane walked sadly back to her horse, disappointed she hadn't had the chance to hold her children or tell them how much she adored them, but at the same time she was so relieved to be free of that life and far away from it. She sat by the river side, in the blissful balmy summer sunshine watching the bees flitting about their business and all the life teeming around her as the water trickled its way out to sea. She comforted herself knowing that her children seemed happy and apparently not missing her at all. Had she really hoped to just wade into their lives, after all this time and expect a welcome ? Jane nodded to herself, for she felt sure that her children would have given her one but her husband and Kathryn, not so much, a feeling of despair and confusion came over her. Throwing a stone into the water she gathered her thoughts and decided to come back a different time, more announced and expected. Not today, the mere sight of that man had given her chills and filled her with dread, she couldn't shake off the heaviness. Jane was relieved that it was Kathryn who now had the pleasure of being at Broome's side, thanking God and all that was holy, that it wasn't her. Taking one last look at the water's edge, Jane dipped under the blossom and threw herself on her horse, riding in the direction of Holdenby Manor, to implement the plan that she hoped would expose a traitor and may even save the King's life.

The road to Holdenby was agonising and nothing like the swift and easy ride she had had to Holton. It was a jagged journey with stops and starts, inspections, hold ups and every delay possible. Jane was annoyed, not only had her impulse visit to spy on her children been a total disaster but so had every turn since then. It was exhausting. So much so that Jane rested her horse and took a coach for the final stage of her journey to give her a chance to gather her thoughts and free herself from the uncomfortable feelings that had since hampered her day. It was a mistake, she realised to rush off to her children like that and it was horrible to see her husband. Holton held nothing for her but in all honesty what was she expecting ? Jane gazed out of the window of the carriage as it wound round the lanes to where she would alight. It was still a long way from Holdenby but she was forlorn, heavy with thought and regrets and hoped the walk would shake the confusion and despondency from her.

Jane hardly noticed the beauty of the Northamptonshire countryside, she felt wretched, completely off key, awkward and itchy. As she came upon the house, it seemed as if everything had changed. The guards were doubled and more intense, it was only because a captain recognised her that she was able to enter the grounds at all, despite having all the proper papers. Her resolve returned, for she knew that nothing could be accomplished with such a down trodden demeanour. She took a deep breath before turning the door that led through to where she thought the King would be. He wasn't. The army had moved him to somewhere more secure apparently but Jane knew full well that this was a tactic to unsettle him and it usually worked. She made her way to the staff's quarters hanging up her cloak and taking an apron to set about busying herself. Washing her hands in the sink she looked out over the beautiful manicured grounds where army men were marching oblivious to the beauty around them, just as she had been earlier.

"Aha, hello Jane, so you came back, you found good news I trust ? Be a dear and help us with the supper, there's more mouths to feed, as you can see." Said the cook pointing out of the windows. "Seeing as you're already at the sink, wash those would you and pray we have enough," winking she added, "we always do, God provides."

The kitchen had become suddenly busy without Jane even noticing she was so lost in her thoughts and up to her elbows in vegetables.

"Ah, Mr Firebrace Sir .. may I have a moment ?" Jane called out as she hastily wiped her hands on her aprons. Henry Firebrace of the King's chamber was a parliamentarian with a cavalier heart. He had known Jane's stepfather well and was always kind to her.

"Of course," he replied, turning back.

"I wish to speak with His Majesty ... if I may ?"

"Aye, seeing as it's you, you may, he'd be glad to have a visitor I'm sure, if you come this evening it'll be me on duty so I can give you a little more ... privacy," he added quietly.

"Thank you Henry I'd be glad to, I shall ask the cook if I am to bring his dinner but if not I shall come directly after."

"Till then Miss Ryder." He nodded, turning and waving a hand up to cook as he left.

♛

Jane was the last in the row of maids that took the dinner trays along the narrow corridors and up countless stairs to His Majesty's rooms. He had been moved to the very top of the house so no longer had the luxury of space or the light he had been used to. The girls tiptoed silently in single file until at last arriving at the King's quarters, a guard sat idle outside and he was given a bowl from the first maid, who then knocked upon the door. It was Firebrace who opened it and allowed them all in. The room was quite a bit smaller than Jane had expected and mostly in the attic with low beams and even smaller windows, there was barely room for anything let alone the King. The girls set down their trays, curtsied and promptly left, until it was Jane's turn, Firebrace said in a loud voice which he in all honesty couldn't help for he was a giant of a man. "Miss, the King's visits are to be an absolute minimum, so I would ask you to stay so as to return these trays 'ere to the kitchen." Jane looked up to see him wink back at her.

"As you wish Sir," Jane replied, setting her tray upon the table. Jane couldn't help but pity the King for this was no place for him, cooped up like this. Jane looked out through the very small window in front of her and got a birds eye view of the beautiful rolling hills and tree tops. It was then a door closed behind her and Jane became aware of His Majesty's presence, she swung round nearly knocking a glass to the floor. Jane had been taken aback by the room but she was positively shocked at the sight of the King.

With her eyes to the floor she did a deep curtsy and tried all she could to keep herself from crying.

"Miss Ryder, how charmed I am that you have come to visit me and even more so that you are still in my service. I am truly most thankful to know I have a friend about me. Please, won't you sit and take sup with me ?"

Jane smiled broadly for she was indeed honoured by the King's familiarity with her.

"Forgive me Sire but I suppose, as a kitchen maid it would be improper for me to..?"

"Nonsense, I ask you as your King. I am still the King aren't I ?" He enquired softly.

"Indeed you are Sire," replied Jane firmly.

"Good, then please take a seat, you would do me a great honour, it is so tiresome always eating alone, I would like it very much if you were to stay, I'm sure Firebrace has no concerns, do you Henry ?"

"No Sir, I do not."

"That's settled then." The King waved his cane signalling to Firebrace to pull out a chair for Jane and he happily did so.

"You may be here in service Miss Ryder but you and your whole family are friends and have always been dear to our heart, now let's see what delights we have here."

Jane was most amused thinking of the gossip that would be flying around the kitchen, let alone amongst the guards, which in some way soothed her sadness at seeing the King so defeated. Although he tried to hide it, he looked tired and hollow, his face drawn, a shadow of the majestic man Jane knew him to be.

Firebrace poured wine for them all and sat back to eat his food while Jane and the King sat silently at the table looking out across the world, his Kingdom.

"Yes, a bird's eye view, albeit a caged one," said the King as if answering Jane's thoughts. Firebrace brought his empty bowl and placed it upon the tray before leaving the room. Jane, aware that Firebrace had afforded them a few moments of privacy, sat up right and made straight for the King's ear.

"Your Majesty, I have reason to believe as you must, that it's someone close to you that betrays you."

The King shot her a glance and whispered in a startled tone, "Firebrace ?"

"No I don't think so, but I have a plan to discover who."

"You do ?"

"Yes, is there anyone, anyone who would be brave enough, daring enough, to pass you a note, in exactly the same way as the Queen's messenger hoped too ? Only this time it will be a blank piece of paper, therefore they would be in no actual danger but it could reveal to us who if we tell only those we suspect of our plan. Is there anyone you suspect sire ?"

The King looked sorrowfully at Jane saying, "If not all, most."

Jane was so saddened by this.

"Well, Your Majesty, I am boldly asking you to trust me."

"Miss Ryder, I trust you with my life and all my worldly goods," he added, a nod to the cabinet he had entrusted her with in Oxford.

"Which I assure you is still safely hidden in Westminster Sire, at the home of my dear friend, Elizabeth and her husband William who are as you may recall trustworthy and loyal. Actually this plan was their idea, we wish to help you find the one that betrays you."

The King laughed in a hopeless way and said, "unfortunately my dear it seems that all of England and Scotland are against me."

"That is simply not true, Your Majesty you have much loyal support but clearly someone here informed parliament of the Queen's messenger, the guard was expecting him and were certainly prepared for him. I for one, don't think it's Firebrace, but if you do or if you have suspicions of any others who are close to you, let us set a trap for them. What if we play a little game, we pretend there is a messenger who wishes to impart information and you would need to take a carriage to meet with them ? But firstly we would need someone brave enough to be willing to get caught, which they no doubt will be. If we tell only those we suspect of our intentions, we could then, possibly discover who it is." Jane spoke quickly, aware that the kindness Firebrace had given them was a brief one.

The King thought for a moment.

"Hmmm, so you want someone to pass me something that would turn out to be nothing. How cunning. There is Mary Cave, perhaps, her father is a parliamentarian so she would be dealt with cordially. I believe her to be close by and I know her to be a good woman, as long as she would come to no injury for I couldn't bear the thought of her being harmed for my sake, we've seen quite enough."

"Perfect, I will find her and ask her first and if she is in agreement, we could set the trap. Something here isn't right, wouldn't it be helpful to know who it is that betrays you ?"

The King rolled his eyes, "I do so like Firebrace, he has been good to me, I would be so bold as to swear it could not be him, but dear child what good would it do us ? I have already been denounced, so they tell me"

Jane cast the King an empathic glance. "That is simply not true Your Majesty, there are a great many who are and always have been loyal to you and the crown, it breaks our heart to see what's happening to you, to England."

"As it does mine," sighed the King.

There was a moment of silence as they both turned their sights to the far off horizon reaching out of the tiny window that framed it, it was a golden evening with the sun near on setting, casting a golden glow over everything. The King sighed again as it would have been a perfect evening for a stroll but this was no longer allowed since His liberty had been restricted, which reminded him of that fateful day with the Queen's messenger and that he still had no idea what it was the Queen wished to tell him. Jane could see how much he missed his wife, he seemed all the more human but it saddened her to see him so visibly unsettled.

"Perhaps, that's what the message from the Queen's messenger brought news of, her suspicions. The Queen obviously wanted you to know something important and she also wanted me to come to you quickly. Perhaps the Queen knew that someone of your immediate household is a spy and is intent on either betraying you or heaven forbid, harming you."

The King held the locket that contained the miniature of her that was painted by Rubens and by all accounts was a perfect resemblance, "My dear Generalissimo," he smiled as he remembered her heroics in assisting him at every turn. The King loved his wife dearly, he missed her terribly not just her company or her love but her unwavering loyalty.

"Are there any here with you now whom the Queen knew ?"

The King thought for a moment. "Sadly, most of those that I trusted, much like your stepfather, have since left me, hence even I do not know all of the people presently here with me, let me think. In the bedchamber there is only Jack…Ashburnham, a cousin of dear old Buckingham, coincidentally he was, until very recently, with Her Majesty in France, then there's Henry of course."

Just at the very moment the door flew open making Jane and the King almost jump up out of their seats.

John Ashburnham, who was known as Jack, smugly knocked at the door despite having already charged in.

"Your Majesty," he bowed, not taking his eyes from them, "Miss."

Jane instinctively got up and over acted flustered giving the impression she had been caught in a compromising situation, she feigned embarrassment, while the King nodded to greet him.

"Funny, we were just talking about you," said the King.

Ashburnham sneered, thinking he had caught Jane and the King canoodling, an assumption which Jane willingly allowed him to think.

"All good words I trust, excuse me Your Majesty, I was led to believe you were taking sup alone, no one said you had a visitor." He eyed Jane up and down, which made her feel uncomfortable.

"Ah, my dear Jack, Miss Ryder here has been helping us in the kitchens and is the daughter of Maxwell, you may speak freely." There was a distinct change in atmosphere, Jane sat down again, slowly, acting coy and demure but never taking her eyes from Ashburnham, who was equally as observant of her.

Ashburnham had come with information that the King would soon be moved, that Cromwell had already sent men to collect him and transport him back to London. The King pondered the words spoken to him, then gracefully wiped his lips with his napkin before placing it carefully beside him.

"Has he, indeed ?" A long silence followed and Jane took this to be her que to leave and began imitating a shy girl from the kitchen.

"If it pleases Your Majesty, I shall return to the kitchen now, unless you have any further …need of me ?" She turned so that only the King could see her face and winked.

The King was too deep in thought, far too distracted to notice or pay her any attention. He rose to his feet, waving his napkin towards the door.

"No, thank you, thank you Miss Ryder, …You may go…I must …" He muttered to himself and made his way back through the door that led to his private chamber, leaving Ashburnham and Jane alone. Jane waited till he had left the room then began tidying away the dinner plates onto the tray. Rather startlingly, Ashburnham came up behind her and grabbed her by the breast, making grunting noises over her shoulder. Jane froze as fear gripped her guts.

"I could make good use of a pretty girl like you," he garbled into her ear.

What a disgusting man she thought to herself as her strength returned, he repulsed her but this amused Jane for she was a woman of a certain age and here he was carrying on like she was some naive child. Ashburnham reached up for a strand of her hair that had strayed beneath her bonnet and began twisting it round his fingers. Jane could feel his heavy breath on her neck, then just as she sensed him to be as close as she could stand, she smashed a plate on the floor and jumped back in alarm using all her force to smack the back of her head fully into his face, causing him to recoil and shout out in pain and surprise, Jane immediately fell to her knees to pick up the shattered pieces, apologising profusely, while Ashburnham nursed his bleeding nose and crushed pride. Jane hung her head in mock shame secretly pleased with herself, it had gone far better than she expected, she hadn't meant to draw blood but perhaps that would be a lesson to him. Ashburnham, holding his nose, trying to stop the flow of blood, held out his hand asking for a napkin. Jane, who was enjoying this turn of events far too much, saw the chance to extend the performance and decided to ham it up further.

"Here you are Sir," she said, picking one up off the table then swung around with such force the back of her hand punched him in his face causing further pain and anguish. Jane was in her element fussing and overacting with sympathy and concern, "oh my goodness, forgive me, forgive me Sir."

She became even clumsier as he took a seat at the table, still holding his nose she saw an opportunity to pull on the table cloth, therefore pulling everything set upon it into his lap ! The commotion and clatter of plates and cutlery brought the guards running into the room but even they had to stifle their laughs at the sight of him. What a pandemonium.

"There is nothing to see here. All is well. All is well, the King rests," Ashburnham huffed, crossly.

"Damn you, we're here to guard the King, not you Jack," said the first guard, turning the rest of them out of the room.

Jane kept her head bowed to hide her satisfied smile as she gathered up the smashed and broken remnants of supper. Ashburnham swept the clutter from his lap along with any dignity he had left onto the floor and sat back into the chair the King had been sitting in moments before, holding his battered and bleeding nose in the air.

Jane made another attempt to 'help' but he flapped her away.

"Away with you woman… look what you've done …away with you."

It served him right, no other man had ever been so disgustingly inappropriate towards her. He behaved most undignified and ungentlemanly, what a rat ! Having a moment of clarity she quickly decided to set the bait for a trap.

"Forgive me sir," she said, pretending to cry. "I shouldn't have been here and then none of this would have happened, please won't you forgive me ? If only Ms Cave hadn't asked me to deliver that message to His Majesty, I wouldn't have been here at all."

"A message for the King ? What sort of message ?"

"I've no idea Sir but Ms Cave said it was important that she had an urgent message for him, I myself think it's from the Queen. Anyway Ms Cave said the next time His Majesty was out, in his carriage she was to give it to him. But alas now that His Majesty is no longer allowed to take carriage rides, so I suppose that would be impossible" Jane could see and sense his interest and she knew she had lured him.

"Ms Cave, would that be Mary Cave ?"

"Why yes sir, it is the very same," Jane cleared everything away swiftly without looking at the man she now believed to be the one who had betrayed their King. Was he the one whom the Queen wanted to warn her husband of, having so recently spent time with him in France ? Could it be him ? The very man who had been placed in this most trusted position by his cousin, the Duke of Buckingham. Jane hurried the last of the broken pieces onto the tray and curtsied before leaving the room. Ashburnham who was now deep in thought, didn't acknowledge her leaving which only enforced her perception of him. Jane passed the guard and made her way back to the kitchen where she met Henry Firebrace on his way back to the King's chambers, he was clearly alarmed to see the shattered plates and Jane so flustered.

"Everything alright Miss ? The King ?" He swept his eyes from Jane to the corridors behind her.

"Yes Sir, the King is well, safe and retired. Mr Ashburnham joined us, alas, it was I that did this and what's more, I am sorry to say …I may have hurt him." Jane hung her head. Henry did all he could to hold his humour, having relaxed knowing the King was unharmed.

"Did you now ? I wouldn't worry, I'm sure he'll recover, I'm sorry I left you for so long, I got talking see. I should go and look in on things. Good evening Miss."

♛

Jane spent the whole night obsessing about her interaction with Ashburnham and his atrocious behaviour towards her. She decided she didn't like him but hoped that wasn't clouding her judgment, she overanalyzed every detail until she saw the changing colours of the sky and heard the first songs of the birds as they welcomed the sun. It was most disturbing that ladies in service had to tolerate such men and Jane vowed never again to present herself as anything less than the lady she was. Surprisingly energised for one without sleep, she was up dressed and beyond the guards by day break. Having saddled her horse she rode in the direction of an old Inn not more than a few miles away which she knew to be the home of rebels and loyal men.

Jane was a welcomed visitor as a great many knew of her stepfather. Finding Mary Cave was easy and when Jane told her that the King himself had suggested her as a trusted friend she was more than happy to help and swore to do whatever she could for him. Jane smiled deeply at her new found friend and they sat together perfecting their plan to possibly unveil this traitor. There was no time or date set, they would rely wholly upon opportunity.

♛

Now all Jane had to do was tell the King that she had laid bait for Ashburnham and that Mary was in agreement, but frustratingly she had hardly seen him. He was confined mostly to his attic rooms, even the maids that brought the King's meals now had to be parliament approved or rather Cromwell approved. The King was desperately alone, missing his wife and family and although he showed no weakness Jane knew this to be one. He was however permitted the companionship of his chaplain. Jane was most surprised when she saw them both striding across the lawns, accompanied by a guard and quickly ran out to meet them. "Your Majesty," she called breathlessly running after them.

"Ah, Miss Ryder, it is indeed a day of pleasant surprises. How wonderful to be seeing you in this beautiful summer sunshine. Ashburnham has negotiated some small freedoms for us which I am most grateful for, I was so terribly bored. A walk in the park today and tomorrow a ride out on the carriage. Small mercies I know but still, one must keep a thankful heart. Please walk with us, I trust all is well with you ?" The smiling King directed them all forward to carry on with the brisk walk he was clearly enjoying.

All the things Jane had wanted to tell His Majesty now seemed superfluous, Ashburnham had taken the bait.

"All is well Your Majesty, I …just wanted to say, it's good to see you outside."

"Thank you, I must say it certainly feels good to be outside ! Now if you'll forgive me, I wish to take in as much of the garden as I am permitted, good day to you Miss Ryder,"

"Good day Your Majesty." Jane curtsied as the King tipped his hat, then he and his chaplain, who tottered behind in a gallant effort to keep up, made haste towards the huge honeysuckle hedgerow that tangled round the fragrant rose bushes.

♛

The following day Jane saw the carriage being brought round to the front of the house and she knew that this was it. She watched as the foot man brushed down the horse, then stood awaiting his passenger who Jane knew to be the King. Sure enough within moments, the guards opened up the side doors and out stepped His Majesty with cloak and cane looking every inch the regal Lord that he was. The footman stood to attention and opened the carriage door to him and his chaplain, who was right behind, the footman then shut the door and was soon atop and at reins. Accompanied by a heavy guard, Jane watched as they rattled up the driveway. It was a perfect summer day for such an outing, all bright and beautiful. Jane closed her eyes and prayed, prayed for the King and for Mary Cave and prayed that their plans would be successful otherwise she would be praying for forgiveness.

Jane wandered the grounds and meadows of the house, lost in the beauty and the silence. All she could hear was the beat of bird's wings, the chirping of crickets and the delightful buzz of all the many insects flying around her, but the thunderous sound of the entourage returning soon broke her bliss. The guards came charging in shouting commands while the King's carriage came abruptly to a halt behind. The guard escorted the King from the carriage to his quarters, signaling to Jane that Mary had been successful, successful at being caught.

The plan had gone like clockwork, when the King's carriage had gone past the blacksmiths, his son had run to Mary's house, she then made her way quickly to the Inn and caught up with the King's carriage just as it turned to head back to Holdenby, as she knew it would. Mary joyfully waved for the carriage to stop but the guards who were all expecting her, leapt down from their horses shouting at her to move back. Mary raised her hands and stepped back as they moved in and apprehended her. She was then savagely manhandled into the Inn, unfortunately they didn't anticipate the brute force of the guards placing her under arrest. News soon filtered down to Jane of the events. It confirmed everything Jane had suspected, she had told no other than Ashburnham. Mary was arrested but insisted she had wished only for the King to bless her, everyone was taking it all very seriously. Jane hoped Mary would have the strength to stand up to these bullies and knew that because of who her father was, she wouldn't be a prisoner for long.

The following morning Jane was awakened, along with everyone else at Holdenby house by the tumultuous clattering of hooves and the alarming shouts of men, it sounded like the whole army coming into the yard. Jane scrambled out of bed to see the lawns swarming with soldiers, this could mean only one thing, they had come for the King. She dressed quickly and without thought slipped down the stairs just in time to see a red faced man so typical of these army men, shouting instructions, they always looked as if they were about to explode. Jane carefully hid just out of sight but with a full view of the whole goings on, watching as the spectacle unfolded. Apparently these men had come to escort the King to London but the King was unimpressed and had returned to bed, which made Jane laugh so loud she nearly gave away her hiding place. It had quite the opposite effect on the man who was in charge who was now clearly on the point of boiling over. He had gone back and forth making his demands, but could do nothing until the King was better rested. Jane understood she must act fast and retracing her steps through the house she wound her way round to the King's quarters that were naturally heavily guarded. Jane made use of a laundry basket she had found in the kitchen and used it as a prop to gain access to the King's rooms. All too easily she thought. The first person she saw was the giant Henry who was looking concerned.

"Miss Ryder," he whispered, surprised.

"Henry, what's happening ? I hear the King is leaving for London ?"

"Aye, apparently so Miss," he said looking at her sadly, "and I'm not sure this will end well, ruffians the lot of them."

"You go too, I take it ?"

"Aye, you can be sure of that."

"Thank God. I shall come too, please let him know, I will no doubt hear of your whereabouts and I will come, I swear it."

"Yes Miss, you have my word and my honour, now if I were you, I'd get out of here and fast, make sure you are well off the road before we get on it !" He gave her a knowing glance indicating the door. "Go now and go swiftly, things are changing fast around here."

"Thank you Henry, I will."

Jane curtsied and knocked the door to be let out again of the guarded entrance still carrying the basket of laundry, she made her way through the corridors leaving the basket back where she found it. Running back to her room, she hastily gathered her effects then went briskly out to the stables where she swiftly saddled a horse. Swinging herself up onto it she made her way quietly to the back of the house and through the fields that led out to the London road.

♛

Jane rode like the wind back to the city. She had no time to contemplate the obvious deceit of Ashburnham, she thought only of the King being taken to London, what could this mean ? What were those treacherous parliamentarians plotting ? Jane knew the King was not giving in to any of their demands and refused to accept their assumption of authority, but for how much longer could he withstand them ? There must be something Jane could do, a way to serve him better and above all protect him from these animals, no they were far worse than animals.

♛

It seemed like no time at all when Jane crossed the river and trotted up the Westminster road she knew and loved so well. All at once her mind drifted and was filled with thoughts of her father and the endless summers of a happier England. She led her horse to the stables at the back of Scots yard and made her way to Elizabeth's house. She was covered in dust and dirt of the road and looked more like a guttersnipe than a lady. Jane let herself into Elizabeth's warm and cosy kitchen, which was so comforting, it was as if she had never left. She flopped into the welcoming fireside chair which was still warm and started to take off her boots, alarmed by her hands that were sore and bleeding from holding the reins. Falling back into the chair, she closed her eyes and within minutes she was sound asleep.

So sound asleep, she didn't even stir when Elizabeth came back and let out a scream at finding some scruffy street child curled up in front of her fire. She was just about to beat her out with a stick when, thankfully she recognised her friend. Seeing the poor girl's hands and her face half covered with filth, she quickly set about with kettles, potions and lotions to be ready for her when she awoke. It filled Elizabeth's heart that her friend was back safe, albeit dirty but she now relished the opportunity to polish her friend back to the diamond she was. Jane slept like a log, while Elizabeth sat patiently waiting for her to stir.

♛

Jane was eventually roused by the bells of Westminster Abbey and the hushed tones of her friends Elizabeth and William whispering at the dinner table. It took her a moment to remember where she was, then feeling happy to be there she stretched and joined them at the table hoping there would be food and room for one more. The smell of Elizabeth's fine cooking made her belly ache.

"Ah ! At last !" exclaimed Elizabeth, "I've been waiting all day," she ran over to put the kettle back onto the stove and to pull her friend a chair. William stood up and welcomed Jane to the table.

"Come, sit yourself down, but let me tend to your hands first," fussed Elizabeth excitedly. Jane offered up her sore and dirty hands that were covered in dried blood.

"Aye and then your face, honestly Jane, if I don't know you better I'd be thinking something terrible had befallen you."

Jane sat at the table while her friend tended her poor cracked hands soaking them and wrapping soothing balms around them, bringing hot water and cloth to wipe her face, like a mother fussing her child. She enjoyed the kind care and attention of her friend and felt greatly comforted by it. Elizabeth with all the swiftness of a well seasoned nurse had her looking and feeling like a lady again in no time.

"Tell us everything Jane, we want to hear it all, don't we Will, did you catch the rat ?"

"Not exactly, we didn't catch him, but I believe we know who it is now thanks to you two. You were right and we did exactly as you suggested, we laid a trap. A lady called Mary, bless her she was brave enough to be the bait and it happened like we knew it would. I'd only told one man, Jack Ashburnham. He's a cousin of Buckingham can you believe, but nothing like him not in the slightest. But then this Joyce chap turned up with what looked like the whole army to bring the King back to London, the King was peeved, said it was far too early and went back to bed. It was so funny, well to me at least, the army chap was furious ! So there was no time to expose Ashburnham or act on what we knew as everything changed so fast and .. and well here I am…again."

"Here you are, so that's why your hands are in such a state. You see William Wheeler, it turns out you do have good ideas ? " Elizabeth beamed at her humble husband.

"So what now Jane ?" Will asked.

"Now, they're bringing the King back to London apparently, so we'll just have to wait until we hear further news I suppose. In truth, I just don't know but dear friends, it looks like I am very much in need of your help and hospitality once more."

"Oh Jane, you never need to ask, does she …Will ? No, this is a home for you whenever you need one. Our door is always open to you." William smiled at his wife who as usual had answered for both of them. They ate together sharing gossip and good humour, Elizabeth suggested a day of rest and Jane had to agree there was nothing she could do today, her legs were tired and saddle sore. Her hands still bound in Elizabeth's healing treatments, so she gave in to the stalemate of her situation and made her way to the room her friend kept for her with its soft and comfortable bed, where she immediately fell back to sleep.

♛

The new day brought with it a new fresh feeling and clarity which Jane craved. Her body felt stiff, but her mind had been revived. Her hands had made a miraculous recovery and were barely recognisable from the crusty bleeding state they had been but yesterday. Jane found a change of clothes laid out for her which brought a smile to her face and a sweetness to her heart. She really was so very thankful to have such a kind and true friend.

The kitchen was empty when she found it, still warm with bread and fresh milk in a jug laid out for her, which she helped herself to before stepping out into Westminster. It was a far cry from the happy bustling streets she remembered. Folk seemed too afraid or too ashamed to take any time with each other and were mostly nose down about their business, harsh, busy, soulless folk moving silently so as the army wouldn't suspect them of anything. Jane wound her way through the streets, hoping to see James when she happened upon an Inn she knew to be frequented by Royalists but was shocked upon finding it boarded up.

"You'll find no one there. Long gone they are, the army came for them, swept them all away," a haggard woman spoke to Jane from the corner across the street. Jane made her way over to her.

"Who is it you're looking for, my love ?" The woman asked.

"Oh I wasn't really looking for anyone," she lied, "but, where did they all go ?" Jane's heart did a leap as she thought of James, hoping he hadn't been swept away.

"Well you look like you're looking for someone to me. No one knows anything, no one talks anymore round here lass, look at 'em. They're all trying to forget. The only one who knows what's going on around here is that star gazer, Lilly, do you know him ?"

"I know of him," said Jane,

"Go seek out the astrologer then, maybe he can help you, tell you what's happened to them all. He's got his hands in all the pies, if you know what I mean, he's the only one who knows what's happening around here, but he'll make you pay handsomely for it." She laughed before retreating down the side street leaving Jane once more alone and looking up at the empty building. "William Lilly, why not ?" Jane said to herself. Finding a coach, she instructed the driver then climbed aboard.

♛

William Lilly's house was a tall thin place sandwiched between two huge imposing buildings on either side. Luckily for Jane the coach driver had pointed it out otherwise she could have missed it all together. She stepped from the coach handing over her coin to the coachman and made her way to Mr Lilly's door. There was a long rope which Jane took to be for the bell, she pulled on it twice and took a step back in anticipation of someone coming to the door. She didn't have to wait long. The heavy door creaked opened an inch and a pale, nervous looking girl peered out. Without making eye contact she said in an awkward accent, " you 'ave a point ment ?"

It took a moment for Jane to understand before she replied that she didn't, but wished to make one. "By way of introduction would you be so kind as to tell Mr Lilly that I am... Mrs Whorwood, the Black Rod's daughter and friend of the gentleman Elias Mole."

The waif repeated what Jane said then raised an eye telling her to wait while she checked with the master. Jane waited patiently out on the street for what felt like a very long time, eventually she heard the sliding of bolts as the heavy door opened to her and the young girl motioned for her to come inside. Shutting and bolting it behind her.

Jane's eyes darted about the place that was adorned and decorated with all manner of interesting things. Horns, feathers, many types of butterflies, talismans, tusks, teeth and claws, it was as if the whole animal kingdom had been through the corridors and each of them had left something of themselves about the walls.

"Ziss way," the waif said, leading Jane up the stairs to a small velvet covered stool much like a perch in the corner.

"Wait 'ere, ze master will send for you." She waved a finger towards the spot she wished Jane to fill. Jane blended into the decor being careful not to leave any part of herself behind. From her perch at the top of the stairs she could see all the way down to the doorway she had entered by and along the corridors which no doubt led to the lair of Mr Lilly. It was a cluttered and chaotic place with piles of papers, stones and skulls that made Jane think this would be as close to a wizard's workshop as she was likely to see. She was unafraid but curious as her eyes moved around the hall taking in all the very odd things that were assembled together. It felt like a very long time before she was called in to meet the man himself. She had heard much about him, not just from Elias, Mr Lilly had a reputation for being a respected man of astrological science. Jane stood up and straightened her skirts, politely thanking the girl who showed her the way to a room where Mr Lilly was sitting at a small desk in the back under a huge pile of papers. This room was stuffed full of more things than before. It amazed Jane that one could have so many possessions. There were birds chirping in cages and bright green ones that flew freely around the room, over filled bookshelves with piles of books and papers everywhere. Jane stood still waiting for Mr Lilly to invite her in further. He didn't, so she coughed, he was clearly aware of her, why else would the girl have shown her in ? William Lilly was a man of great self importance who, no doubt adept at his craft, had become unbearably aloof and difficult. He looked Jane up and down with disdain and then went back to his paperwork. Jane was unsure as to how she felt by this obvious snub. She took her purse from her pocket and allowed the sound of the coin to draw his attention, which it did. "Mr Lilly ?" Jane saw that despite all his self importance he still sprung like an organ grinder's monkey for the sound of pence, which amused her.

"I was told you would know what became of the White Hart Inn on the Charing Road, the one no longer there ? More importantly, what became of the men there ?"

William Lilly snarled and looked at Jane offensively.

"Why would you think that I would know of such a place or the whereabouts of such men ?"

"A woman suggested you would," Jane was miffed.

"Madam, I am an astrologer, I read the heavens not the minds of drunks, I know nothing of this Inn ? Less of the men that frequented it. Good Day to you." He pointed his quill towards the door and went back to his papers. Jane stood her ground because she had decided to follow advice that led her here so she believed there had to be something of value in her visit. Thinking fast she whispered.

"Well, actually Sir, in all truth I have come seeking your counsel regarding His Majesty the King." He lifted his eyes, fixing them upon Jane as she spoke with increasing confidence. "I was told you would be able to guide us, as you alone know what is happening in the world, so would you make a chart for him and divine what our best move should be for his safety and ultimately his liberty."

"Liberty ? His Majesty is a prisoner of parliament is he not ?"

"Well, yes I suppose he is, currently. Yes he is in the custody of Cromwell's men and word is they are bringing him back to London so, if it is indeed possible for you Sir, would you advise us, as it were, of what we could best do to …serve His Majesty at this time ?"

Lilly stared at Jane for an uncomfortably long time, causing Jane's hands to sweat. One of the green birds flew past her face causing her to step back and Lilly to return to his charts.

"Come back, in a week, I shall gather what messages there are amongst the heavens and then I shall advise you, but, I'll have you know it's not cheap, my consulting the constellations." He said without looking up.

"Sir, I did not for one moment think that it would be," replied Jane sweetly.

"I shall expect…twenty pounds."

"And I shall gladly give it to you now," smiled Jane, reaching for the money from her purse. She moved forward in order to give it to him but he winced as if she was about to strike him. Jane, not wishing to frighten the poor man, corrected herself and placed the money on the only free space amongst all the clutter before her.

"Until then," she said, turning to leave.

"One week from today at 12 o'clock, precisely, I am a very busy man."

Jane closed the door behind her and made her way to the door through which she came and the street outside of it, what a very strange man she thought.

♛

The grey and dusty streets were in complete contrast to Lilly's colourful and unusual abode. Making her way to the Inns of Southwark, she hoped to find news of what happened at the White Hart or fresh news as to where His Majesty had been taken. Upon finding another old tavern frequented by Royalists and glad it was still open she made her way inside. In a crowded back room she crammed herself into to hear what was being said in the hushed tones of those who were now considered rebellious. It turned out His Majesty had indeed returned to London and had been taken to Hampton Court Palace, which pleased Jane a little for at least it was a palace. There was talk regarding Cromwell and his sniveller Ireton, kinder words spoken of Lord Fairfax, who it turned out was trying to distance himself from these crazed fanatics, fears of assassins, heated words and fearful talk of what would befall the King if they stood by and did nothing. It erupted into further harsh words, blaming, finger pointing and as far as Jane could tell, all noise and very little action. She looked about the many men there, some of them burly, some of the gentry, all of them Royalists and most of them afraid. Jane, having heard enough, was about to leave when someone grabbed her arm. "Excuse me …Miss ?"

Jane spun around to see someone vaguely familiar, at first she did a double take for it could have been the King himself but then she simpered as remembered those eyes and that smile.

"Jane …Ryder ? It is you !" He whispered, igniting all of her senses.

Jane could feel the heat rising in her cheeks and the swirls in her tummy, she nodded, smiled and giggled, childishly lost for words.

"Huzzah ! I thought it was you. Come on, let's get out of here."

Jane offered no resistance, besides she was leaving anyway, holding on to his arm as he guided her deftly around the tables, out of the Inn and on to the river side.

"Ah, thank god for that, for you," he said, " I thought I'd suffocate in there."

"Hello Mr Shirley," she smiled.

They both looked at each other and laughed.

"Please, you can call me James. Shall we?" He held out his arm again and proudly promenaded her along the river bank. Jane couldn't believe her good fortune in not only finding James but now being upon his arm which was a feeling she adored, she loved the way his body felt next to hers. There was something so mischievous and marvellous about him, she felt elated, it was the most lady-like she had ever felt. They glided along together and he cheerfully pointed out the birds and the blossoms as Jane hung on his every word, transfixed by the way he twirled and moved with such perfect poise it was as if she was in one of his grand performances, she was spellbound and quite breathless just listening to him.

"So, do tell me Ms Ryder, what kept you so long ? Where in the world have you been ? I heard that you were in the North but that was weeks ago. Does that mean you were in the presence of His Majesty, all this time ? Please tell me all, for I am so very hungry for adventure and it seems to me that of the two of us, it is you that has been living one !"

"Oh, there's nothing to tell really." She stammered shyly, much preferring the sound of his voice. What she really wanted to tell him was that it had been her he had made love to, that they had a child and that she had thought of him every day, she desperately wanted to find the courage but she just couldn't, suddenly all the feelings of joy were washed away. James sensing and seeing her turmoil took command of the conversation so as not to embarrass her further. Jane realised that no other man had ever been so concerned for her feelings, he really was adorable.

They walked and chatted aimlessly, finding a comfortable spot under a great willow tree with branches that lapped the shore. There they sat watching the dragonflies dancing in the dappled sunlight that sparkled off the Thames. Jane, feeling relieved and relaxed, began telling him all about her time at Holdenby and of William Lilly's strange and interesting house. James listened intently and marveled at Jane's fantastical antics, in what had only been a matter of weeks. There was an impressive silence as he shook his head in disbelief.

"I don't know what to say…How daring of you Miss Ryder, truly astonishing ! I mean really, you are astonishing. What an amazing adventure and what an incredible tally of events you've been party to ! My lady, you astound me, how honoured I am that you would speak so freely with me. Incredible."

Jane blushed for she hadn't told him to impress him and not for one moment had she considered any of her actions incredible.

"Sir, I am embarrassed."

"Well you shouldn't be, I feel incredibly proud to know you and to be in your company, truly you are an exceptional woman, really you are. I on the other hand have much to be embarrassed about for I do nothing, nothing whatsoever. You see before you a broken man, poisoned by this dull and ghastly putrid world of shame, but then… then I have the good fortune to see you, again. It's as if God wills it ! You have done more for His Majesty than many of those men shouting about it back there." He said waving his hands towards the Inn they had just left.

"I am inspired by you and I want to help, tell me how can I help you to help His Majesty ? For I am to the core of my being, still and evermore a Queen's man." He sprang to life and bowed before her in one of his graceful theatrical bows that Jane remembered so deliciously.

"My lady, I am from this moment forth, at your service. Now what would you have me do ?" He lifted his head showing a glint in his eyes through the dark curls that covered his brow.

Jane couldn't stop smiling and instinctively clapped her hands in approval and applause. "Sir, would you really be willing ?"

"Willing ? Madam I am begging you, please save me from this dire, tedious life I am currently living, I beseech you, please let me help you ?"

"Well in that case," she said slowly but thinking quickly. "Sometime ago I met a gentleman, Sir Lewis, a larger than life character, who was …a guest at the Tower, he suggested that the best way, in fact the only way to help the King would be to spirit him away. Having witnessed for myself how he suffers I tend to agree. So perhaps, between us we could… devise a plan, to somehow free him from this misery and spirit him safely away ?"

"Oh dear God. Yes ! Yes, a hundred fold yes, what a splendid idea, let us do just that, let us imagine new and wonderful ways to free His Majesty, let us call upon the divine for inspirations and interventions. I must tell you I already feel invigorated and more alive than I have felt in weeks, come let us walk some more."

Jane was only too happy to oblige, she felt equally enlivened just being in his presence, she didn't want to be anywhere else. They talked and walked well past sunset, discussing all plausible and even the impossible, plots and plans for the King's escape. The stars were appearing in the sky when they realised how far they had walked together, letting their imaginations run wild. James suddenly stopped as if he had just had a revelation.

"But of course, why didn't we think of it earlier. I'm surprised no one else has, I mean it is the most obvious ! Do you remember, way back when we lived far happier lives, there were stories of a Prince, I think it was Edward, I believe he was the son of the Tudor King Henry ? Anyways it became the stuff of legends, it really was a fabulous tale of him swapping places with a pauper and the hilarious and somewhat dangerous adventures they had while living each other's lives ? Do you remember it ? Well, why don't we use that rather perfect idea, it worked so well before and most importantly it worked out well in the end, so what if ? What if I were to switch places with His Majesty, what if somehow we could get him just far enough from the guards so that he could escape and I could step onto the role of the King ? If it happened before it could happen again, only better… it might be fun."

Jane looked at him a little startled.

"Fun ? James, wouldn't it be dangerous ? What if you were discovered ? I mean, who knows what those parliament men are plotting or what they might do. You would be putting yourself in a most precarious position."

"Fortunately, dear lady, the precarious position is my favourite," he winked at her. "Damn them, let them do their worst for they already are aren't they ? I mean just look at things, look at London. It's a world away from the generous, gracious elegant town it once was. The soul has been ripped out of it ! You said yourself we must do something and this could be it. This could be our chance, after all, isn't the King's life and liberty of the foremost and utmost importance and in all honesty, this could well be the performance of my life. I would rise to the challenge and in all truth who else but me could do it ? I've done it before, you know ? I have performed as His Majesty, admittedly in jest, but still, I believe I could do it, I believe I could become … A King." He laughed as he began slipping into a regal character. "Even if they did catch me and make me a prisoner, they would still think I was the King of All England, so I'd imagine I'd be treated quite well, quite graciously in fact."

"Perhaps," mused Jane, "I could …acquire some of His Majesty's clothes from the laundries."

"Perfect, there we have it, we have the actor, a damn good one if I do say so myself and we have the costumes. It already has the beginning of a fine performance, wouldn't you say ? I promise you that if you were to dress me as the King, my dear I would perform as one, as him. I beg of you to place your faith in me, in this is the plan, this is inspired, cunning and quite daring, it already has all the makings of a most delightful performance. Besides, as it's already been done quite well before, we'd just revive it ! You have given me a new thrill for being and have saved my life and who knows this may even save the life of the King, nay God will save him and bless us all." He said gallantly, raising an imaginary cup. "Miss Ryder, I swear I will not let you down."

"But what then ? What happens when we've made the switch ?"

"One act at a time my dear, who knows but the King would be far safer and would he obviously then be in a far better position to gather troops or whatever it is His

Majesty wishes to do. Oh, yes we could definitely have fun with this ! The King could instruct me as to what he'd have me to do and say. Should it all get too much, just and come get me. I trust that you'll come for me ? You would come for me, wouldn't you ?" He looked at Jane earnestly pulling at all of her heart strings.

"Yes, I would come for you, nothing would keep me away." She replied tenderly. "Perhaps you could escape too, I mean if the King is able to get away, why not keep going ... to France... to His Queen ?"

Jane's imagination and spirit was stirred too and not just by being tantalisingly close to the one she adored. It did seem a perfect plan, albeit a daring one. They were eager to put forth their ideas, inspired and sparkling with possibilities as they made their way to Westminster in what seemed like moments, before stopping outside of Elizabeth's house. Jane said she would gather as much information as she could and James said he would perfect his Royal role. They stood looking rather longingly at each other, neither one wanting the moment to end.

"That's settled it then, we have ourselves a rather grand performance to prepare for, thank God and thank you, Miss Ryder. Jane, I owe you my life, for you have invigorated my soul and saved me... from being bored to death. One week from now, from daybreak I shall be back at the willow tree awaiting you, you can be sure of it, the devil himself could not keep me away." James took her hand and gently kissed it.

Jane smiled, unable to speak, her heart was pounding so much she thought it might jump out of her mouth. She had never known or even dared to allow herself to feel such desire. Her hand was tingling from his touch, how she wished that kiss had been upon her lips. She let out a huge sigh as her fingers slipped from his warm hand and he turned to the darkened streets of Westminster. "Adieu," he smiled as he walked briskly away, with her hands next to her heart Jane watched him saunter out of her sights.

♛

Fluttering with joy, Jane breezed into Elizabeth's kitchen, dramatically flinging herself into the chair in front of the fire. Elizabeth, who had been expecting her friend, had everything made comfortable and ready for her. Jane, sighed dreamily into the fire as only a love struck fool can. Elizabeth smiled knowingly at her friend and set a plate of food beside her.

"Aha ! I know that look, Jane Ryder."

Jane cast her friend a side eye and smiled knowing full well she couldn't hide the delirium that was beaming out of her.

"Oh Lizzy ... I've had the most perfect day ... you wouldn't believe it ?"

"Aye, go on then !" Smiled Elizabeth, "you bet I will." They both laughed the childlike laughter they had always shared as Jane told her everything.

♛

In the days that followed Jane had a spring in her step and set about her tasks with renewed enthusiasm. Firstly, she confided in her dearest friends, Elizabeth and William who both offered their assistance and had every confidence in James's plan. With Lizzy's help she managed to sequester an entire outfit of the Kings from the palace laundry with cuffs and ties, despite the whole place being overrun with Army men. Jane then took these to the house where James had performed his Triumph of Beauty and left them with the small chap with round glasses. It all looked very different in the daylight. Every day the plan became more real, more convincing and more possible with great timings and connections that seemed to confirm they were undertaking God's work. William suggested she should write to the Queen for advice and visit the King's chaplain who was now in the Tower, so she did, again with absolute ease. She enquired about Sir Lewis only to be told he had escaped, much to her delight. It was whilst seeing the chaplain within the Tower walls that Jane was brought back to the harsh reality of the seriousness of the King's situation. She knew she could trust this man, so she asked his thoughts regarding their plan to liberate the King.

"Don't be ridiculous, child, what then ? What may I ask, do you intend for His Majesty to do when he has his … liberty.. as you say ? For I think you will find he shall be far from free, what's more, you will have infuriated Cromwell's army, already hell bent and mad with fury. You'd be driving them into more of a crazed stupor, if that could even be conceivable to the devil himself ! What then ? If, as you say, His Majesty is somehow sprung from his gaol, where would he go ? Who would be willing to harbour him ? He has no army and as far as I understand he has very little money, he has a spattering of loyal men yes, but nothing, I say nothing," he said looking sternly at Jane. "Nothing in comparison to those brutes of Cromwells despicable so-called army, who now run this land. I tell you they will hunt him down and there is nothing kingly or chivalrous about being hounded for your life and then you will have played into their hands as they will have every reason to kill him."

Jane gasped in horror.

"Oh yes my dear, if they haven't already made plans and plots to do so, they certainly would if he dared, or somehow managed to outsmart them. They would absolutely hate that, so I fear this liberty you suggest would have no effect at all, only God can save him now. I should think very carefully before you go rushing in with a handful of good intentions, for even if you do find honest, loyal men they shall all end up by their necks and as for you, well that doesn't even bear thinking about my dear ... I wouldn't trust Cromwell's men with a fish."

"The King could go to France, to his Queen ?"

"To France, how pray do you imagine he would get there ? Cromwell would have every port shut down and searched immediately ! France ? No, the French are still licking their wounds after their own wars and certainly wouldn't welcome another poor relative, no my dear, as much as it would please me to offer you ideas or support yours, I suggest you make your way back to your own family and forget this folly, may God bless you and your heart, for I can see your intentions are earnest and true, I shall pray for you."

"And I shall pray for you." Jane sat back defeated and deflated, it had seemed such a good idea when she and James had imagined it up but then she realised that any idea she thought up with James would feel to be a good one.

♛

Jane left the Tower by the way she had come in, sighing to herself as she walked along the riverside making her way back to Westminster. Seeing the sun set upon the water was another reminder that time was slipping and the King's fate was in the balance. The walk back was slow, Jane was forlorn it had not been the meeting she had hoped for, oh what to do ? Seeing Elizabeth's house in sight she stopped, she didn't feel like walking in on them in such a useless state so she took a sharp right and headed for the Strand, desperately wishing to see James. Her wishes were soon granted when she walked past the Stags Head and he fell out.

"Forgive me madam…Aha, could it really be …Miss Ryder, you seem to be forming a habit of coming to my rescue." Staggeringly drunk, he stumbled into a gracious bow at her feet, then wobbled attempting to regain his composure.

"Thank God it is you ! What amazing good luck, how very, very wonderful to be seeing you, may I ?" He held out his arm for stability and Jane helped him hook his arm into hers as he raised his cane saying 'forward' as if guiding a horse.

"My dear girl, this is the confirmation I needed 'tis kismet, timely and clearly blessed by Fortuna herself. How lucky for you also Miss Ryder for I have a little surprise for you. It was already becoming unbearable waiting to see you, I'd have been out of my mind if I had to wait all week. The Gods must have heard me. Come, come, I want to show you something." A few steps further they reached a tumble down cottage, set back from the road.

"Here, in here," he motioned towards a small doorway. Jane, thrilled by this unexpected turn in events, instantly forgot her woes. The door was already open, so they made their way into a very small and cosy sitting room. Three chairs were placed around the fireplace and there were various piles of papers but other than that it was quite sparse. James invited Jane to take a seat as he lit several candles before ducking under a curtain that led into a back room. Jane waited patiently on the most comfortable looking chair while several clangs, bangs and all sorts of noises came from out the back. She was so completely intrigued as to what James was about to reveal to her.

"Are you ready ? Prepared to be amazed ?" James shouted.

"Yes… yes I am," said Jane in delighted anticipation.

James pulled the curtain across and stepped through to show what or rather who, he had transformed into.

Jane gasped in astonishment. Miraculously the ill effects of alcohol had worn off and there, right before her very eyes James, slipped effortlessly into character and became the King himself. Every inch of his demeanour had changed, he looked positively regal, having somehow acquired the signature moustache and beard that graced the King's face and with his hair loose, under the wide brimmed hat, he was a convincing double for His Majesty. When he spoke Jane had to look again for he had perfected the King's speech right down to the faint Scottish accent and the slow directness of his words. Jane was flabbergasted and James was enthralled by her reaction, he carried on with the performance speaking with such authority and elegance that Jane could have sworn that this was the King himself.

"How, how did you do it ? You've perfected him, in every way, I can hardly believe it."

"Well I am an actor my dear," winked James, " a professional one …whom I may add, was lucky enough to be in the presence of His Majesty for many a year, so if anyone were to play the part of him, I would much rather it be me. Wouldn't you agree ?"

"Why yes I would," whimpered Jane, bedazzled by his impersonation. "It's amazing, you really do look like him .. I mean ..it's truly incredible."

"Why thank you, I'm rather pleased with myself. The clothes were a massive help of course, thank you for that. I've been practicing with some of the other Queens men, who by the way, aren't aware of our endeavour but I know they'd be happy, nay, eager and on hand for absolutely anything, anything should you need them." He reached out to kiss her hand without slipping from character. Jane joyfully obliged because she did so like him doing that. His resemblance to the King was striking and she couldn't take his eyes from him.

"Oh .. but James .. I mean Your Majesty, I almost forgot, I have just come from the Tower and a meeting with one of the King's chaplains, who is incarcerated there and he has warned me, sternly warned me, against our idea."

"My dear lady, he would say that wouldn't he ? He not only has the fear of God but he is in prison. Pay no heed to that miserable incarcerated man, freedom is what we all crave, freedom and life ! We want to live ! To feel alive, we don't want to wither and die under this horrible puritan regime. Men are scared, tired and yes it's hard to know who to believe or trust out there," he said waving his cane to the door. "But, we are not of that world. I am a Queens man and we ARE loyal. To each other and the crown and what's more we love to perform, and this, my dear girl, is the performance of my life, thank God for you ! I can think of no greater honour to give to His Majesty and his Queen than to offer him his freedom, so dear heart do not give up on our plan because of the words of someone who has already been caught, it simply means that his own plans weren't that good." James sniffed indignantly. " Now, if I may be so bold, may we share and go over the designs of our plan which, Miss Ryder, it is our heavenly duty to implement, for I assure you, I am not about to back out or surrender now."

"Yes Your Majesty, if that is your wish ?" Jane beamed proudly.

"Absolutely it is Miss Ryder …absolutely."

"I've yet to visit the King at Hampton Court, so my thoughts are still to go there."

"Absolutely yes, you should go straight away, tell the King of our rather grand and brilliant plan and trust that he will be in agreement with it."

"Do you think it wise ? So early on ? I mean he has just arrived and are we really ready ?"

"Jane," James looked at her with seriousness. "We must seize the opportunity, there isn't a moment to lose. The King's life could be at stake and I am eager to get going with my rendition." He said with confidence.

"What shall I tell him ?"

"Everything ! Tell him we are ready, able and willing to spring him from this nest of vipers and get him far away from those that betray him, if he would place his trust in us."

Jane shivered at the recollection of Ashburnham and hoped to God that Mary Cave had not suffered, things had moved so quickly since then. James was right, there wasn't a moment to lose. "And then," James continued, "If he is in agreement of course, which I sincerely hope he is, then we ... You and I will be waiting with two good horses, we make the switch, you and the King gallop off and I make my way to France. Perhaps it would be helpful if he were to bring someone that knows the road to guide me so I'm not galloping round in circles. If perchance a loyal servant is available, insist that he brings wine." James laughed.

"But what if they raise the alarm and recapture you ?" asked Jane, worried.

"What's the worst that will happen ? I'll be taken back to Hampton Court for a life far more luxurious than the one I am living now, they'd probably just give me extra guard and it would give us extra time to devise an even grander plan. Or I could beg their forgiveness saying they've made a terrible mistake at having brought back a drunk opportunist." He smiled at Jane to reassure her, although he clearly hadn't thought this part through.

"My intention is obviously not to be apprehended at all but to make my way to France, as swiftly as possible. Once it is declared that the King is free and safe in France, there will be huge uprisings and a crushing blow to Cromwell's army who will have to...well who knows what they'll do, but they'll obviously stop looking for the real King ! I imagine all the roads and ports will be closed once they know him to be at large, so I must make haste, when they hear that the King has made it to France it will be terribly embarrassing for them."

"Perhaps we could ask if a servant could meet you further down the road, but do we need a back up plan, just in case. I mean what would you do, what if they... capture you ?"

"What would I do ? I will perform of course, for then the performance would truly begin, have no fear for I have been blessed with good humour, as well as this charm and dazzling intellect, which has saved me more than once. They may have the might but they have very little mirth. They shall not hurt me, I simply won't allow it, and besides I do have back up, the very best in the business. The Queens men. Fear not, just focus fully on getting the King somewhere safe and far away. Whatever happens I promise to give the very best performance for as long as the King wishes it. I trust that my audience will also be willing to allow me to do so for, well, for as long as one can. Tell the King that our main objective is to liberate him and this is how we'll do it. What happens after that ? Who knows, we will throw ourselves at the mercy of fate and fortune, makes it all the more exciting wouldn't you say ?"

Jane was in awe at the lengths James was willing to go and was invigorated by his loyalty, how she wanted to fling her arms around him. In the silence that followed she couldn't help but stare at him, James did look incredibly convincing, he even had the King's mannerisms down to a T. Every nuance had been taken into account and James embodied His Majesty in a very convincing way, it was astonishing and besides, Jane liked looking at him. James had captivated her for what felt like her whole life and now knowing more of his daring and courageous nature, she was positively besotted.

Jane, aware she was fawning over him, tried to regain her senses by stringing some words together about going to Hampton Court. She coughed to sound serious, "then I shall go at first light." James agreed, never once dropping his Royal character.

"Until then Your Majesty," Jane curtsied, making sure to avoid his eye, lest she start blushing again and promptly left the same way she came in.

"Adieu Miss Ryder."

♛

Back out on the bustling Strand, evening had fallen, the road was busy with carts and people, all shouting to make their way. Jane was flustered, she took several deep breaths to ground herself. She was bewitched by everything about him, hopelessly, ridiculously, consumed by him and in a flush of passions. While standing on the edge of this euphoria she reminded herself that she harboured a secret and in her usual act of self sabotage, she stopped this flow of blissful feelings and replaced them all with guilt. Guilt because she knew she ought to tell him and shame because she hadn't, these thoughts would always, without fail bring her crashing back down to earth. Why did she always do it to herself ? Why couldn't she allow this happiness to flow through her ? She became aware that she always stopped and tried to control these feelings and berating herself was the most effective way for her to do it. Try as she might she couldn't get back to the elation she was feeling but moments before. She made a mental note to herself to never try and control these emotions again, to let go and flow with the excitement that she always felt around him, no other man could command such rapture in her. She told herself that one day there would be the perfect time to tell him, but it wasn't now or any time soon for that matter, wrapping herself up against the evening chill and she made her way back to Westminster and in the morning she would make for Hampton Court.

👑

Jane, having slept well, was up and out early, she hadn't seen Elizabeth or William that night, as they had got back late and she left before either of them had awoken. The sun hadn't even risen by the time Jane was stepping across the cobbled streets of Westminster. There was a freshness in the air but she was not cold, she was positively glowing, James had rekindled that fire within her and she could think of little else. Every time she closed her eyes he was there and it sent her pulse racing again, making her wildly restless. It made sense to move with this energy rather than be ravaged by it so Jane made her way to Scots yard stables, it was still warm enough for the stable hands to be sleeping outside and she gently rolled one of the boys awake.

"Aye Miss," yawned the young lad she'd woken who sprung into service immediately.

"Would you saddle me up a horse, I have urgent business in the name of the King."

The young boy didn't need telling twice and nimbly set about the task Jane had asked of him. Of course she could have done the job herself but thought it more polite to ask, she passed the young fellow a handful of coins, which she knew was overly generous but then she had woken him up and he had bought her a fine horse in moments.

"Thank you Miss" said the urchin bowing to her and smiling from ear to ear, Jane smiled in return and was glad she had blessed him. "God bless you," she said as she swung her leg ably over the horse's back.

The young boy was assounded for the second time, for rarely did he see ladies mount that way, he rubbed his eyes then, looking sideways he whispered, "Aye Miss and may God save the King."

Jane smiled, adjusting the reins she gently kicked her ride into step and they trotted out of the stable yard.

♛

The road to Hampton Court was one Jane knew well having spent so much of her younger life upon it. It inevitably brought back fond memories of her much missed father, King James and the Duke of Buckingham. Jane knew deep in her heart that of all the men of the other worlds it would be these three she wished would be beside her now. How she wished, with tears falling down her face, that these three great and sturdy men of her childhood would somehow reach down from heaven and help her, help the King. Jane mused to herself that none of this nonsense would be happening if those men were here, not one jot of it, but then Jane reminded herself, a great many of the men who had turned on King Charles did so because of their grievances with King James. They envied his intelligence and despised his quest for peace. What sickening, snivelling, shit pots the lot of them.

Jane rode into Hampton Court Palace with her head held high making no apologies for her Royalist loyalty. The main gate was guarded by some of the men Jane knew from Holdenby, who acknowledged her politely. She asked to be granted access as she was expected by His Majesty. Her boldness threw them off guard so they allowed her to ride in. Once inside the court yard she was greeted by more serious guards who wished to search her and see some sort of paperwork which she didn't have. Another of the guards offered to escort her to the parliamentary officer in charge just as the great voice of Henry Firebrace boomed across the square.

"Aha ! How good to see you Miss Ryder, I'll be right down," quelling the officialness of the guard who stood alongside her.

In no time at all the great man himself came out of the kitchen doors behind them.

He nodded to the guard and greeted Jane warmly, "Come with me Miss, the King is at prayer but we can get you by a fire with something warm to drink or eat." He tutted, fussed and flapped saying loudly, "and not one of these men has the good manners to take your horse ? No manners, all muscle and muskets, no brains. Honestly, this way Miss Ryder, follow me."

"Thank you Henry," said Jane as she followed him back to the kitchens.

Jane was delighted to see so many familiar faces bustling about in such familiar surroundings. It was as if the madness of the outside world had not penetrated the kitchens of the palace and it comforted her, even though everyone looked purposeful and not understandably, as jovial as Jane remembered.

Henry made a place for them at the end of the long kitchen table, pouring hot tea for them both. Jane loved Hampton Court, it was like a red brick wonderland nestled in marvellous forests that held a great many of her childhood memories. She was at ease just being here. Henry filled her in on all the events of the past week and their road here. Which had gone surprisingly smoothly, thankfully the King was still being treated with the utmost respect and the household had made the move easily and swiftly, everyone looking forward to being back within palace walls, even if under different circumstances. It felt hopeful.

The King still had certain liberties and no doubt appreciated being back in more suited accommodation but he was noticeably anxious, under enormous strains and pains. He had no word from his wife the Queen which grieved him. Her long absence was affecting him terribly, Lord Fairfax had arranged for him to see his children on route which had broken his heart and reminded him of how alone he was.

Jane was saddened to hear that he was in such despair but then how could he not be ? She asked if she could see him and asked Henry how she could best help.

He whispered under his breath, "perhaps a letter from the Queen or his children ? I feel it would greatly swell his spirit …if you ?"

Jane shook her head sadly for she had neither. "Alas Henry, I have not come bearing gifts, I bring only my allegiance."

Henry smiled admiringly, "He could do with more men like you Miss Ryder. Come, His Majesty will be back in his quarters by now. I'll take you to him if I may ? He will, I'm sure, be pleased to see you." He led the way to the King, following two kitchen maids who were taking trays to him, moving silently along the regal corridors. Henry courteously went ahead of the maids to knock at the King's chambers and the King's footman opened the door letting them all into the library where the King sat waiting. He was not expecting Jane to be there and was overjoyed throwing his arms wide in welcome as if his own children had come.

"Oh how splendid, what a wonderful surprise, welcome Miss Ryder, please ?" He gracefully signaled for an extra seat which was immediately bought for her, the King had lost none of his command but he looked gaunt and frail. Jane fell to her knees.

"Your Majesty."

"Come, come dear heart… on your feet lass."

Jane greatly appreciated his over-expression of Scottishness and rose to her feet with the help of his hands.

"Will you join us Henry ?" He asked, as Jane composed herself and took her seat at the table.

"No, thank you Sir, I have business elsewhere. May I leave Miss Ryder with you ?"

"Yes you may, gladly," the King smiled.

"Very well then, Miss Ryder." Henry bowed to them both respectfully and left Jane and the King silently smiling at each other.

The King looked upon Jane as a long lost daughter, "I must tell you how pleased I am to see, a friend."

"That I am Sire and I am mightily pleased to be seeing you," said Jane, "I am equally glad to see you back in the palace, surroundings you are accustomed too."

"Yes, you and I agree there," the King wryly smiled.

Silence fell about them as the King looked forlornly into the distance, the crackle of the fire brought them back into the room. The reality was Cromwell's men had taken over Hampton Court and despite the regality of their surroundings, it was obvious that the King was a prisoner in his own home.

"May I speak frankly Miss Ryder ?"

Jane nodded silently in agreement to the King's earnest request.

He focused his misty eyes upon the leaping flames of the fire.

"All is lost …My crown …My Kingdom … My family … everything." His eyes swelling with tears as he spoke of those dearest to him whom he undoubtedly missed desperately.

"You may think, much as I do, that I was foolish to respond to that puritanical parliament as I did and engage in this God forsaken mess, well that's what they'll have you believe. Unfortunately I had very little choice, they had stripped me of all means, forcing me to raise taxes, to surrender my friends, worse still, to sign their death warrants. Which… will haunt me for the rest of my days I assure you. I can only tell you that I did what I thought to be right at the time, wholly in the name of God and of Liberty. The liberty of all, not just my own but then they attempted to force my hand towards ideas which were not mine and therefore not, in my eyes, of a divine nature. There are a great many other minds at work here and not everything is as it seems or as they will tell you. Propaganda is a powerful tool. My intentions were always for the highest good and for the people. I understand that Cromwell believes otherwise but then he is not the King … well …not yet anyway, he is a brewer," he half laughed to himself in resignation. "I know not what designs he has for this country or the world he is intent to drive the people towards, but it is not one I wish to see." The King turned towards Jane, his eyes tired and pink, his hollow face etched in pain.

"I am neither fearful nor a fool Miss Ryder, I know they, those puritan men of parliament wish me dead and will, no doubt use unscrupulous means to accomplish it. As you see I am already living as a prisoner whilst my family are exiled from their home and thrones. They've destroyed every ideal of beauty we were hoping to achieve. These fair isles are about to be taken to hell in a hand cart with the brewer banging the drum. This is how you find me…In ruin …In what was once my favourite palace is now my less welcoming prison… I can trust no one and …In all honesty Miss Ryder …Death is …"

"No, no no Your Majesty, " Jane gasped.

"Come dear heart, I am not seeking pity, it won't do for the pair of us to be in misery, come now." He smiled and offered her his hand.

"I was lucky enough to know your father, he was a good man. An honest and decent man who served my father faithfully, men like that were hard to find in those days and even less so now. Your mother is also a fine woman and here you are the product of such excellent breeding, much like your fathers horses." He chuckled to himself and smiled kindly at Jane.

They sat silently and stared into the fire, Jane lost in memories of her beloved father, mother, King James and happier times when the Stuarts flourished as they watched the dancing flames. Thinking of King James triggered the thought of the other King James, the one that was currently perfecting his impersonation of this King sat before her and in Jane's mind doing it exceptionally well. Jane turned to look at the King, there was definitely a striking resemblance between the two men, more so now Jane had the opportunity to observe them both so closely. James had even perfected the King's soft Scottish lilt.

"Your Majesty," Jane said slowly as if daring herself to utter the words she had come to say.

The King turned to her, smiling from his weary face.

"We have got to get you out of here, out of this misery away from this place and these people that hold you prisoner, you must escape ?"

"And how would you suggest I escape Ms Ryder ?"

"As it happens Your Majesty, I do have a plan." Jane smiled.

The King, who trusted Jane well, sat back in his chair and returned her smile, "do you ? Well in that case, you have my full attention."

Jane cleared her throat, "Well," she began searching for the right words.

"Your Majesty, forgive me ... I'll just say it as it comes and I trust we shall make some sense of it at the end. It is the reason that I came to visit you today. Seeing as we find ourselves in a most ridiculous situation, would like to hear a ridiculous idea ?"

The King was amused, "what could be more ridiculous than this ? Carry on my dear, by all means." He cast his eyes back to the fire.

"I have a...friend, a man... someone I believe in wholeheartedly, that I trust, who happens to know you quite well."

"Does he ?" The King raised his eyebrows.

"You may remember him, James ? James Shirley ? He was, or I suppose he still is, one of the Queens men. He performed and indeed wrote many of the wonderful masques for you and Her Majesty the Queen ? Well ...we've had this idea, by we, I mean Mr Shirley and I." Jane couldn't help but smile and neither could the King as they were both transported back to the lavish and wonderful memories of Whitehall.

"Ah yes, of course, how could one ever forget, a wonderful writer and a fine actor." The King closed his eyes, remembering those fantastical times.

"Yes, the very same. Well James is, that is to say, he has lately become, most respectfully of course, an impersonator of ..."

"Of ?"

"Of you, Sire."

"Of me ?" Smiled the King, bemused.

"Yes, and may I say wonderfully so."

"Oh I see," but he didn't.

"Yes James, wishing to be of service to you and of course the Queen came up with a rather brilliant idea and feels now is the perfect time for it. He is at this very moment perfecting your manners and polishing his performance. It really is uncanny when he is dressed… oh, perhaps I ought to ask you to forgive me further Sire, for I have … procured…" Jane chose her words carefully and looked coyly up at the King who was following her every word.

"Procured ?"

"Yes, forgive me but I have borrowed a few items from the Royal wardrobe at Westminster and when James is clothed in them …"

"Performing as me while dressed in my clothes ? … Miss Ryder I'm not sure I'm following ?"

The heat of embarrassment was rising within her,

"Forgive me," she repeated, "I will try to explain with greater clarity."

"Yes, would you ? And could we get to the point ?"

"To the point Sire, yes, in that case, James who is .. or was .. as I mentioned,"

"Yes, yes I understand thus far. Mr Shirley…in my clothes, but I'm not sure where this is all leading ?"

"Mr Shirley, James wishes, quite earnestly so, nothing more than to be of some assistance to you and especially to the Queen, whose kind and gracious patronage he has never forgotten. Between us we …James and I." Jane blushed when she revealed they had been together but carried on quickly, lowering her voice, " We have devised, what we feel to be an infallible and most fantastic plan."

"Yes, I do recall you mentioned a plan," smiled the king, who was a very patient man. "Ah to escape ?" He whispered, raising one eye towards her, having thought of it many times himself.

"Yes, Your Majesty, to help you escape." Breathed Jane who realised she was twittering and making very little sense.

"Here's our plan," Jane took a calming deep breath as she poured out her ideas.

"James is willing to take your place, to trade places with you, so that you might escape this treachery. We wondered if there are times when you are able to shake the guard somehow, get away from the palace and into the woods so that you and James could switch places ? James could be a decoy and charge forth for freedom, while you could go someplace to gather yourself with clarity and without these constant threats looming over you. For your part Sire, we'd need you to watch the guard's movements and note down, changes, times, possible opportunities when you feel you might be best able to slip their attention, and then if there is a chance, we take it." Looking out of the window for inspiration to add to the scenario playing out in her mind, she added, " What about you taking a boat ? What if you crossed the river, wouldn't that be far easier and quieter ? If somehow you were able to get across the river, on an arranged night, James and I could be waiting with horses, there on the other side for you. You then trade places with James, with him riding as you for France. It is the most obvious place, is it not ? Believe me Sire, James will be easily taken for you, he is a very good actor, but he will need help. Could you employ a couple of men to ride with him ? But only tell them on that day, so they have no time to raise an alarm or betray us, then they can all make their way to France. We arrange to meet these… trusted ?" They looked at each other knowing that it was impossible to tell who could be trusted, surrounded as they were by so much treachery.

"Arrange that you will meet these…men ? A little further down the path from where we will be, giving us ample time and opportunity to make the change, James will play your part all the way to France and once he is safely with the Queen, all concerned will believe that you're in France therefore their guard will be down. We believe once it is discovered you are free and are at large… the whole country… especially the ports will be impossible, so James must cross the channel before the

193

alarm is raised. I have asked the astrologer Lilly, his advice. I was recently at his house and I am to return there as I asked him to draw a chart regarding your ... liberty. Forgive me, it seemed like the right thing to do at the time, I thought him to be an odd fellow but perhaps it's because of all those dead things he keeps about. He's sure to think we will follow his advice, so if by chance he does see in the heavens and should he alert parliament men, it would be advantageous to tell him our plans are quite the opposite to our real intentions." Jane mused thinking aloud.

Jane scanned the King's face for clues as to what he was thinking because he said nothing although he was clearly contemplating the pictures and plans Jane was planting in his mind. She continued in hushed tones.

"I shall travel, if I may, with you, to somewhere far away, far away enough to be safe and unaffected by the inevitable hallaballo which will no doubt ensue when they discover you are at large. Forgive me but I have already written to the Queen seeking her guidance and her blessing."

The King smiled upon hearing that Jane had consulted the Queen first, so she continued with more enthusiasm, looking to the King for reassurance but his eyes were closed, his hands clasped against his chin as if listening intently or deep in thought.

"With James safely with the Queen in France, they would no longer be looking for you. When the whole world knows you are free and safe with your Queen, Cromwell and his cronies would be trembling with fear, for they know the country is with you. I hear there are many uprisings happening Sire, many people, all over the country are calling for an end to this, for your return, for you to reclaim England, for your freedom. When the people know you are free, that you have escaped, I believe it would spark an almighty rebellion, the likes that not even this army could contain. So that, Your Majesty, is our plan."

There was another prolonged silence but Jane had become accustomed to these whilst in the presence of the King.

"Well I must say it sounds very dramatic but dare I say it, not impossible ? Alas, you must forgive me Miss Ryder, for I have very little faith in men at present and although I hope that Mr Shirley is, as you say a trustworthy fellow, I would have to put my life in his hands, which begs the question, is he truly willing to risk everything, risk his own life in such a dangerous way ? And where would 'we' go ?"

"Somewhere safe and far away, as for James, yes, I honestly believe he is more than willing, he is determined. I have seen him, as you, Your Majesty and may I say he is absolutely convincing, in every way. He needs only to make his way to France, quietly and quickly. No one would be able to tell the difference, especially in the dark ? Under a cloak ? No one would think it was anyone other than you, why would they ?"

"You make a great deal of assumption Miss Ryder, what if God forbid he is caught ? What plan does he have for that possibility, for it is one ?"

"He has considered this… a bit, but he is intent on getting to France, he will whatever happens continue with his performance as he calls it, he is neither concerned nor afraid. He wishes only for your liberty, that is what drives us both. You would be in a far better position to observe the unfolding events from far away. You could advise him, should it come to that. Once it is all over and they welcome you back to Westminster, to your throne, we will switch you again and no one would be any the wiser, although you will have been a lot safer."

"What of assassins ? People that would attempt to harm him ? Every day Miss Ryder there comes another threat, another fear, I couldn't live with myself knowing that a good man has endured what I could not."

"You have endured Sire and it is exactly this constant threat that we wish to relieve you of. James is fully aware of the potential dangers but he is as committed as I am in assisting you to regain your liberty. I am willing to put all my faith in him and this plan. We only see what we expect to see, much like the masques. Remember how our beliefs were suspended by Inigo Jones's wizardry at each and every performance ? I saw with my own eyes how easy it is to be, well, … deceived is not the right word but influenced certainly, influenced to see, think or believe a certain thing or person or tale to be true. Anyway, no one knows what to believe these days and no one dares to say what their true beliefs are either."

"I agree, it certainly sounds like a performance I'd like to be part of, one with a far happier ending."

"Yes with a, happily ever after. Your Majesty, I assure you, you have a great many men still loyal to you. Although they may not be fighting men, they are true Royalists at heart and they have no place in Cromwell's England."

The King looked deep into Jane's eyes, he knew as well as she did that the puritan world that was creeping over England would be a death toll for them all.

"Well, Miss Ryder, you do surprise me and I do not doubt you. You have already proved yourself to me, and I have never questioned your loyalties, probably because our families have been together since way back, all the way back to Scotland." They smiled at each other.

"And, it may surprise you Miss Ryder but it appears I currently have no other ...engagements. I wonder, to be absolutely clear, what is it that you would ask of me ?"

"To trust us Your Majesty. You must decide on a day or preferably a night that you could easily slip away, unnoticed. Do you think it is possible for you to get away ? To the other side of the river ?"

"I do, I have access to the river and a boat." The King smiled, at last his interest was stirred.

"Where do you believe it would be best for James and I to wait for you ?"

"Mosley, the trees give cover and from there it is a clear ride through the forest."

"Good, for we shall need both." Jane smiled as they sat silently together for a long while each lost in their own thoughts.

"Miss Ryder, you honour me with your ingenuity and your courage. Like your father before you, you are a brave and loyal friend . Thank you, we will see to it that you are greatly rewarded."

Jane smiled with tears welling up in her eyes as she looked at the King and remembered her father.

"I seek no reward or recompense, Your Majesty. It is my belief that this inspiration comes directly from God and it is by his design. My only wish is for your safety and to be of service to you and to Your Queen. I truly believe this plan to be possible, that this is our chance, even though I know it sounds fantastic."

"Yes dear sweetheart, but aren't the most fantastic tales all the more ... wonderful ? I must tell you, I feel inspired. I will certainly give your ideas some further thought."

"Your Majesty, I, we would be honoured if you would even consider them. I understand plans may change but of our devotion you can be certain. We are in a perfect position to escape from here, after all this is still your palace and you know the lay of the land well, as do I. We must at least try, I feel the universe will support us, we know that fortune favours the brave and brave we will be, for who knows what parliament or Cromwell's army will call for next. Let us seize this opportunity for freedom, for your liberty."

"It does sound possible and certainly desirable, I shall ponder and let you know my decision, in a few weeks ? By then I will know clearly and concisely, having prayed and collected myself. I will know if it is the right and just course of action."

"Thank you, Your Majesty."

"Now Miss Ryder, I do believe it to be time for something, will you join me ?"

The King rang a little bell and in moments Ashburnham appeared, he looked taken aback to see Jane sat at the Kings table, although he must have known she was there.

"Mrs Whorwood," he nodded in his greasy oily manner, instinctively rubbing his nose and remembering the pain of their last meeting.

Jane smiled knowingly, which unsettled him as he was someone whose life was filled with lies. The King requested wine and if they permitted such joyful things some cake to be brought for them both. Ashburnham sheepishly nodded and left the room, while Jane and the King continued to sit in the silence they were so accustomed to. It showed that they were both at ease in each other's company and also that there was no agitation, irritation or other unpleasant currents between them. The King who had lost a great deal of trust in what men and women for that matter, knew he could always be sure of how he felt. At this particular time, in Jane Ryder's company he felt comfortable and at ease which were sure signs that she was wholeheartedly on his side but then the King had always had a soft spot for the wild barefooted child of William Ryder with her red highlander hair and bonny smile, she had won over all of their hearts long ago.

Ashburnham swiftly returned having knocked at the door and entered without waiting for the King's beckoning. He set the tray down and poured the wine, placing plates with dry fruit loaf ahead of them asking if he could join them. Jane and the King looked at each other as Ashburnham had clearly already made this assumption.

"Why of course Jack," said the King.

Ashburnham cut himself a wedge of cake and dropped down into a fireside chair with all the elegance of a lead weight.

"What news have you, Jack ?" Enquired the King.

"None, nothing that I'm sure Mrs Whorwood here hasn't told you already." He replied in his sneering way.

"Unfortunately Sir I know nothing that an esteemed gentleman such as yourself would not know." Jane took her cup and sat back focusing her eyes to the fire.

"Then what is it that brings you here Madam ?"

She was taken aback by his blatant rudeness which the King found amusing, Jane however did not.

"Now, now Jack, you've no need to be jealous of Miss Ryder, her family has always been at our side, thank God and had her dear stepfather not so recently retired, I believe he would still be here. I am however most fortunate to have Miss Ryder still visit with me." He playfully placed a hand above hers, "Actually, we talk very little Jack." Ashburnham raised his eyebrows and drank his wine, then he began wittering on nervously about trivial things, happenings in the kitchens, nothing of any interest or consequence.

Jane half listened as did the King, the energy in the room had changed and they were both aware of it.

Jane cared little for Ashburnham, he had exhausted all goodwill from his family connections as far as Jane was concerned and she undoubtedly knew him to be the traitor within the King's camp. She tried hard not to show him the contempt he was due, but this just made it uncomfortable being in his company so it wasn't long before Jane made her excuses to leave. The King fussed over her like his own daughter and sent Ashburnham to call a carriage, Jane thanked the King but asked if she could have a horse instead, this brought a swell of pride to the King and a look of disgust from Ashburnham, who muttered, "as you wish," before leaving.

"I will return in three weeks, Your Majesty," whispered Jane.

"I trust that you will Ms Ryder," smiled the King as he helped her into her cloak. Jane felt compelled to tell him of her discovery and misgivings regarding Ashburnham and the events that led to Mary Cave's apprehension.

"Your Majesty," she began rather coyly.

"Jane," the King interrupted as if reading her thoughts.

"I am well aware of your dislike and mistrust of Ashburnham," he said in lowered tones. "Have no fear. I know of his part in the trap laid by yourself and Madam Cave," Jane saw a twinkle in the regents eye.

"I still have an ear to the ground, you know. Mary was freed with no further trouble. However it appears you were right, the whole debacle did reveal something. In times like these, much as I would like to keep what friends I have close, I keep my enemies closer."

There came the knock with Ashburnham's impatient face poking around the door after it.

"Your horse madam," he retreated, fearing he had caught the pair of them in some clandestine embrace.

The King smiled and nodded at him as Jane curtsied and gave the King a last lingering look before following Ashburnham out the door and along the corridors to the yard where her horse was waiting for her.

♛

The King's peace was constantly disrupted by threats of assassination and whispers of betrayal meant to keep him unsettled and frightened which indeed it did. The sense of doom and foreboding greatly outweighed the cordial treatment he received. It was becoming increasingly clear Charles Stuart was no longer considered King. His long standing allies had drifted, a great many of them shifting sides to suit, the brutality of betrayal was laid bare in every case. Without his Queen or his children to comfort him and unable to place any trust in those around him the King's thoughts constantly led back to Jane and her daring plan. Should he place his life in her hands ? She had kept hidden his effects from Oxford, therefore unlike a great many others she had proved herself to be trusted. The King cast his eyes above for his thoughts now turned to his friend and Ashburnham's cousin the Duke of Buckingham it was the only reason he still tolerated him. The King knew that absolutely none of this treachery would have occurred if the Duke and Lord Stafford still lived. How he wished for their counsel now, if only those two stalwart, strong and brilliant fellows would come to his aid. But then the guilt crept into his soul for the King had never forgiven himself for allowing Lord Stafford's demise. Parliament had forced his hand many times but this was the most dastardly, tears rolled down his face. The King had never felt so alone, so lost and utterly broken, he sighed heavily, what was to become of him ? Was this the end of the monarchy, was he really to be the last anointed King of Great Britain ? Had he really taken everything his Father had done to unite these isles, to ruin ? He cradled his head in his hands as visions of his father and his dear mother filled his mind, with them memories of far better times, the King knew he would now never be able to fulfill the dreams his father had. The King wrestled daily with the torment of his incarceration within his own palace and the madness of it all. There came a knock at his door bringing him abruptly back to his present and current situation and he composed himself at once. In his heart he knew that whatever the circumstances, he was, as his breath confirmed, still alive and therefore still King. He took a moment to wipe his eyes and adjust himself then allowed whoever it was, admittance.

"Ah, Ashburnham, do come in Jack. I was just thinking of you, well your dear cousin George and how much I, like you yourself, miss him ?"

Ashburnham bowed low and entered, closing the door behind him. As if sensing his black heart, the fire spat as he walked over to it, making him jump. He reached for the poker and stoked up the flames before adding some more logs, then dumped himself into the chair behind him, whatever he was, he was no gentleman.

"Aye, the handsome Duke, my mother thinks of him more than me," he sniffed, glaring into the fire as it roared back to life. "But," he continued without taking his eyes away from the fire, "I shall always be grateful to him for placing me within your court, Your Majesty."

The King smiled curtly, for it was obvious he wasn't grateful in the slightest.

There came another gentler knock at the door as the King's supper was brought in by a flurry of maids, who laid it perfectly and silently at the table. The King smiled as they placed down the dishes prepared for him, some of the girls had been part of the household for years and had covered many miles in service to his needs, he nodded in appreciation to them all.

"Won't you join me Jack ? For I am so sick of dining alone."

"I'm not hungry Sire."

"Well," sighed the King, "my appetite is waning too and yet, it does smell very good and there does seem to be an awful lot of it, are you sure you won't join me ?"

"If you insist."

"Wonderful," smiled the King, as he invited Ashburnham to take the seat on his left and sat himself down at the head of the table.

"Now you can tell me what news there is of the outside world, anything that might be interesting or in the least distracting for an old captive such as I."

Ashburnham moved himself to the dinner table shaking out the napkin and placing it into his collar as the ladies flitted about them.

"You do bring news, I take it ?" Asked the king as he surveyed his dinner.

"None that you'd be happy to hear," said Ashburnham, heaping food on his plate despite his lack of hunger, the King sat back concerned.

"Well why not tell me anyways dear chap, do forgive me ladies but it has been so very dull here of late."

Ashburnham waved his glass to be filled. "Well .." He began taking a big swig of wine and promptly asking for another as he wiped his face. He then poured out his news from Westminster which was heavily laced with parliamentary propaganda.

The King ate slowly and silently as Ashburnham relayed all the horrors of the potential threats and told him of the hideous crimes he was being accused of and how his father was being slandered, while Cromwell's had moved into the palace at Whitehall.

This made the King slam down his fist in fury. He excused the serving ladies as Ashburnham, with his hands greased from the fat of the King meats, fumbled with a glass implying his want for more. His glass was duly filled by the last maid who then floated silently from the room and quietly closed the door behind her.

Ashburnham continued to slurp and feed his face much in the manner of an animal all the while delighting in sharing the very worst of the gossip from London. The King pushed his plate into the centre of the table as Ashburnham, who noticed that the maids had kindly left the wine jug, stood and poured himself another in a most grotesque display of gluttony. The King listened and watched this unworthy creature as he filled the room with fearful threats clearly limbered up by the wine. Ashburnham shared all he was meant to and some things he wasn't, the King observed the buffoon with nonchalant indifference. When Ashburnham began repeating himself, having exhausted his tales and vocabulary, the King swiftly rang the bell summoning Henry Firebrace, who escorted him back to his quarters and put him to bed.

Once more in the peace of his own company, without the wittering, simpering snake Ashburnham, the King reminded himself to eat alone in future. He drank his wine and then headed for his desk to compose a letter for Miss Ryder for if Ashburnham's loose tongue was to be believed, even slightly, his life was in grave and unthinkable danger. The King would begin at once to monitor his captors movements.

As October came to a close the King was feeling more and more anxious, even though he had been treated well and was glad of the conversations with the giant Firebrace, who had fast become a friend. There was a rather sickly haunting feeling that now saturated the palace, Ashburnham had put this down to the Tudor King or rather his many wives who were said to walk the corridors undead but the current King emphatically felt a darker, more sinister situation unfolding, which indeed it was. He no longer felt at ease or able to rest so high was the sense of threat, he committed himself to Jane's plan, believing it to be the only remedy to his dire situation.

Jane had used her time wisely, she had raced back to London and to William Lilly's house. Her appointment with him was brief as it appeared he too was taking his leave of the city, hurriedly he gave her the charts she had requested.

"Here, I have no wish to have any part in your fanciful ideas Madam, I have read the constellations and should you wish as you say to liberate the King I would be swift, as you may know the debates in Putney have become heated. I would suggest making use of the fortunate aspect at the full moon."

"Where should we go, should we be successful in our attempts ?"

"Madam Whorwood, if you have seriously no idea as to what you should do next, I suggest you rethink this folly, for it sounds to me an ill thought out plot and as I told you, I wish to have no involvement in these foolish, badly orchestrated plans."

"Would you be so kind as to suggest the safest path for him to take Sir ? You do after all have a better insight."

"Maybe, but I do not align with your intentions at all and I've probably given you enough to incriminate myself already. Head east, towards the rising sun for all I care. I have my own neck to think of, now take what you have paid for and leave."

Although she was stunned, Jane was also amused by him and his bluntness.

The three weeks passed quickly with Jane conversing with Elizabeth and her husband, running errands and spending as much time as she could with James. In no time at all she found herself back at Hampton Court Palace waiting to see the King.

"Your Majesty," she curtsied to the floor with the grace of a lady who had been doing so her whole life.

"Ah, Miss Ryder, how wonderful it is to see you. Do come in, you are a most welcome guest," the King motioned for her to close the door behind her.

"Now," he lowered his voice.

"If you are still keen in assisting my liberty, and I sincerely hope that you are because I would like to accept your kind offer and place my trust in you and Mr Shirley entirely and immediately. I have been giving it a great deal of thought but in all honesty I now have very little choice. I have been observing, for my part, the movement of the guards which I've written for you here," he passed Jane a small piece of paper which she unfolded.

"You will see on the map I have given you, where I can get to. I have noticed a small boat tied here and it has been there these past weeks, so I've every reason to believe it will still be available to me, if I act quickly. I believe the most fortuitous day to implement these plans would be Monday. There are fewer guards that evening, giving me a better opportunity to make for the river where I will easily be able to get to Moulsey Hurst, already a hunting ground giving us a clear path to ride on. Therefore, if it is still a possibility, I will meet you there, this Monday at what I believe to be the best time, for me at any rate, which is seven o'clock precisely. It will be dark but as the moon will be full it will hopefully be clear enough for us to see. Once I land at Moulsey Hurst, God willing, I will be at your mercy and luck. This is of course if your plan to assist my escape is still agreeable to you ?" He looked at her with hope as Jane listened and looked at the note with instructions and places clearly marked out.

"Monday," she mused, "that's the day after tomorrow ?"

"Yes, forgive me, I know I have sprung this upon you but I am now desperate to be free of this place. Unfortunately, for me, there is a dark foreboding cloaked over me, a prevalent ill feeling that is permeating everything. I can no longer trust anyone or anything, not even the food. So if this is still in agreement with you and Mr Shirley of course, which I trust it is. I shall have faith and see you both at Mousley Hurst. You can see clearly on this map, where I mean, where there are other boats tethered, at seven o'clock, Monday. Well, I shall certainly have taken to the water by then, if you would look out for a small boat ?" He held Jane's hands around the note she held, looking deeply into her eyes. "There is terrible gossip of treasonous plans they are concocting at Putney. I fear if I do not leave quickly, there will be an attempt made upon my life, I feel awkward and unsafe."

"That settles it then, Monday it is. Mr Lilly mentioned the Putney debates and he also suggested when the moon is full. I asked his advice and rather flippantly he said to head east for all he cared. Therefore Your Majesty, I suggest you and I head west. You have my word as God is my witness that we, James and I, will be ready and waiting for you at Mousley Hurst, Monday at seven o'clock. We shall not hesitate or waiver, we will be there and at your service, I promise you."

"Thank you," the King breathed a huge sigh of relief and returned to his writing desk.

"Now, do sit down Miss Ryder and tell me news of my friend, your dear stepfather, for we will not be alone for long," as Jane sat the door swung open with little reverence or respect. It was Ashburnham.

"Oh Your Majesty forgive me, I wasn't aware you had company, Madam Whorwood," he nodded, enjoying how much it irritated her to be called by her married name. Placing the tray upon the table, he said, "I'll fetch another cup."

"Bring two, my good fellow for won't you join us ? Madam .. Miss Ryder here," the King quickly corrected himself, " brings news of Maxwell."

"Very good Sire," said Ashburnham, bowing out of the room, leaving the door open. Jane smiled when he returned and thanked him kindly as he placed the cups and poured wine for three.

Monday and the full moon duly came, the King had battled all day with the necessity of leaving his faithful dogs. Following dinner, the King had calmly left his quarters when he knew the guard to be lax for a walk in the Privy garden. The boat was still as he had hoped tethered by the shore, he swiftly untied it and cast it out onto the river. He climbed in quickly, giving all his strength and determination to the oars. They silently dipped and glided through the flowing moonlit waters, rowing for freedom he focused fully on the other side of the river. In no time the little rowing boat ran aground and the King leapt from it. He began heaving it ashore when a further set of hands helped him, making him jump as he turned to see a smiling face of someone he recognised.

"May I help you, Your Majesty ?" Whispered James.

The King was so surprised he promptly slipped on the river bank, his nerves being so understandably frayed.

James easily lifted the boat out of the water hiding it behind some bushes as Jane appeared and offered her hand to the King.

"You made it," breathed Jane clearly elated.

"As did you," remarked the King brushing himself down.

"May I introduce you to...yourself Your Majesty ?" Said Jane proudly as the King and James firmly shook hands and quickly began to change clothes.

"My word, it's remarkable."

Even in the dark the King could see that James did look very much like him.

"Am I really that handsome ?" He asked, smiling at James while handing him his coat. "I am indebted to you Sir. You certainly look the part now I am trusting to act the part also, I leave the weight of the crown of England upon your shoulders, I ask only that you make haste and please portray me with the integrity and the grace you would expect from your King."

"Your Majesty, I give you my word, I will do my very best to exude your values."

"Jane, I did as you suggested and told two fellows of my plan to escape and I told them only today. They are in accordance and I hope they will accompany you to the coast. I have no reason to mistrust them but one can never be too careful, but after that .. it's very much up to you, I trust you will make your way to Paris as fast as you can, Godspeed."

The King handed James his cane.

"I am never without it."

Suddenly the King was overcome with fears and doubts as he looked at James showing such courage and he embraced him.

"Your Majesty, we must go," said Jane, pulling him out of his sadness. He mounted his horse joining Jane who was already seated and raring to go. Everything suddenly slowed, becoming silent and still as they all cast hopeful determined glances amongst each other. Jane looked desperately at James, not saying a word, for they had agreed not to say goodbye. The moment they had long planned for had finally come but now they felt so unprepared, engulfed by the danger of their endeavours and the realisation that they might not see each other again. If it were possible to fall in love in an instant then this was the moment, when they both knew that they belonged together because the thought of being without each other was suddenly unbearable. Jane's heart was thumping as she turned away and focused on the road ahead. She gripped her bridle and tucked her heels into her horse." Sire, we must go."

The sound of galloping hooves were racing towards them, "Away with you and may the road rise to meet you," said James as he slipped into his regal character.

"May God bless you." Jane said over her shoulder as James waved the King's hat and raised his cane with charismatic enthusiasm while Jane and the King charged off in the opposite direction.

"God bless you," echoed the King.

"God save the King," said James to himself as he wrapped the King's fine cloak around himself and made his way further down the path. The moon was rising making everything silvery and the air was crisp and clean, James didn't have to wait long for the pounding hooves to come to a stop, "Sire …sire we must make haste." Stirred from his lingering thoughts of Jane, James silently nodded and climbed upon the horse they had brought for him and followed on. An able horseman James easily kept pace with the man in front. They hadn't gone more than a mile when they collected another horseman and rode as four. James dared not ask who he was or where they were going, he simply kept up and kept quiet.

♛

Thankfully the men said very little as they galloped along, with the moonlight leading their way. They had, James felt, covered many miles by the time they came upon an old Inn in the forest, the men stopped and talked amongst themselves, James was nervous, apprehensive of the men and unfamiliar with the road.

"Sire, we must rest the horses and get some sleep ourselves or else we'll be dead before we get there." James dismounted and wondered where 'there' was, the King said he would be accompanied to the coast but this didn't feel like the road to Kent. He then remembered William Lilly had told Jane to head east but this was no road to Essex either. He felt slightly disoriented as they secured the horses, making his way around the trough, he followed the three men into the rambling Inn covered in ivy. It was dimly lit but a smoking chimney signaled someone was awake.

The door creaked open and there in the corner was the remains of a fire still warm but reduced to embers, all four men headed towards it with their numb hands outstretched. James pulled down his hat and found a seat next to the fire while one of the men headed to the bar.

"Sir, are we welcome here by your fire ?"

"Aye you're welcome to what's left of it. Can I get you …" He surveyed the company, "gentleman, anything more ?"

"Yes, ales if you please and your senses serve you well …we are indeed gentlemen …we carry grave news and must be upon the next tide …have you by chance fresh horses ? We can pay...handsomely ?"

The man poured large mugs of ale from a barrel eyeing the speaker with an air of suspicion.

"Horses ? No …but I can have the boy bring yours round a fresh net .. and there's plenty of water ... I dare say by morning they'll be fit once more and you are welcome to rest here… I'm no parliamentarian, no puritan either. The world's gone mad if you ask me …I'm happy to serve all ... if they lay their money down," nodding to the King's man to place his coins upon the counter, which he duly did. In their place the host served up four mugs of ale then went out back, no doubt to kick some poor boy, telling him to see to the horses, then returned with more logs for the fire.

"We don't get many late night visits…upon this road …mostly carriages during the day, so you'll have the whole place to yourself. First light is hours away yet, I'd wager you could do with the rest ... here." The landlord handed out some blankets, James' companions accepted his generosity without saying a word, nodding in appreciation. The host nodded in return and left them to their business by the fire.

"I know you may be wondering how we come to be upon this path, but I have an idea."

James shone an eye out from beneath his wide brimmed hat.

"Go on," he purred in his first performance as the King of England, he waited with bated breath to see if he would be discovered, but the man continued.

"Your absence will no doubt have been discovered by now, I think we should we take a little rest then head to the Isle of White. I have reason to believe the governor there will be sympathetic and will give us sanctuary."

James immediately felt uneasy as a second man interjected, "the Isle of White Jack ? To Governor Hammond are you mad ? He's a roundhead, the Isle of White would turn into our prison ... No, were not looking for sanctuary. Isn't the plan to get to France ? We must have a better plan that …or else ?" He looked over at James, "all will be lost, Sire, this is madness, we should never have stopped and that would be more madness, we have been foolish to put our faith in Jack's plan. We should keep going."

'Ah, so this is Jack, Jack Ashburnham,' thought James, who had already been warned of his duplicity.

"Well no one else has a plan, other than this wild scramble through the woods ...get to France yes but... I have reason to believe.." Jack continued

"Believe what Jack ? That if we slowly plod to the Isle of White the Governor will take pity on us ? I believe that Hammond will turn us in as soon as look at us ?" It appeared that neither of the other men supported Jack's ideas.

"Look, we had very little choice, we all needed a rest. I say we sail to White and then…"

"Not as much as we needed to get to the coast, you've held us up at every turn, you've had us going round in circles and now you've got us tucked under blankets for God's sake…What is your obsession with getting to the Isle of White ? … Sitting ducks that's what we'll be there, why not make straight for France as planned, let's get to France." Jack ignored him and addressed James directly.

"Look, there can be no doubt that the whole of Hampton Court knows you've escaped by now and by morning London will be in uproar the ports will be closed, we have no time. Hammond's father, you remember, was once one of your Chaplains." Ashburnham was desperately seeking reassurance from James, hoping he would think it was a good idea. "Look, Your Majesty," he whispered, with much anguish in his voice. "Surely… surely you trust me, and at a desperate time such as this you would first seek out and put your faith in one of your own Chaplains ... wouldn't you ?"

"Well …" began James, who had already been warmed not to trust him.

"Your Majesty, I want you to know that I will follow you and I am your man, but if you are thinking to put your faith in Jack's plan, I beg you to reconsider. Let it be known I think it a preposterous idea, I have no faith in any of parliament's men, even if their father is a priest."

"Chaplain," chimed James and Jack together.

"The alarm will soon be raised, if it hasn't already, no one will think of looking for us on this road or on the Isle of White, besides we are already halfway to Southampton." Ashburnham was clearly distressed.

"Tis folly I tell you, let us get to France, let us go …now." Said the most doubtful of the men shaking his head.

James looked over their frightened faces and saw he needed to take charge of their fears somehow. "Sadly, there was no time to consider or plan, we must devise one from where we find ourselves to be now gentlemen and that is apparently halfway to Southampton. It would be folly to turn around so let us rest a while and then continue our course to the coast and see what presents itself there. We may find passage directly to France if God wills it. May I thank you all for having the courage to accompany me this far." James whispered as he raised his cup, carefully looking for their response but they were lost in their own thoughts and not one of them doubted that he was the King. James relaxed, pulling his hat down and blankets around him as all four men drank their beer silently and stared sleepily into the flames.

♛

Jane's and the King had charged west and were now in comfortable rooms at St Mary Bourne. The horses were as fed and watered as they were.

"Your Majesty, all will be well, we have made good time and already covered many miles, we shall carry on at first light, so let us be ready for an early start. I think it is time to tell you, I have very clear and direct instructions from the Queen." She passed the King a letter she had been carrying since London.

The King eagerly broke the seal and read the letter then placing it close to his chest he cried.

Jane looked away so as not to see this tender moment of the King of England whose contact with his wife had been restricted by the men who had kept him a prisoner and who he was now a fugitive from. He stood up gracefully and silently headed back to his room clutching the letter from his wife.

♛

The moon had long set but the sun had not yet risen by the time Jane awoke, she dressed quickly and went to the King's room across the hall. She could see the flickering of a candle underneath the doorway so knew he was awake, she tapped gently.

"Come in," came a soft reply.

The King smiled broadly, "come in, come in child," he whispered, "and close the door."

Jane smiled and knelt before him.

"Oh ! No, no, this will never do, 'tis I who should kneel before you. I am indebted to you and I owe you my life. I am eternally thankful to you and I would be honoured if you would think of me as your father as we travel together from this moment on."

Jane nodded, "the honour would be mine ... father."

They smiled at each other as the King put on his boots and James's cloak. He picked up his candle and they left together Jane following down the stairs. The King had paid with pence from his pocket and enjoyed performing as a common man, he thanked their host and they made haste to their horses.

"To Glastonbury, ?" Jane asked.

"To Glastonbury." The King replied.

♛

By now London was ablaze with the news of the King's escape. As Jane expected, William Lilly had been visited by Cromwell's men. He had told them he believed the King would take a route toward Essex, driving a large part of the army east in pursuit. Thankfully giving the fugitives more time.

After little rest but many arguments it became apparent to James that his companions were terrible company. They had risen before the sun, taking another long ride en route to Southampton. After getting lost again in the New Forest and fighting amongst themselves, Ashburnham placed himself at the helm and fully in charge of their situation. He found an Inn where he suggested James should wait while the others went to secure their passage. James felt apprehensive as he waited alone for the best part of the day, he had very little to do except wait and drink, It did however give him time to think. It was now clear that Ashburnham was the fellow they had picked up further down the road. Perhaps one of the younger men had confided in him for the King had only said there would be two riders. James had no trust in him and by all accounts neither did the other two but they were now all at his mercy. Hours passed, testing James's nerve and his patience. Ashburnham returned first but without the others and to James' amazement he came with Colonel Hammond, the Governor of the Isle of White. Why had he brought him here ? Ashburnham gleefully explained that the Governor would welcome them to the Isle, but James could see he was clearly a parliament man and had his own interests. The gravity of the situation fell upon James like a ton of bricks. As he listened to them, he could see Hammond was filled with a mixture of sadness, obligation and opportunity. James's other companions appeared soon afterwards, they too were surprised by this turn of events. Whatever Ashburnham and this Hammond chap suggested made the other men sadly shake their heads, confirming to James that all was now lost. Before long they were all joined by the Governor's men who had very kindly come to 'escort' the King to the Isle of White.

James's heart sank, "Jack ...you have outdone me ?"

♕

James shouldn't have been surprised at how quickly this Jack had turned on him and effectively handed him over, he had been warned but the disappointment no doubt seeped out of him. Had the King really been surrounded by such useless, worthless and treacherous dogs ? Ashburnham, seeing James dissatisfaction, sprang up and became quite another character, he clearly didn't know himself or his own actions. He lent forward, his face contorted with the pain and torment that was no doubt inflicting his mind and his heart. His eyes were wild with panic and he was beginning to sweat. "Or I could kill him, Your Majesty, I could kill them all, right now, is that what you want me to do ? Shall I kill them ?" James was stunned, surprised at the man's audacity and the ridiculousness of his statement as they were quite obviously defeated, surrounded and outnumbered, perhaps it was a pathetic last ditch attempt to redeem himself. James sighed and looked at him with pity, shaking his head, he then picked up the King's cane and stood knowing that now his performance would really begin. James held out his hand for Hammond, who didn't take it but motioned for James to follow him out of the door. They took a carriage down towards the harbour where Hammond's boat was waiting for them. Jack and the other men who had that morning ridden by his side were made to stay behind at the Inn and James did not look back, his attention fixed fully upon the Isle that appeared through the sea mist.

♛

After a whole day's ride Jane and the King arrived in the sleepy little town of Glastonbury. They tethered their horses and made themselves known to the boy that would look after them at the back on the George, then Jane following a little map the Queen had sent her, led the way up past the church of St. John towards the Bluebell Inn.

Ma Gollop had spent the whole day cleaning, dusting, polishing and making sure everything was in its rightful place. She was thrilled to be expecting such an esteemed guest. She had tried to keep it to herself but her joy was hard to hide.

"Not sure what's got into you," remarked Joseph.

"Not you," shot back a deep voice from the other end of the bar and the two old friends laughed out loud.

"Hey, you two should know better, I'll have none of that rough talk, thank you very much and certainly not when we have visitors." Ma Gollop looked at them sternly across the bar.

"Oh yes, she's having visitors, Martin."

"Oh, visitors, you say ?"

"Aye, and by the way she be fussing, I'd say it be a gentleman."

"O really now, Ma Gollop, who could you be expecting save Joseph and I ?"

"That would be telling, besides it be none of your business" sang Ma Gollop over her shoulder as she directed the girls who were sweeping through upstairs.

"Well whoever it be, she's being thorough and I do love a thorough woman," laughed Joseph.

Ma Gollop who knew both men well and long, took no notice of their jibes, she was happy in their company and happy to ignore them. She carried on with her preparations and was greatly satisfied seeing the whole place sparkle and gleam.

"Like a palace Ma," said one of the girls, taking her penny and skipping off home.

"Aye sweet heart, like a palace," smiled Ma Gollop.

Ma Gollop sat awaiting her guests with the fires lit and the shutters pulled. Joseph and Martin had long left, leaving her alone, half asleep but with an ear for the door.

Jane and the King looked around to make sure no one was following as all fugitives do and tapped gently on the huge heavy oak door. It wasn't long till they heard a soft singing, which Good Wife Gollop always did as she opened doors in a kind, welcoming way. They stood back as they heard the latch lift and the door open, they were expected so the door was unlocked.

"Ah, there you are," smiled Ma Gollop broadly, showing them in, "at last… come in, come in my loves, come in and rest." The travellers smiled back gratefully accepting her welcome and following her direction went inside.

In no time at all Ma Gollop had taken their cloaks, poured out some cider and served hot soup with fresh bread, which the King and Jane ate heartily, happy and thankful that they had reached their destination safely.

♛

James was deep in thought, wrapped up in the King's cloak, as he was rowed through the mist towards the Isle of White. He silently berated himself the whole way for having missed countless opportunities to take flight. The reality of his situation became more pronounced with every turn of the oars. He was now the King. He must perform as if his life depended upon, which indeed it did. Although he was well aware of the potential dangers, he hadn't thought he would have been betrayed so soon or apprehended so quickly. Why didn't he leave the Inn when he had the chance ? He had been there all day. Fear had taken over him as had the wine. He was however impressed by the respectful and kind treatment he was receiving from everyone. He began to feel like an esteemed guest. As they landed at Yarmouth a comfortable carriage was brought to take him on to Carisbrooke Castle, which delighted James as the whole crossing he had filled his mind with thoughts of Newgate prison and thankfully this appeared to be very far from that. As he sat in the comfort of Governor Hammond's carriage, he reminded himself that he was no ordinary prisoner and breathed a huge sigh of relief.

It was the first time James had been to the Isle of White, so he took great interest in his surroundings watching the countryside roll past. It was much bigger than he imagined, he saw the famous Needles in the distance as he made his way to the heart of the Isle, Carisbrooke. The ride up to the castle gates was bumpy but beautiful, surrounded by ancient trees. It was as if you could see the whole Island from there. He alighted in the Castle courtyard surrounded by its high walls and was swiftly directed to his sumptuous new quarters, which greatly surprised him. It seemed that Colonel Hammond was going to great lengths to make him feel comfortable. James was delighted and highly relieved, he had the feeling he was about to enjoy being the King of the castle.

"And this," Ma Gollop announced proudly with a sparkling voice, "is the very room where your daughter was born." Coincidentally the last time she had been this excited for a visitor was when the Queen had come all those years ago.

The King with tears in his eyes surveyed the room and walked about it quietly touching the furniture and soaking up the ambiance.

"No one has stayed in it since, I promise you, so it's just as they left it, well, you know we've kept it clean, swept the cobwebs. Now it can be your room."

"Bless you Good Wife, I believe we are indebted to you for her safe arrival, I owe you my heartfelt thanks, for I have yet to meet my youngest child, Henrietta Anne. How, how …very kind of you .." The King, overcome with emotion, stumbled on his words.

"Ah, well here's hoping you'll be seeing them both very soon. She was a bonny babe, with the dark hair and eyes of her mother, but now I see you, I see she will be every inch her father's daughter. Beautiful they were the pair of them, I can see them now, sat over there, mother and child at peace, just beautiful."

The King sat in a nursing chair that faced the window, where in a different time the Queen had sat with their new born daughter in her arms.

"May God forgive us and protect us all," he said, raising his wet eyes to the roof.

The ladies bowed and quietly left the room, leaving the King to his thoughts and his memories. Ma Gollop then showed Jane to her room a little further down the hall.

"Thank you for taking us in and for welcoming us, I know it is a great risk you are taking, having us under your roof. The Queen must trust you greatly, for it was her that suggested we come straight to you."

"Aye, bless your heart, the dear Queen and the King have great faith in you too young lady. The Queen wrote to me, she was hopeful you might make your way here. I am so very glad you did. Nothing short of a miracle. But then, Glastonbury is and has long been a miraculous place. The Abbot gave my kin this roof so that we would always offer rest and a welcome to those in need. So that's what I do and my mother did before me. I never thought in all my days we'd have such esteemed guests, honestly I'm still surprised by this town, you just never know what might happen. Sleep well my dear, you are safe here and you are loved. " Ma Gollop bowed and smiled before making her way back downstairs. Jane ran after her and hugged her for she was already fond of her. "Thank you."

Jane gently closed the door to her room, she had a full belly and a comfortable bed and had achieved the unthinkable, the impossible. There was a certain amount of satisfaction she granted herself knowing the King was safe and far from the treachery of the city but for how long ? Jane couldn't tell, this war had made sure that nothing and no one was taken for granted, but for now, right now, it felt good to be far away from London and Oxford and all of those other places and palaces that parliament was salivating over. Their minds and their hearts had been turned, taken over by a great sickening and not just the plague. Jane comforted herself with the thought that James would surely be in France by now and if not already with the Queen at least on his way to her and it swelled her heart. She prayed and gave thanks that they had all arrived safely, for Good Wife Gollop and for the sanctuary and ancient shrine of Glastonbury. Then she blew out her candle and drifted into a sweet and well deserved slumber.

♛

It was mid November so the days were short and the light was low. It was also incredibly cold. The King stayed by the fire in his room and wished to be left undisturbed. Ma Gollop had the girls take his meals up, they were simple but nourishing, sometimes he ate, other times they were left untouched. Jane was unfazed by the weather and did some exploring, guided by Ma Gollop suggestions with strict instructions on what to say and to whom. Ma Gollop knew everyone in the town almost as well as they knew themselves, if not better. Glastonbury was a kind town, still coming out of the shadows of the reformation, having suffered so terribly from it. The old folk still lamented the long ago loss of the great church, the dear Abbot and the livelihoods of everyone about town who had relied so heavily on the pilgrims and their purse. Somehow even after the total devastation of everything holy and worthy, the bones of the place had carried on, the folk held themselves together and quietly thrived. Some visitors still came of course but mostly they were stopping over on their way elsewhere. In that sense it remained the pilgrim place it had always been, transient. Folk were more than interested in the striking figure of Jane who was a handsome woman and a stranger to these parts. Ma Gollop would introduce her then blind them with such intricately woven details that their enquiring mind would come to a staggering halt, she would then wish them a good day with her beaming smile and walk away leaving them confused as to what happened and why they asked in the first place, it made Jane laugh, a lot. Ma Gollop was so very easy to be free with. Jane and the King had rested for only two days when the news came that the King was at large and inevitably it quickly became the talk of the town. Judging from the people's views this news was well received which greatly warmed the heart and restored the King's faith in his people, the very people he had wished to protect but feared had turned against him. To hear people now rejoice in his freedom gave him fresh cause and enthusiasm. That day they spent entirely planning, discussing, waiting ! So very pleased with themselves that they had successfully achieved the impossible and also won the support of the people.

There was however little time to celebrate as only days later another boy came, bearing news that shattered their joy and gave them completely different feelings as by all accounts the King had been apprehended and was now a prisoner, again ! Naturally this news altered the mood dramatically. Their minds immediately raced with thoughts of James and the circumstances he must have faced. The King was fretful, why hadn't they discussed and planned for what would happen in such a situation ? Were they foolish in thinking he could have escaped their clutches ?

"Have no fear Your... father, I trust James, I know he will uphold his side of the bargain, in fact he told me he was beyond excited to be performing again, so that's how I would like to imagine him."

"My dear child, didn't we already imagine him to be free ? This agonises me, I am ashamed of myself, that I have so willingly allowed another to take my place. I should have made my way to France myself and not accepted this folly. I have endangered him and you. What am I to do now ? I have no advisors and I am even further from my wife and my children."

"I understand your concern but we mustn't give up hope so easily, you have my word James will be in his element so we should be, are we not well housed ? You are safe here, I trust Good Wife Gollop and I trust you to find peace, I must find out where they have him and go to him, find out what happened and what we can do now."

Without delay it was agreed that Jane would return to London and gather what news she could while the King would remain with Good Wife Gollop.

"God willing, I'll be back before you know it."

♛

At the break of dawn Jane went to collect her horse, the weather was atrocious, wild and wet, she had made the commitment to leave so battled through the elements. Her horse was well rested and more than ready for the road.

"You don't want to be going out in this Miss, I'd wait for the weather to pass if I were you, that's if you were thinking of heading out today." Said the groom who tended the horses. Jane had to agree she probably wouldn't make it far anyway, so she took refuge inside the Pilgrims Inn. She found a place near to the fire where she could dry off and gather her thoughts but she was restless. The innkeeper's wife made her way over under the guise of cleaning but really she came to gossip.

"Ah hello love, you're the Good Wife's niece aren't you ?"

Jane smiled in agreement and nodded proudly for she loved to be thought of as Ma Gollops family. It also reminded Jane that in a small town, everyone knows everything.

"Taking cover from the rain dear ? Well I can't say I blame you, not a morning to be out, said to brighten up later, mind. You'll be more than welcome by the fire till it clears my love. We're not expecting many today, especially not now God has opened the heavens. The Lord moves in mysterious ways .. none more mysterious than the things he be putting our dear King through .. breaks my heart to hear .. so it does, after everything.. I mean, I didn't see sense in that war .. the troubles, you know.. but he's nothing like that horror of a man .. Cromwell .. just terrible .. he's nothing but a usurper if you ask me .. the King, his life and family all scattered everywhere .. I mean .. the Queen .. must be mad with worry.. her being so far from him across the water .. and not so long ago having had another baby .. she must be at the end of her nerves I'd wager .. not good for a woman to be so far away from her husband like that .. and as for his Majesty .." Jane was amazed by the woman's ability to talk without taking a breath but there was something comforting in her relentless voice. Jane nodded periodically, said a couple of ah's and Oo's and very little else as the woman busied herself overwhelming her with words.

"Well, I expect you've heard the news, can't be anyone in all of England that hasn't , it turns out it's been a right eventful week up in London."

"Really ?" Jane replied nonchalantly.

"Aye so it has, first came the news that the King had made off and escaped, at large so they said and I'd hoped Miss, really hoped he'd made a proper run for it, you know got somewhere safe and good, ha ! If there be such a place left in this land. I ask you, keeping the King a prisoner ? Have you ever heard of such a thing, what nonsense."

"Here seems safe and good, " Jane smiled.

"Aye and so it is, Glastonbury is a kind town always has been Miss but it's been a long time since we've had Royalty here, what with that Tudor King Henry's men being so brutal about the place, and them shameless roundheads making such an unholy mess of it. It was a very different town when the Abbey was still standing, full of people it was, so my granny used to say. Perhaps he should have come here but who knows what thoughts be filling his head, I mean I do kind of understand it because in all honesty where's the King to go ? They've smashed up all the Palaces or taken them over for themselves. The gossip is he's been deserted by those that stood with him, poor man. You ever thought you'd call a King a poor man. He was sold by the Scot's can you believe, for silver I heard, him being of Scottish blood as well, but apparently that's where all the troubles started for him. Something to do with his prayer book and the bishops apparently, I wouldn't have trusted them again after they'd already sold me once, I'll tell you that for nothing. Who knows why he went to them ? My husband says I shouldn't be so interested as I'll never know what goes on in a man's mind or anyone else's for that matter, and you know he's right but it is interesting isn't it ? Our King sold so it's said and it was the army that bought him … probably with his own money. Then it turns out, they, Cromwell's men, Parliament or the army or whatever it is they call themselves. I call them monsters. They held him prisoner, you heard me right, had the King a prisoner and he made off ! Can't I say I blame him, I would have done too if they made me a prisoner in my own palace, not that I could call this place a palace mind you, but you know like my husband always says, a man's home is his castle. So anyway, he made off from Hampton Court. But then..." The innkeeper's wife finally stopped her incessant talking, drawing a deep breath.

"But ?" Asked Jane, who was now caught up in the woman's monologue.

"Well, that's the saddest part. My husband says he's a clever man that Cromwell, I don't think there's much clever about this war do you ? He had his army on the King's trail straight away and now they've captured him again, hunted him down in no time .."

"Really ?"

"Oh yes really and in no time too. Almost straight away someone said. Someone caught him or handed him in, I can't remember exactly what they said. Now what they're saying is, he's being held a prisoner on the Isle of White of all places, can you believe it ? It makes no sense does it ? I didn't even know there was a prison there or maybe Cromwell has made the whole Island a prison, he seems to be doing pretty much what the hell he likes everywhere else. The Isle of White ? I ask you… Who knows.."

"The Isle of White ?" Echoed Jane jumping to her feet as her heart began thumping wildly in her chest. Why was James on the Isle of White ? It made absolutely no sense. Her mind was a whirl, she had to get to him quickly, interrupting the innkeeper's wife, who clearly still had a lot to say, she apologised and made her excuses to leave. Jane's head ached from the woman's endless talking and now her mind was a tangle of thoughts. The rain had eased as she thanked the groom and mounted her horse, kicking in her heels, she rode out towards the coast.

♕

Jane rode hard, in what felt like all weathers, her mind raced almost as fast as her horse did. Try as she might, she just couldn't clear her thoughts. It took her days to get there, arriving at the dock Jane heard news of the week's events and easily found passage across the still waters to the Isle of White. She found that most men wherever their loyalties lay still had respect for her as The Black Rod's Daughter and were happy to take her money.

Jane took a carriage straight to the castle and was greeted warmly by Colonel Hammond, who undoubtedly knew her pedigree.

"Ah, Miss Maxwell," Hammond assumed, holding out his hands, "Welcome."

"Why thank you Governor Hammond." Jane smiled, without correcting him.

"I trust all was well with your crossing," he mused, clearly affected by her beauty. The niceties continued until Jane was quite tired of them, prompting her to get to the point.

"I understand that His Majesty the King is here ?"

"Yes. You are correct Miss Maxwell, terribly unfortunate business. I have, as you will no doubt appreciate, a certain amount of loyalty to parliament and what with General Cromwell's…" he drifted off. " I found myself in a most awkward position, one of the men came looking for me, you see, asking for my help. Well, as soon as he told me who he was travelling with, I was obliged…I had no choice but to inform the authorities."

"Inform ?" Jane retorted.

"Well yes, like I said I had very little choice. His Majesty and three men were seeking sanctuary, having so recently taken flight from Hampton Court and what with the whole country looking for them, if I'd have done anything differently I myself would have been dealt with most severely."

"And so you apprehended them ?" The severity of her voice betrayed her nonchalance.

"Well not really apprehended, I like to think it was an invitation. His Majesty, he is now our guest. I know not what happened to the others but I insisted the King come with me. I had very little choice Miss Maxwell, the gravity of the situation I'm sure you will appreciate was beyond grave. If I had not done so, immediately I would have put everyone and possibly the Isle itself in terrible danger. If General Cromwell had discovered that I was aware or knew of His Majesty, if I had turned the other cheek … well … he could of razed the whole place to the ground. Truly I was in an awful predicament and the safest option for all of us was for me to alert parliament and bring him here."

"Yes, I understand, but why did he come here ?"

"I've no idea and I certainly had no knowledge of them ! A man came across and sought counsel with me as Governor, I hastened to meet them as that is a requirement of my position. When I was in his company, he said they needed help and revealed the King was with them. Miss Maxwell, what else was I to do ? I felt this to be the best option and I assure you I have nothing but the best of intentions."

"The best," echoed Jane sarcastically.

"Yes, I assure you the very best of intentions. I initially offered His Majesty protection, but now as you may be aware, I am effectively his gaoler and His majesty is in custody, of sorts. The King has so far been content, he is comfortable and looked after very well. He has a certain amount of ... shall we say freedoms and as long as he doesn't break these conditions there seems a very good hope that these terrible times might come to an end and that Miss Maxwell I'm sure you will agree would be of great benefit to all of us." He searched her face for approval, Jane smiled and placed her cup back on the table and asked calmly,

"Would it be possible to speak with His Majesty ?"

"In private ?"

"Yes, why not, yes please, I suppose it would be totally within your powers of Governor to permit such a thing wouldn't it ? And I would greatly appreciate somewhere to freshen myself and sleep if there is room of course ? Only I have travelled so very far you see, but only if you considered it to be appropriate ?"

"Of course, Miss Maxwell, follow me."

Jane was led to a quaint side room along the corridor.

"You are our guest, please make yourself comfortable. I shall be back to escort you to His Majesty's rooms presently." Hammond was slightly bewildered at his new found occupation and unsure of proper protocols he was however enjoying himself.

Closing the door behind him, Jane was left alone to appreciate every detail of the sweet and dainty surroundings. There was fresh water with which to wash and fresh towels, everything was pleasant and most agreeable. She was bubbling with excitement to be seeing James again, even with these unforeseen turn of events, it seemed everything was working out favourably. Having washed and feeling fresh she couldn't help but wink at herself in the mirror and laugh as a light but determined knock came to the door. Jane was ready ages before so jumped eagerly to answer it."Governor Hammond."

"Miss Maxwell."

"Please call me Jane, all my friends do," she smiled as she waltzed past him, well aware she was leading him to believe her to be a woman of ill repute and it was working.

"Very well, this way please, Jane," he said uncomfortably as he wondered how a woman with such a wealthy father would be in such a position, he convinced himself she must be the King's mistress.

She followed him along the corridors, up a sweeping stairway and around corners until at last they arrived at the great door which divided her from him. There was only one young disinterested guard outside but other than him Jane hadn't noticed much in the way of the military or militia and she was impressed by this lack.

"Here we are, and should you need any .."

"I shall not hesitate to ask Governor Hammond," Jane fluttered her eyes, enjoying every moment, "thank you."

Hammond stoked his beard then tapped at the door.

It was answered by Firebrace who was delighted to see her, he bowed and opened the door wide. Hammond, seeing that they already knew each other, bowed and left as was fitting for a gentleman.

Henry Firebrace, that esteemed servant of the King who had become a faithful friend, had instantly noticed the man held in custody to be an imposter but he had never betrayed him and continued with his duties as normal. The other men who assisted in the escape had been remanded on the mainland and the King led to the castle alone, meaning there was no one on the Isle who had actually known the King or seen him of late except Firebrace. Despite him turning a blind eye at Hampton Court he was still trusted by Cromwell's forces and sent immediately to the Isle of White to be groom for the King.

Henry closed the door behind Jane and gave her a bear grip hug.

"Hello Henry," smiled Jane, equally pleased to see him.

"So, have you come to tell me just what's going on here ? And who that chap in there, masquerading as the King actually is ?"

Jane breathed a huge sigh of relief and giggled. "Fine choice of words Henry, for isn't this all a masquerade ! I thank God that it's you, thank you Henry, you are a true knight and you shall be greatly rewarded for your sincerity and your loyalty. I was unsure up until this very moment as to what I would find here, but now, oh thank god. I assume then that you are … keeping up appearances ?"

Henry laughed, "Yes my lady, it appears I am. I was sent for as soon as they apprehended him, I knew something was afoot at the Palace, the King himself said he may be a changed man if I was to see him again," he winked at Jane.

"He made a good run for it," Henry said solemnly. "Your man here, who by all accounts trusts that I believe him to be His Majesty, so let's not spoil it. By the way, he is really very good, I could have sworn it was him, if I hadn't so recently been with the real King, he's a wonderful actor and I dare say he is enjoying the part. They got all the way to the coast but .."

"Ashburnham ?"

"Yes sadly it was, it seems parliament got to him a while ago, sequestered his home and lands and basically held him to ransom, so he's not wholly bad Miss, just weak, frightened. The young men the King entrusted confided in him at the last minute and he made it his business to join them, unfortunately. They made a good pace but it appears Ashburnham had insisted they come here all along. Why they didn't head straight for France I don't know."

"I didn't know he was being blackmailed, it explains his actions I suppose. The King wouldn't give up on him, probably because of the Duke being his cousin or him being so very alone, who knows."

"Who knows ? He did well to get away, but now we are here, a prisoner once more, at least this chap is …may I ask who he is ?" Henry whispered.

"Is he not the King of England ?" Jane replied kindly.

"Of course he is Miss. Am I permitted to know if the other fellow is well and safe and by God's grace with his Queen ?"

"By God's grace and with thanks to you dear Henry, he is safe and well, you have my word," Jane clasped her hands over his giant fingers as he offered them up in prayer and in thanks. "God blesses us all."

"Now, if you'd be so kind, Firebrace, may I be permitted to see His Majesty ?"

"At once Miss, he's been expecting you," Henry knocked, then slowly opened a further door, which opened into a warm and well lit room dressed with beautiful tapestries. By the roaring fireplace, with a large wine in his hand, regally and elegantly stood James, dressed impeccably as His Majesty.

"Ah, well hello, how very good of you to come Miss Ryder," he smiled and raised his glass in welcome.

Jane was astonished by his likeness to the King and taken aback by the sight of the man she loved, " Your Majesty," she whispered as she curtsied before him, all the way to the floor. Henry bowed and left the rooms, closing the door behind him, smiling to himself and happy to leave them alone.

Jane lifted her head and they stared at each other in breathless silence until they heard Henry shut the outer door, then they both burst into nervous laughter. James eventually broke his gaze and placed his now empty glass upon the mantelpiece.

"Of course… you may call me James, but only you," he said with a wicked smile looking very pleased with himself. Jane couldn't help but look upon him adoringly,

"Damn, I can't tell you how happy I am to see you and may I say how beautiful you look."

Jane blushed like a maid and giggled nervously, James had the ability to send all her senses wild.

"Obviously I wasn't expecting to see you so soon, things took a turn quite early on and well here we are. But ... We did it Jane, we saved the King, just like we said we would, we fooled them all, I trust the King has his liberty ?"

"Yes but poor you, now you are the prisoner, forgive me for we didn't think or plan for this as well as we should have, it pains me greatly to know you are confined this way, I am so very sorry."

"Don't be my dear, for in all honesty, I am having the time of my life, a most grand and jolly time. What was I doing before ? Nothing ! Nothing but rolling around the gutters and back streets of London, I was succumbing to a dismal existence. Now, I am performing for my life every single day, in a castle no less and I am loving it. I am treated exceptionally well, fine wine, fabulous food. In fact dear heart everyone treats me like a King," he winked at her. "So please pity me not, for this is by far the most fortunate turn of events that has happened to me in ... in years ! The Governor is even setting out a new bowling green, just for me ! Can you believe it ? So really, do not worry, I feel more alive than I have in ages. If anything I am sincerely thankful to that Jack chap, he's done me a huge service."

Jane laughed, relieved he was alive and evidently so extremely well, she indicated towards the bottle of wine on the mantle. "In that case, Your Majesty, I think we have every reason to celebrate, may I join you ?"

"Indeed you may, Miss Ryder, for your presence fills me with joy and yes we do indeed have cause to celebrate, come," he swiftly poured her a full glass of the finest Port from Hammond's cellars, both beaming broad smiles as they raised their glasses to the King and their blessed good fortune.

They dined and sat together closely and completely at ease beside the roaring fire exchanging tales of their adventures. Jane told of Glastonbury and what a charming little town it was and how perfect Good Wife Gollop had been to them. How she came straight away when she heard the news and how delighted she was to find him in such good spirits. James had very little to say of the treachery which had befallen him as he had been treated so well since and excitedly told of all the kindness he'd received. He promised to continue his performance or service as he saw it for as long as the King desired him to or until the parliamentarians came at him with guns ! He was however under no illusion, knowing full well he was playing with his life, but in his eyes it only made the acting more thrilling ! He swore to serve the Royal cause faithfully and if need be to the death !

"It must be God's will, for how else can we explain the good fortune I've found and the safe passage you had all the way to Glastonbury ? It is nothing short of a miracle, and I swear to you, I too feel miraculous. It is as if I have been born again, I was dying without the stage and the theatres, I was nothing, forgotten, forlorn," he shook his head. "But, you trusted me, the King trusted me and you've brought me back to life. Now I drink the finest wine and everyday I am brought a fresh shirt ! A charmed life I lead, I don't see it as a prison, I feel as if I am on a jolly little holiday, all in service to the King and the dear Queen. I assure you I thank God every single day and if I do say so myself, I do believe I am portraying His Majesty rather well. No one suspects in the slightest and if anything they have aided me all the more by removing those scallywags who accompanied me, you see how everything has worked in our favour ?" He raised his glass, " God saved the King."

♛

After all the wonderful wine had been drunk and their conversations had, like the fire, died down, they looked at each other yearningly for far too long.

Jane broke the silence and the gaze, "I should...I must go." She stuttered.

"Must you ?" Whispered James as he leaned forward.

Jane let out a sigh that came from the very depths of her soul as she felt every bit of her being tremble with want. She swallowed in a vain attempt to keep her feelings inside and hidden, suddenly she felt very shy, hot and embarrassed.

"I…I …I'll go, I… I Good night," she mumbled as she clumsily got out of her seat and made for the door, hoping to run from her feelings, only to find James, somehow magically in front of her and in front of the door. Jane turned away covering her eyes, knowing full well that if she looked at him now she would never be able to look away again. She stumbled back, unsteady due to the wine and mystified as to how he had come to be before her so quickly.

Jane blurted out the words she was so desperate to hear, "I'm in love with you," she said, surprising herself. It was as if her words were alive and wanted to make themselves heard. She was so shocked she immediately covered her mouth hoping to put those words back in or at least stop any more from falling out, she stumbled backwards and silently asked herself, "am I ?" Had she at last discovered what that meant ? She dared not look up at him as she was so overcome by the passions and deep feelings she had harboured for him her whole life. Flooded with memories of the night they shared and images of the son he had fathered. She placed her hand on her head hoping he wouldn't be able to see inside, taking tiny steps back, "oh no, no, no, no."

She felt her back come up against the cold of a wall, without opening her eyes, she sensed James to be incredibly close to her but found herself totally comfortable with that feeling. "Do you know who I am ?" She whimpered with no idea where her words were coming from and she felt ridiculous, blindly she searched the ethers for him and his response. The memories of that night came cascading down between them as Jane remembered saying those very words to him and for an instant in her mind they were transported back to Whitehall and a plump velvet cushion. She smiled knowing James was so close as their breathing became harmonised, a warm fuzzy glow of pure joy engulfed her, flushed with euphoria she giggled and turned to face him but quite suddenly, Governor Hammond knocked then abruptly swung in through the door waking Jane from her enchantment. She gasped and opened her eyes wide as if she had been exposed. She breathlessly excused herself and slinked past Hammond, knowing she had to get out of that room.

♕

Jane slept very little that night, despite the copious amounts of wine, she was restless and felt ridiculous replaying the evening over and over in her mind. She had to move, to run away from these thoughts and feelings that were overwhelming her, surprisingly alert for one who hadn't slept she would have slipped out of her room and the castle unnoticed had it not been for Henry who was already up and loading logs.

He startled her, "Oh Henry," she said, relieved it was him.

"Leaving so soon Miss ?"

"Yes, I must, my feelings have gotten the better of me and I can't think, my heart beats so fast, I must leave urgently, please say I have urgent business... back in London," she said quickly.

"Aye, don't worry, I'll make sure he knows. I don't think he's going anywhere. Come inside and I'll have someone come and take you to the ferry," he smiled comfortingly.

"Yes, yes please, that's a far better idea. I've ridden so far and so hard and it being so cold."

"Be easy Miss, it's no trouble, anyways I'm sure His Majesty would insist upon it." He winked.

Jane blushed as she followed him into the guardhouse.

"Here Miss, have a seat." Jane sat close to the fire warming her hands while her mind raced with thoughts of James. In what felt like no time at all a simple trap was waiting outside with a young lad checking the harness.

"Ready when you are Miss Ryder. May I enquire if you will be ..?"

"Yes, for certain Henry, God willing I will be back in a matter of days. Whilst the King is a guest here, I hope very much to be a regular visitor and I shall look forward to seeing you and His Majesty... soon as soon as can be." Jane looked up to the King's quarters, taking Henry's hand she climbed up onto the seat and held it firmly whilst she sorted her skirts to sit.

"God be with you Miss."

"And with you dear Henry and with you."

The sound of the horse brought Colonel Hammond out through a side door on the other side of the courtyard. "Ah Good morning Miss … Jane, you're leaving us so soon ? I trust everything was to your satisfaction." He called as he made his way over to her.

"Indeed it was Sir, thank you for your kind and gracious hospitality, I must go but I would very much like to return, if I may ?" Jane replied.

"Yes, indeed you may, there will always be a welcome for you on the Island and especially here at Carisbrooke."

"Sir, you are too kind, I shall be happy to pass on the good news that the King is well, may God bless you."

"Thank you, go well Jane."

Hammond held up his hand a little embarrassed at his new position of King's Gaoler. The boy took Hammond's signal to slap the horse, turning the cart quickly on its axle, steady and slowly heading out of the narrow main gates and down into the town. Jane waved to the men behind her and secretly blew a kiss to the one she loved.

♛

James was woken by Hammonds staff which was something he was getting used to. They pulled back the curtains, laid out clean clothes for him and set a tray with fresh tea upon the bed. James sat up while they moved silently about him, it occurred to him that it must be late in the day as the sun was already high.

"Ah Firebrace, my good fellow, where is Miss Ryder ? Will she be joining us for.. ?" He sighed, wishing she had been the first thing he had seen.

"Your Majesty," bowed Henry, playing his part faultlessly, " Miss Ryder left on the first tide, she said she had urgent business …in London." Henry began building a fresh fire and called for the maid to take the King's tray.

"I see." James tried to hide his disappointment and was quickly distracted seeing Hammond outside, busily and very kindly having this new bowling green laid out, just for him. The actor was amazed, he was well used to performing for royalty, but he was absolutely thrilled by the performance he was giving AS royalty and by the rewards it brought him on a daily basis. If this is to be my prison there will never be a happier prisoner than me, he thought to himself.

"Do you suppose she will be back, Firebrace ?" He asked nonchalantly, looking out of the window and trying desperately to ignore the hollowness he felt.

"Undoubtedly, Your Majesty," Henry nodded to reassure him and smiled knowing full well the look of lovers, he bowed and left James alone with his thoughts and his fire.

♛

Jane's infatuation with James was now totally encompassed and replaced by guilt. If he had remembered her and had known it was her that fell into his arms that night surely he would have said. Why was she so embarrassed and why didn't she have the courage to ask or tell him ? What he couldn't possibly know was that he was the father of her child and how could she now keep it from him ? She was overwhelmed by all the whys and wherefores. What a mess and what's more her guilt was completely eclipsing their current far more serious situation, of James being a prisoner no matter how much he was enjoying himself and of the real anointed King hiding in a boarding house in Glastonbury. It all felt as if she was caught up in the most bizarre drama and if she was honest with herself it was, as James had said, certainly thrilling. She knew she had to get news to the Queen but she suddenly felt an urge to be with her children. Obviously that would mean having to face her husband, which unsettled her but now she had finally admitted to herself that she was in love with James, she no longer felt any fear of him besides there was never anything but obligation and habit between them. Her mind was a kaleidoscope of questions and her tempestuous emotions were making her feel raw and raggedy, it was the most insufferable carriage she had ever taken.

♛

In no time at all Jane arrived at Cowes, taking the first ferry to Hill head and with seamless connection, coaches all the way to London, giving her plenty of time to exhaust the demons plaguing her mind. She nimbly made her way through the streets she knew well. She made her way to the laundries and easily found Nell, who told her that getting a letter across to France would be damn near impossible right now and a reply might take even longer. Jane's heart sank for she only intended to be away from James for a couple of days at the most. Nell suggested she wait a week at least. This hold up hadn't occurred to Jane, having so easily made it on to the mainland, she assumed everything was flowing freely, but apparently not. There was nothing to do but wait. The images of her children filled her head and heart, it had been so long since she had seen them, held them. These feelings of longing were soon overridden by the memories of how awful it was for her to actually be in the house she hated. She just didn't know what to do. Wandering back to Westminster she made for Elizabeth's house which was surprisingly empty. Letting herself in she found it cold without her friends there, but she was glad of somewhere to rest. She easily got the fire going in the kitchen and got comfortable in the chair she loved so much, it was the perfect place to hide away and gather her thoughts, which were inevitably about James. This terrible war which had devastated and laid waste to much of the England she had known had also saved her life, for which Jane would be eternally thankful for. It had saved her from her loveless marriage and delivered her into the hands of her beloved, again and again.

♛

December passed quietly but with all Christmas celebrations being banned, it really was a bleak winter. London was icy cold but Jane was motivated and moved quickly. Busily making her way to Nell who thankfully had received news from France and gladly gave her the much anticipated letter and told her that Elizabeth and William had left the very day she arrived to be with the King on the Island, which pleased Jane greatly. Nell then gave her further instructions to meet up with the King's network of supporters who wished to entrust her with letters to be taken to him. She endeavoured to meet with them all. It felt unreal, like everything was happening at breakneck speed and she was sure she must have walked half of London as the whole day was filled with coincidences and conspicuous meetings.

She was happy to pass on all the correspondence she collected but she alone knew that this would mean travelling to Glastonbury first, which would in turn mean a further delay to her reunion with James.

♛

Carrying the healthy bundle of letters from the King's supporters, Jane slipped out of town taking various carriages and coaches with ease and made her way safely back to Somerset. Glastonbury had a timeless charm about it, a world away from the harshness of the city, Jane was glad to be back and reassured to see everything was exactly as she'd left it. The Bluebell inn was as just as she remembered it, relaxed and spotlessly clean. Ma Gollop was delighted to see her and greeted her warmly, fed her belly with delicious food and her ears with all the gossip, then insisted she went to see the King, or Harry as he now liked to be known. Here Jane found a most profound change, Harry, the King had cut his hair short and removed his moustache entirely. He was dressed in simple clothes and looked much like a monk sat at his writing table. His room was still bare but now looked lived in with some books and some plates and cups on a tray that had clearly been there a while.

"Ah, daughter, welcome, I am so, so very pleased to see you safe and well, do come in," even without his royal costume, he maintained a graceful presence. Jane half bowed and half fell to her knees.

"Dear heart, don't give the game away now," he said kindly, " come in, come in, for I am eager to know what news you bring, dear sweet Jane."

"I bring news from France and these from your friends," she held out the letters she had bought, as he indicated for her to put them on the table.

"Friends ?" he said doubtfully.

Jane then sat opposite him at the table and burst into details of all that had happened since she left, except her evening with James. The King was dismayed but, like her, unsurprised by the disloyalty shown by Ashburnham. He was however most pleased to know that Firebrace could be depended upon and found it all quite amusing from the safety of his rooms in the little town of Glastonbury. The King suggested Jane rest as a way of letting her know he wanted some privacy to read his letters and would be happy to have dinner with her and Good Wife Gollop that evening if Jane would be happy to stay. Jane was more than happy and delighted to be staying at the cosy Inn that Ma Gollop made so warm and welcoming. Jane retired to the room prepared for her and looked out of the window at the Abbey ruins which always encouraged her to imagine how magnificent it must have looked all those moons ago before it was stripped from the sight of mere mortals.

♛

The King did not join them for dinner, he stayed up in his room and asked to be left undisturbed. Jane and Ma Gollop respected his wishes and took their dinner together downstairs where Ma Gollop could keep an eye on the comings and going's. Which amounted to some men playing dice, Martin and Joseph finding something to argue about, keeping the fire roaring, and a young girl who was still busy with her work. Ma Gollop told Jane loud enough so all would hear, that her father was recovering well and was hoping to be able to take some short walks when the weather improves, it still being winter and so cold and wet. One thing Jane noticed about the air in the West Country was how damp it felt.

Jane and Ma Gollop finished their meal whilst making up wild stories imagining a past they might have shared, more for everyone else benefit, Ma Gollop knowing what gossips they all were. Jane kissed her good night and went up to rest in her room, which was down the corridor from the Kings. Upon hearing her he looked out of his door and invited her in.

In the dim candle light, the King gently expressed his concerns at the gravity of the situation that he and this innocent man, meaning James, were in. He wanted to be absolutely certain that he could depend upon him and his performance. Jane was touched by his so obviously desperate pleas and again reassured him that so far, no one had suspected, other than Firebrace who as she had said was wholly reliable and unswerving. The fact that James had been isolated has only served their situation, for no one on the Isle actually knew the King personally or if they did they hadn't seen him in years. The King was greatly pleased and confided in Jane that other than a wonderful letter from the Queen, which he was so thankful for and to which he had spent the afternoon and long into the evening replying, there was other news that had stirred his spirits. There was news of a possible uprising from the Scottish army in support of the English Royalists, should they invade as they said they would, the King must give James clear instructions as to how to act as he himself would do, while he made immediate plans to return.

"Unfortunately I have been let down by the Scot's before so I do take this news … rather tentatively, but …should they strike with a force to be reckoned with, there are men on the Isle of White who are willing to lay siege to the castle until I/Mr Shirley, are released, therefore I must be in the vicinity to switch with him, lest our deception be revealed. I understand it to be a big possibility but I must know that I can count on you to assist me in travelling to the Island and in making sure this news reaches him/James beforehand."

"You have my word."

"Jane, you save my life again."

♛

Plans were enthusiastically put forth for the King and James to be switched again as soon as the troops could be raised and the King able to command a victory. This meant Jane was about to be very busy and it thrilled her, she now knew the roads so well. Driven by her excitement at seeing James she made it speedily but safely to the dock and eagerly awaited a ferry to the Isle. She was happily greeted by Governor Hammond who had come to meet her himself and was pleased to be seeing her again.

"Welcome back Ms Maxwell, Jane, I trust you had a pleasant journey."

"Indeed I did thank you Colonel, I trust all has been well with you since I saw you last ?"

"Well, yes, the King is still very much our guest so everything is pretty much exactly as you left it, do come and see for yourself. He is in good spirits, more so when I told him I was coming to collect you." He smiled.

Looking out at the rolling countryside it reminded Jane so much of Somerset. She made idle chit chat with the Governor who spoke very highly of the 'King' telling her how fond he had become of him.

Jane felt giddy with excitement, becoming hot and flustered as the walls enclosing Carisbrooke castle came into view. Politely agreeing with Hammond although in all honesty she was oblivious to his conversation. Stepping down from the carriage her eyes and heart were fixed firmly on where she knew James to be. Hammond led her over to the King's quarters and they were greeted by Firebrace who was also glad to see her. Jane followed him to the stone steps in the centre of the courtyard that led up to the King's rooms, he knocked upon the door and opened it for her. Jane curtsied as Firebrace left and closed the door behind him.

James was still standing by the window, having watched her arrive. They looked longingly at each other as their smiles became wider causing them both to burst out laughing. Jane instinctively covered her mouth lest someone should hear her as James deftly made his way over to her, taking her hand, he gently kissed it.

"I'm so glad you came back, I can't tell you how happy I am to see you."

"As I am …so happy to see you." She mumbled eventually, unable to take her eyes or her hand from his.

Suddenly there came a knock at the door bringing them both back firmly to the ground, James kissed her hand again before he slowly let it slide from his.

A maid came with fresh tea for them both, James thanked her as she set the tray down and poured before leaving them once more. James composed himself and Jane regained her posture, knowing they had been dangerously close to giving into passions.

"So ?" James smiled playfully, looking ridiculously handsome. She was so deliciously and easily attracted to him.

"Oh yes," Jane giggled as she snapped back to her senses and the far more important business of relaying the King's messages. She handed him the letters she brought which he began reading at once, changing the very energy of the room.

James was surprised that things were moving so quickly and that his performance would soon be coming to an end especially as he felt it had just got started ! Having read the letters he put them into the fire.

"Damn it, already ? I mean, splendid, wonderful news that the King has a plan and trusted men to implement it. Of course I will be ready, at a moment's notice, but …if my Royal life is about to come to an end, I, by that I mean we, really ought to make the most of it all wouldn't you agree ? Come on let us have some fun, I'd like it very much if you were to stay. For a while at least ?"

"I'd be more than happy to stay, Your Majesty," Jane smiled, knowing she would be happy to stay with him forever.

"Good, then allow me the pleasure of showing you around this fair island. First the bowling green and the rest of the Castle, then who knows ?" He held out his hand for hers and she was only too happy to oblige.

The days that followed were frivolously fantastic as James playfully led Jane around the castle, then the whole Island in pursuit of mischief. They revelled in the hilarity and the pleasure of being in each other's company once more. The Isle of White became their playground as they childishly found great amusement in the most unlikely of places and circumstances. High spirited they flirted outrageously, finding humour in absolutely everything. Every day was joyfully filled with reckless abandon and every night was spent looking for stars. They took long rambles on horseback exploring the beaches and countryside and took evening carriage rides into town where James held court or dinner theatre as he liked to call it. They regularly met with Elizabeth and William who, although in the King's service, were staying outside of the Castle walls, James even publicly Knighted William making Elizabeth a Lady to wondrous applause. Everywhere they went erupted with riotous jollity encouraging such good feeling and sympathies amongst the people of Newport that an uprising took place in the King's favour. James took great pride in these performances and the people's response delighted him but it inevitably upset parliament and meant his freedoms would unsurprisingly, soon be quashed. The army were swiftly sent in to dampen and thwart any further merrymaking.

♛

It also meant that Jane was advised to leave, for the moment at least. Hammond was embarrassed as he had allowed the King these freedoms so now he felt he had to prove his efficiency to parliament as a competent and effective gaoler. James was to be confined to the Castle grounds, like a naughty child and be more closely guarded. He watched sadly from his windows as Jane climbed aboard the carriage that would take her to the mainland and away from him, again. Jane too was overcome with misery, she tearfully looked up to the windows where he stood and blew him a kiss as he whispered, "adieu sweet Jane, until we meet again."

♛

Having Elizabeth in service on the Isle meant Jane was still able to relay the King's messages across to James easily from the mainland without drawing attention and without crossing herself. There was a flurry of excitement as Royalist supporters on the island and mainland demanded the King's freedom. These uprisings, which at first so encouraged the King, were soon floundering, inevitably crushed by Cromwell's army. It soon became heartbreakingly obvious that no Royal victory was on the horizon. Furthermore, as time passed and the King's hopes were consistently unrealised, the comfort of his simple life became all the more appealing. As it became more obvious that the uprisings were futile the King became more and more withdrawn finding comfort and solace in prayer. Good Wife Gollop found him books of the Benedictine that were once from the Abbeys great libraries, which he devoured. His days were spent alone and in silence as he retreated from the horrors of war altogether, realising that as he had no chance to defend himself and absolutely no interest in fighting, he would surrender all to the Glory of God.

♛

James continued to perform for his captive audience and made the most of his time on the Island. The year sailed by with the army unsure as to what they should do with their prisoner while Cromwell, irked by Ireton, (who was such a persistent and gnawing little man having nothing but bitterness cursing through his veins,) was determined to put the King on trial. Ireton had whipped up a frenzy of men already twisted by the wrongs of war and the injustices they were convinced of, vengefully taking matters into his own hands fuelled by hate and a grievance he'd been born with. In the end he demanded men put their name to a document insisting that the King be tried and brought to, as they called it, justice. These events abruptly turned the tide on the fun and games that James and Jane were enjoying. There were various negotiations between James and envoys sent from Cromwell, but James had to wait for instruction from Glastonbury via Jane which made the opposing forces believe him to be difficult and stalling, enraging them all the more, but there was nothing he could do. The King was weary, so weary of what felt like an impossible impasse and totally disheartened. He said he had little energy left for such things and had given his life to the Lord. He suggested James escape but they had planned escapes before with Jane waiting several weeks aboard ship upon the Medway, only for the plans to be jeopardised, even with Firebrace' sturdy encouragement. The King was unmoved by news of further uprisings and displays of loyalty, the people wanted an end to their troubles and a return to some sort of normality. It was becoming more and more obvious that the world Cromwell had promised to deliver was far removed from the one they were inhabiting. With more restrictions and higher taxes, the puritan zeal was becoming unbearable. The continuous fanatical and relentless destruction and pillaging of everything sacred and beautiful had devastated the hearts of the people, tired of so much ruin and waste. They wanted the return of their King as England and the King were one, no matter how much the puritans raged about being Godly, it soon became obvious they were far worse than the tyranny they were meant to overcome.

♛

"Good Wife, I am troubled. I have walked all the way around the town and the Tor but still I am unable to lift my spirits. I heard men talking, they say that even God has abandoned the King, it has upset me a great deal." Said the King, sadly returning from his evening walk.

"Ah bless you dear, now there's a thing, simple folk upsetting a King ? It's up to you if you listen but I wouldn't give those unhappy thoughts a dwelling place. Do you know what I've often heard ? They say that this is a madhouse, and that we're all mad here, it makes me laugh all the more. Ha, those puritans just can't bear the thought of anyone being happy so they'd rather think us mad. I'll tell you it makes me glad because it means they'll stay far away but it doesn't mean that God has abandoned us. Come sit and be easy, you're just in time, I'll bring us some dinner." Chimed Ma Gollop with her usual infectious cheerfulness. She was always unfazed by misery and couldn't help but see the very best in all situations and people. Ma treated him the same as everyone else, which the King admired and appreciated. Smiling at her resilience, he took his usual seat in the corner next to the chess table where a game was set up awaiting players. People were accustomed to seeing him in the corner of the Bluebell and knew him to be Ma Gollop's kin. Folk often spoke or played chess with him, never once suspecting or realising who he truly was, but everyone knew that his game was very good. The King sat wrapped in the same old, heavy robe James had swapped with him that night by the Thames, always reminding himself of the far finer one he had exchanged it for. Ma brought sup for them both and they ate together looking into the flames of the welcoming fire, while Ma began whimsically thinking out loud.

"I live for moments like these, feeling alive and content, underneath all that worldly noise, war and nonsense. Peace and stillness might not always be an easy feeling, at first, I'll grant you, but it's a blissful one, unmistakable. It's then that you connect to all that is, to life itself, you become the living breathing heart of earth. But people are afraid of letting go of all that worldly stuff, but when you pass through the fear of losing, when you give it all up. What's left ? You are and your connection to all of life and the realisation that you are a part of it all and there's nothing you need to do but allow life to show you the beauty of the paradise that surrounds you. You are a child of the universe and it loves you, you are loved by all of existence. In my mind that's what God is, pure love, love just is and like the sun it shines on us all, all of the time."

♛

That summer saw more uprisings, although quelled by Fairfax, they nonetheless made Cromwell's army nervous. Parliament realised that the people, who they spoke for and represented were tired, having lost faith in the army, they wanted the comfort of their King and were demanding his return. Ireton was furious at this and began taking things into his own hands. He stirred up hatred once more, insistent that the King be brought to his idea of justice. He was so successful at convincing men of their grievances and injustices that they stormed parliament, refusing entry to any of those they considered to be sympathetic towards the King or that disagreed with them. They even held down the speaker by force and treasonously passed an order that the King be brought to 'trial'.

England had deteriorated into a dictatorship.

♛

Jane was in London when these events were unfolding and she witnessed the frenzy whipped up by Ireton and others. Pamphlets of parliamentary propaganda were being distributed en masse to add to the chaos. London was in total panic and Jane knew she would have to make her way quickly to Somerset for the King's response. Gathering up the letters from the King's supporters and as much information as she could she made her way out of town. How had this escalated so quickly ? Jane made the decision to head straight for the coast sending a desperate message to Elizabeth insisting that she help James escape and by any means possible as there were terrible plans being plotted against him. Jane had been forced to keep her distance from James but now she wanted nothing more than to be near him. She hoped the King would be in agreement with her bold move but now it seemed James' safety was paramount, she then rode as fast as she could to Glastonbury.

♛

Jane was heartily glad to be welcomed at the Bluebell and gladder still to be back with the King and the Good Wife. Ma closed the shutters and sent the girls home so they could hear Jane's news and contemplate privately. Jane began relaying the diabolical events happening in the capital and told how she hoped she had got a message to James, the King commended her on her quick thinking, but what now ? They had not thought this far ahead. James had been playfully enjoying his Royal role and the King likewise had been happy in the shadows. Ma shuddered at this scandalous news, "don't like the sound of any of it, not that I understand much of it, mind you," she shook her head. "Well Ma," Jane began slowly, looking over at the King for reassurance. "This means that we have to act quickly. We've been blissfully avoiding all these goings on, but now they, Cromwell and his men wish to …well, to take things further. They've taken over parliament and now, they are treasonously calling for the King to be put on Trial." Ma looked with surprise from Jane to the King, then back again. "What a to do ? Seeing as I know nothing, it's best I say nothing." She smiled leaving Jane and the King together to muse over their next step, they were unsure if James had escaped or if their message had reached him so they now had to work out all the what if's of any and all possible outcomes.

After many hours of questioning, debating and discussions they were still fraught and unsure. "It appears," began Jane, looking sadly at the frail man who was still her King, "that now the army is in charge of parliament, they will undoubtedly insist on this trial Ireton has convinced them all of and is clearly hell bent on fiendishly pursuing."

♛

James had not received Jane's letter, he had already been removed under armed guard from the Isle of White. He had point blank refused two earlier escape attempts, not trusting the men who arrived with horses in the middle of the night and thought Firebrace ridiculous when he suggested taking a boat and giving himself up to God and the elements. Besides he was enjoying himself far too much to face the harsh reality that his life might actually be in danger. James was taken to the mainland, arriving at Hurst house where he would stay for several days not knowing what to do or what would become of him. Although not quite as comfortable as Carisbrooke, he was still enjoying the most wonderful hospitality and the finest of wines, blissfully unaware that an executioner was being sought in London.

♛

Jane, like the King, was fretful and anxious as they conversed well into the night desperately considering their next move. They were painfully aware of the consequences now facing them.

"London is in turmoil. We can surmise, actually there is little doubt, that these beasts, Ireton especially, who it's fair to say has Cromwell on a leash, will stop at nothing until they have their pound of flesh, which if the whispers are to believed, will be sooner rather than later." They looked at each other in horror.

"I have nothing left Jane, we have exhausted all avenues and played all our cards. I am no general and I have no will to fight this monstrosity, this force any more. It is obvious they wish me dead. I know there will be no place for me to live peacefully in the world they are building," said the King utterly dejected. "I must take courage and face them, that is all I can think of. It is the only decent thing to do now. I must surrender to their will and surrender my life. I shall accompany you back to London, where I will give myself over to them and free this poor man from the burden of their hatred. For how can I live with myself otherwise ? I must surrender to them, Cromwell et al."

"No, Your Majesty, we most certainly will not. I have sworn to protect you and I will not be surrendering you to them, while there is breath in my body. We cannot just wander back into London like that. They would be livid, do you think for one moment that they will let James live, especially when they discover he has fooled them … all year ? Do you seriously believe they will let either of you live ? They are not gentlemen, they are hungry, like a pack of wolves, they will rip us to shreds. They will not be satisfied until they have done away with the monarchy altogether. No, no no that's not it. There must be something else we can do, another way. I agree we must help James, we have to get to him before they…" Suddenly a flash of inspiration illuminated her despair.

"Wait, I think, I've seen .. I mean .. I believe we could play our greatest move yet."

"I am always so impressed by your imagination Jane but sadly I fear this time we have no moves left to make."

"But, we are still playing…aren't we ? We still have our King." Jane said slowly.

"Barely." Sighed the King.

"We have our brave knight in James, our rook Firebrace, what we need now are pawns."

"I'm not sure I'm following you Jane."

"No ? We are still playing… aren't we ?"

"My dear child, we have not stopped. But I feel all is now lost and our little game is a monstrous mess."

"It may look like that, but let us not forget we're playing a game and it's not over yet. I have an idea. I've been inspired and I believe, well I can't say where it came from but I just saw it. I saw it all as a grand performance. The army, Ireton, Cromwell and whoever these people are that are peddling this rubbish," she said, throwing the parliamentary pamphlets to the floor and stamping on them. "They are so blinded by their hatred, they cannot see, they cannot see ? They are seeking a public trial to publicly humiliate or worse… But … No one sees. They see only what they want to see. Not one of them has suspected James to be an imposter. He has fooled them all year and he really has had the most marvelous time doing so . He has pushed their boundaries to the absolute limits and has done so brilliantly and clearly convincingly, he understood the dangers he faced should be discovered, but he hasn't been. He, like us, has no place in a puritan world and I believe he would throw himself, as it were, into the ultimate finale ! So... Let's give them what they want, a fantastical final act... with a twist. We will obviously need to set the final scene ourselves, so what we need now are more players, we need pawns, we need actors." She could picture it all so perfectly, playing out in her mind's eye, she knew exactly what she wanted to achieve, just like a puzzle all the pieces were fitting together perfectly, Jane was electrified by the potential of her ideas.

"You have a habit of doing this sweetheart. Of losing yourself in your own imagination. Actors ? Once again, I feel you may have lost me but I know you have a funny way of manifesting these ideas so take a breath and then tell me, slowly, exactly what you have in mind ?"

Jane laughed nervously, thankful the King was wise to her ways. She began pacing around the room as the energy of her idea gathered speed, the images were flashing through her mind so quickly she couldn't clearly articulate what she was thinking. She knew her idea was daring, no doubt dangerous and ambitious but could they do it ?

"What if we go along with their plans ? Let them have their trial, James will no doubt relish in the performance, in fact he'd probably adore it. If it turns in our favour, hurray we will get you swiftly to London to take your place as King. But if not, if things take a turn for the worst, which seeing as it is already farcical, a shameful shambles and treasonous mockery of justice, it wouldn't be at all surprising. James then takes his performance to the ultimate stage as you, the gallows or the block or whatever. He gives a rousing speech to the audience but then we somehow rescue or switch him...again ? Perhaps having some sort of mechanism that allows him to... James once told me, if it has happened once it can happen again, well, let's switch him again, but right in front of their eyes ! Jones. We'll need Inigo Jones and all of James's theatrical friends, the Queen's men, what if ?..." She spoke out loud but mostly to herself as her eyes sparkled seeing the cascade of thoughts that tumbled through her mind falling perfectly into place. It all aligned, it was the most obvious course of action. She bit her lip in concentration as she tried to squeeze and condense into words the thoughts that had just assembled in her mind.

"You see .. it .. there is .. what if ? … I mean what if there was a way of giving them exactly what they want ? What they are mercilessly pursuing, which is an end to the monarchy is it not ? Isn't that their ultimate objective ? Well let's give it to them, on a silver platter. It would of course mean that everyone in the world would assume you to be ... Would you be willing to remain here ? Indefinitely ?"

"That's a mighty long time Jane, Madam Gollop may not be able to tolerate me or my ways for eternity, but yes I am more than happy here. I am safe and I've come to like it a lot. I appreciate the peace and the simplicity. I have always preferred contemplation to legislation. I am content knowing my wife and my children are safe. This is not the England we loved or hoped to lead into an illustrious renaissance of beauty and love. I gave my life to the crown, to England, but here in the sanctuary of Glastonbury I feel I can at last give my life to God. But…I could not and I will not allow another man to suffer in my place."

"I assure you Sire, James has not suffered, nor does he ever intend to. He has been having a right jolly time of it all. He's been treated well, so well in fact, he has lived more these past months than he had the previous years ! You've read his letters, he has been a wonderful King. He has implemented all of your thoughts and wishes precisely as you've instructed, impeccably and he's thoroughly enjoyed himself, I promise you. We knew this time would come, perhaps it hasn't unfolded the way we would have wished for but we can still be triumphant. Now we must focus all our efforts in liberating James, in such a way that the opposition feels they have won, so we must see this through to the end."

"The end ?"

"Yes, forgive me, but what if ? If we allowed these evil forces to believe they have put the King to rest. Let's give them what they want, what they are shouting for, give way to the republic they crave, let the people judge them for their actions. It will of course mean that everyone will believe you to be dead. If they believe the King is no more, it will allow us to prepare for a better future, a brighter future for all, like the renaissance you envisioned. It's just like Sir Lewis suggested, we must get out of their way, the time will come but we must step back from this absurdity, until.."

"Until ?"

"Until, we are ready and better prepared, until the people come to their senses and see this barbarism, this regime, for what it is. Until this nightmare is over and the people cry out for a restoration. You still have many loyal supporters and you have three devoted, strong and sturdy sons, we could put all our efforts and energy into them. Prepare the new generation, the new hope of your sons and rightful heirs back upon the throne of Great Britain. We must lay new foundations, new groundwork, to make Britain Great, the King and the land must be one, much like it was said of King Arthur, who rests not far from where we now stand."

"Go on," encouraged the King, trying his best to follow her train of thought.

"But first, this madness has to play out, it has to finish once and for all, the curtain must fall on the misery of these times, it's the only way. I must go to James, I haven't seen him for so long. I hope he received my letter and has escaped but that's doubtful as he has failed to trust the others we have sent to free him. If you are in accordance with my idea, for him to perform as you in this very public display of surrender, he must know what you'd expect him to do, what to say and how you wish him to act in his final days as King."

There was a long silence between them as the King tried to unravel her ideas and Jane focused more fully upon them.

"My dear, I trust you and I can see that you are inspired and passionate. I am quite happy loving simply here at the Bluebell. I have grown fond of Madam Gollop and the company she keeps, she looks after us all very well. As to my last words, here it appears we are on the same page as I have already composed a whole manuscript." The King went to his writing desk and handed over to Jane the book he had spent these last months writing.

"The Good Wife suggested I write my innermost feelings down. When I was so completely lost in misery I wrote this. A wise woman she is, for not only did it focus my thoughts but it eased my pain, I was able to pour my deepest, intimate and until now hidden thoughts and feelings into it and they flowed with ease. So if I was to die, it would be these thoughts, these words that I would wish to share with the world. It may not be a masterpiece, but it is every word that has filled my mind since I found myself in this …This awfulness."

Jane was deeply honoured to be holding the words so delicately written by her King and now her friend.

"Did you know that my father wrote many books ? I like to think that it was he that guided me with this."

"Perfect, I shall, if I may, take this beautiful book with me to London and ask for it to be printed and distributed forthwith."

"Yes by all means do, take it, share it, give it to the people so they may know a different portrait to the ugly one painted by parliament. I find their brutish destruction so abhorrent, I imagine they have destroyed all the beautiful books, the works of art, I expect there's very little left of the beauty we tried to encourage." The King sighed deeply with regret. "Everything is within this little book and I'd like it to be known forever more as …Eikon Basilike, in homage to my father's gift, the Basilikon Doron." He said thoughtfully, adding his inspired title to the front page in a beautiful flourish.

"I promise you it will be distributed throughout London and beyond, the world will know."

"For the world will be watching, remember that Jane. Now what else do you require of me for this grand finale ?" He looked at Jane with resignation.

"May I be so bold as to press you further to compose some definite last words. The last words as you'd wish them to be known, for this final act as the King." Jane felt uncomfortable making this suggestion but she was confident she had stuck upon the perfect plan so she wanted to have everything to hand.

"Then James can rehearse, for when or if the time comes, that he will speak the last words of the King of England."

"And this poor fellow, Mr Shirley, what will become of him ? Is he prepared for what they might do ? They have so far treated him honourably, yes, but who knows what will happen now that the world, as they say, is turned upside down ?"

"Nothing Sire, they shall not hurt a hair on his head," his beautiful head Jane thought to herself but she carefully omitted this word, although the King who was a lover of all things beautiful clearly saw the light in her eyes.

"Or his neck," she added abruptly.

"I shall leave at first light, would that give you enough time ?"

"Yes, I will have them ready for you in the morning. A man's last words naturally have a certain element of haste about them, I find myself far more fortunate than a great deal of others who are not given this luxury of deliberation."

"But, what if James has escaped ? Are we to raise more troops and …"

"No, no more Jane, I have already surrendered to the Lord, as God is my witness I shall henceforth devote myself to Christ consciousness totally and fully, from a corruptible to an incorruptible crown. If Mr Shirley has escaped and I sincerely hope he has, he may return, with my eternal thanks and blessings to being and living as his former self. Parliament would then be free to concoct whatever story they like as to my demise, they do seem to have a penchant for making up stories."

There was a meditative silence between them. They both breathed deeply, giving all of their trust and their hopes over to God.

"I should begin straight away for if I am not mistaken I feel I have caught the inspiration that sparked within you, good night dear Jane. I trust I will have the right words written for you and James, in the morning. May God save the King."

"Yes and may you be released and relieved, born again," smiled Jane, not taking her teary eyes from him. She curtsied and left the room, running as fast as she could to find Ma Gollop, she wanted to share her thoughts and ideas with the kind and hospitable wise woman but Ma raised her finger.

"Ah no my dear, hush, there's nothing I need to know, nothing that will change things here. What business you have is yours alone, I know and I trust that you will have great success, for I see in your eye and about your person, you have nothing but good intentions and that's enough for me. Whatever happens, we will have the filtered news come down to us in time, it has not much effect on us 'ere anyways.

So go with my blessing dear heart and know that me, and your father," she whispered touching her nose, " will be here carrying on much the same as we have all year, safely, quietly and peacefully, not much changes round 'ere."

"That is why my father would very much like to stay with you, for good."

This was music to Good Wife Gollop ears. "My dear, he can stay as long as he likes, of course, of course, it would be an honour .. no, very much more than that ..if there be such a thing. We've all enjoyed him being here. The place would be empty without him now." Ma said a silent prayer while looking up to the room where the King was busily composing the words he wished to be known to the world as his last.

♛

Jane was fidgety and restless, so Ma Gollop decided to take her on an evening stroll to fetch water from the spring at the foot of the Tor. Carefully they climbed through the low web of yew trees, taking rest by an old oak. Jane breathed in the stillness and finally relaxed listening to the flowing waters. Ma Gollop often came to this spring as this was where legends said St Joseph had hidden the Holy Grail and that's what turned the waters red. The mists rolled about them like a silvery cloak as they quietly collected their water and prayed for success for Jane's journey and for peace. "Peace, because that's all folk really want Jane, when all's said and done, to live in peace with each other and mostly with ourselves, may we all know peace and love of course, may we all love and be loved."

Ma Gollop closed her eyes, breathing rhythmically into the swirling well waters that gargled and bubbled up out of the ground. Holding James in her thoughts, Jane found herself repeating Ma's words, 'may we all know peace and love'. In the silence that followed a most wonderful thing happened whilst they sat at that sacred well. Jane was flooded with a feeling of such lightness and an overwhelming sense of satisfaction, it felt as if her greatest desires had already been granted. She breathed in the magic of the moment and was awash with joy, the feeling swelled within her, lifting her up, making her aware of herself in a new expanded way. These new sensations of indescribable bliss filled her with an awesome awareness that she was a part of every living thing, the trees, the water, the air. She saw a myriad of colours all flying into one brilliant light and knew she was a part of that radiance too, as bright as the sun or possibly it was the sun. This luminosity flowed inside her, sparkling down her spine, swirling through her whole body, till she felt it leave out of her toes and go deep into the damp mossy earth they were sat upon. Jane was amazed as she opened her eyes, everything seemed vibrant, more alive, more real, her eyes found Ma Gollop who was wide awake and smiling one of those warm smiles that reached all the way into Jane's heart.

"Did you ? .. I mean, I saw ..it must have been a dream, but I felt it ...honestly, something strange always happens to me when I'm in nature like this, I mean really in it, it's happened before, I feel such wonderful feelings." As usual a jumble of words fell out of Jane's mouth all at once. Ma Gollop laughed as she steadied herself on a tree and held out a hand for Jane as she pulled herself up and dusted down her skirts. Without moving her lips Jane was sure she heard her say, "sometimes we don't need words." Silently taking their water they wound their way through the trees that looked like giant wise men, willowy and mysterious. Past the hedgerows that were now brimming with life, birds singing all the more sweetly as squirrels gaily chased each other through the branches and Jane was sure she saw the flick of a wolf's tail. Rays of moonlight made the mist look like a tide of tiny stars that gave everything a glittering silvery glow, the likes of which Jane had never noticed before. It was as if they were bathed in a divine light.

Jane was revived yet mystified as they wandered back down to the town arm in arm. "I do so love this town," she thought to herself, then loud as anything, a new voice in her head said, "and Glastonbury loves you." Jane looked around but knew she would see no one, she realised that some things are quite unexplainable and there was a great deal more to this life than she might ever know or understand.

"You're in love dear and love is the most unexplainable yet powerful force there is. The world loves lovers." Ma Gollop giggled and held Jane's hand tighter as if hearing all the thoughts she was thinking.

The morning came round quicker than the sun, Jane and Ma Gollop were already busying themselves but they had yet to hear a sound from the King's room although they both pretended not to be listening out for one. Jane was just beginning to feel impatient when at last there came the unmistakable sound of footsteps from the roof. Ma Gollop adjusted her bonnet and her skirts and Jane double checked the basket they had packed when the door opened and in came the King. Both women turned and curtsied, knowing it would be the last time.

"Good Morning Ladies, please that is a habit you would do well to relinquish," he smiled at them both. He looked different, calmer, less worried, less distant, less haggard. He walked over to the corner table and sat down, near to the fire, it was still early and still cold, Ma Gollop hadn't yet opened the shutters, so the three of them were very much alone.

"Please, join me." The King waved the women over but no one was sure of how to act or behave. He gave them an encouraging glance so they took their seats silently opposite him.

"Jane, I trust you have the manuscript ?" Jane nodded.

"The manuscript, Ma, is the book you encouraged me to write. It is my innermost thoughts and explanations, a baring of my soul as I have discovered it here, in your home and in this most wonderful place that is Glastonbury. I have felt the inspiration of this town and at ease with its people, but most of all I have felt comfortable in your company. Thank you. Thank you for your kindness, your hospitality, your encouragement. I could go on." The King looked at Ma Gollop who began to blush.

"Oh my goodness, thank you. It has been my absolute pleasure, you are and have always been most welcome, Your Majesty."

"Ah no," he raised his finger. "It's been so very long since you referred to me as such, I had almost forgotten and I'd rather you did too. I have been no King this past year, I have been your guest and hopefully your friend. Now I'd like you to put that thought far from your mind and forget I ever was the King and know me now. Here I have a further document I wish to entrust to you Miss Ryder and it contains my last wills and words as King of these once glorious isles," he smiled wryly and shook his head. "The moment I give these to you Jane, that's it, that is the end of that life for me. I have for all intents and purposes died, I shall no longer be entitled to or wish to expect anything more than my fellow man. I shall take my place in humanity and forevermore be known simply as Harry, the name I have very much enjoyed living under," a tear swelled in his eye as he remembered his long lost brother.

"You may not know that some years ago, there came from France four brave musketeers, sent from my dear wife with the very design that you have accomplished Jane and for that incredible feat and for your unswerving loyalty we, the Queen and I will always be thankful to you. I have a deeply personal letter here for the Queen, I trust you to be sure she receives it. For if I am to truly relinquish my crown and my kingdom I must also part with the love of my life, my wife." He stammered, no longer able to hold back the tide of his tears.

"I have loved my people as a father and as God's divine representative here on earth. Now I have surrendered, fully to God and God's will, I seek only peace for my heart and my mind. Where better to experience and feel the essence of that than here, safely far from those that wish me harm and injury. It is as if I have been blessed with another chance at life, I will devote myself to prayer, here at the shrine of our Lady of Glastonbury Abbey, a gentle reminder that all things must pass. My thoughts with the dear man who these past months has been willing to risk his life and who alone was daring enough to play the part of King. He has relayed everything so perfectly, I am obviously greatly indebted to him, there are clear instructions for him in this final act as to how I would conduct myself. You go with my blessing, my eternal thanks and all of my heart." he stood, as did Jane and Ma Gollop and he hugged them both, "God speed."

"Good bye," said Jane thoughtfully, carefully taking the parcel of letters and placing them into her basket as Harry smiled. "You were right Jane, I feel I have been born again !" He said, raising his hands to the roof. Jane hugged Ma Gollop, "until we meet again Ma, Harry, may God be with you both," she left them, making haste to take the first coach out of town.

It was a different London to the one Jane had left. There was a nervousness and a sense of disbelief heavy in the air. She discovered quite quickly from her friends at

Scot's yard that James, the King had not escaped and was still very much a prisoner. Although she was prepared for this news she had hoped not to hear it. She wondered if he had received her letters or if he thought of her at all, it had been so long since she had seen him. Apparently he had been brought back to the mainland weeks ago and he was or soon would be at Windsor. The other widely known secret was that Cromwell's men had been seeking executioners about town and this had set a great unease amongst the people, who were shocked by these intentions. The ordinary men who at first had been driven to fight, had long since lost their faith in the 'cause'. It had carried on too long, the costs were too high and none of the things they were fighting for had come to pass, only leaving folk bewildered and frightened further. Parliament fiercely sought honest men or basically anyone who would be willing to take off the King's head ! Which implied there was not one amongst those vile instigators of this terrible plot who wanted the job ! Jane was unsurprised but truly thankful that no executioner could be found.

The whole of London had descended into Lunacy.

♛

Time was of the essence. Having satisfied herself with the latest news and gossip, Jane's first appointment was with the printer. An old and trusted Royalist that had shut his doors to the whole business of war and the campaign of terror. Jane didn't have to convince him that the manuscript was of prime importance and was diametrically opposed to the hate and propaganda currently being peddled. He saw the value in the work at once and pledged to commit to it straight away. Given the book's size, he said it would take at least eight weeks to assemble and print as many copies as Jane had asked of him. She then made her way to the laundries to find Nell and send the King's last letter to the Queen, before quickly heading out to the back streets of Charing Cross which she knew well and where she hoped to find the man she was looking for.

♛

Inigo Jones was a genius, who leaned heavily on his Welsh ancestry. He was a tall, heavily built, gruff but charming character with ruddy cheeks, he looked well travelled and well weathered, playful and usually drunk, except when he was at work as he was a true perfectionist. His mind was filled with incomparable brilliance and beauty, having designed the Banqueting House and all the fantastic masques, sets and scenes that had been displayed and played there. Although Jane couldn't claim to actually know him personally, she had applauded his wonderful works many times and it filled her heart just remembering them.

"Mr Jones ?" she asked timidly as she came up behind the great man.

"Who wants to know ?" He replied without turning round.

"I do Sir, I am a friend …of a friend and I was or rather I am hoping that he might help me, us. I suppose, I wish to employ you …him."

The man laughed as he carried on drinking, without turning round he answered over his shoulder.

"No one could afford me. My creative days are long over lass, all be for nothing now anyways. Parliament and puritans making damn sure of that."

"I am neither of those but I have admired your work my whole life and Sir you have amazed and delighted me in so many wild and wonderful ways. I am in need of your brilliance and quite frankly I know of no other who could even imagine the things you do, that's why it has to be you, him, the great Inigo Jones. I am in need of his assistance, for a … performance, of sorts, which I trust he will believe to be worthwhile also."

"And well paid ?"

"Oh yes, very well paid, handsomely in fact."

Flattered, Jones drank up the last of his drink then slowly placed his cup on the counter before turning to greet the lady with open arms and a wide smile. His eyes sparkled like jewels in his chiseled face.

"Well, why didn't you say so Madam ? Yes, you have indeed found me, I am the one you seek, Inigo Jones at your service. Take a seat my dear and tell me exactly what it is a lady like yourself might want from the likes of I ?"

"It is a delicate matter, may I ask that we go somewhere more … private ?"

He was most intrigued by this woman, half hidden in her heavy cloak, talking in whispers, something about her stirred him from his idle drinking so he led the way to a booth further back in the tavern. He invited her to sit then sat down himself, taking a good look at Jane's familiar face as she took down her hood.

"Friend, you said ? Which friend would that be ?"

"Mr Shirley."

"James ?"

"Yes, James Shirley, the poet and player."

"Ha, he was a player alright and a fine actor too, he's not dead is he ? I've not seen or heard from him in a while and if my memory serves me, he still owes me money."

"No Sir, he is not dead but alas his life is in danger."

"In danger ? James Shirley, you old scoundrel. Whatever has he got himself into now ? I've pulled him out of many scrapes you know, I wish I could help you but, look at me, all life has been stripped from me, madam you see before you a broken specimen. I'd wager you'd do better seeking assistance elsewhere. Hang on, I remember you, you were always about the palace, aye, happier times. I am far from the man I once was, but I am mightily proud that you remember the thrill of it all, wasn't it a joy to be living ? Now look at us, hiding in the shadows..." He took a big swig from the bottle he bought with him and began rambling, mumbling drunken self pity under his breath, inaudible to Jane who was losing patience.

"Mr Jones, Sir, I have a proposal ...of sorts, that could only be entrusted to you and only you, to save the King and James's life."

A flash went through Inigo's eyes, "Save the King's life ? Ah, I owe him my life and much as I would gladly lay down mine to save him, I think we may be too late, far too late. It's a waste of time thinking we can make a difference now. Much as it pains me to say, for I loved him but he is as we speak a prisoner of Cromwell and make no mistake he wants the King's head and the crown upon it ! He already sleeps in the King's bed, damn him ! As much as it enrages me, look at me, how could I be of any service ? I am no fighter, I am a man of culture and beauty or at least I was, I have no place in their dull and lifeless, frightened world. It is nothing but vulgarity passing itself off as Purity…"

"No Sir, this is not a call to arms, it is your brilliance we need, your designs and your imagination, the very things in which, I know you and only you, do excel. Would you allow me to share my imaginings and then could we discuss the possibility of realising them ? If you feel my ideas to be foolish or impossible, then I shall take that to be fact and bother you no more, but if …" Jane paused, staring deep into his eyes with determination. "If you would take this commission, believe that it could happen then, Sir it is not only possible but I dare say inevitable that we will save our friend Mr Shirley and the King."

"How is it that your foolish ideas have led you to me and what impossible feats do you deem me worthy of ? I do love the words foolish and impossible, especially when they are strung together so eloquently. I haven't the slightest idea of what you are saying to me or what any of this has to do with James, but indulge me, speak freely my dear."

"Thank you Sir, forgive me but I shall just pour out the ideas as they come and together we can then unravel them. Firstly, we will need you and some of those known as the Queens men, to put yourselves forward to be the executioners that Cromwell is seeking. As you know no one is willing, there is no one in the whole of London who wants this despicable task, therefore, I dare say you will be given the job immediately!"

Inigo looked indignant. "I beg your pardon ? You want me or rather the Queens men to be the King's executioners ? Am I hearing you right madam ?"

"Yes Sir, you hear me perfectly well, I am indeed suggesting that you put yourselves forward to be the executioners. Securing that position would allow us, well, you, to stage the greatest performance of your working careers."

Inigo raised his glass and eyes brows affronted, "Madam, I'll have you know I have created and staged many great and marvelous performances in my time."

"Forgive me, I didn't mean, I beg your pardon Sir, I know that to be true. Please forgive my impertinence. I'll start again, I have an idea. Of a performance of sorts." Jane took a deep breath.

"As I'm sure you've heard, they are unable to find the executioner, parliament is quite blatantly planning a beheading, no doubt a very public one !" Jane looked over both her shoulders to be sure no one could hear. "Cromwell and his puppeteer Ireton, are calling for a trial, their intention to cruelly shame His Majesty and then, God forbid, pass some unholy and unlawful judgment upon him. You know, as well as I, that if an executioner is being sought, then this trial they are offering is already a sham and quite frankly a disgrace. But …. What if Mr Jones, what if you were to put yourself forward, you or perhaps the Queens men would be willing to put themselves forward ?" She fumbled in the folds of her skirts to find the heavier of the purses she had concealed there and placed it on the table.

Jane looked at Inigo hopefully but she could tell she hadn't explained herself very well for he looked at her with disgust.

"No, Madam, absolutely not. How dare you even think such a thing, how dare you think such a thing of me ? Shame on you for even asking me, this can't be, I am affronted, you are quite mad and clearly mistaken if you think for one moment I would .." Jane interrupted before he could finish, taking full control of the conversation.

"No Sir, I promise you, it's not what you think, I'm not explaining myself very well and you have misunderstood my intentions, which I assure you are good. I have the highest of regards for our dear King and for James, who has placed his life and well quite possibly his head into our hands. Sir, I implore you, hear what I have to say in its fullness and then tell me your thoughts. For I truly believe and do most sincerely hope that you will agree with me and what's more I believe that only you could accomplish such a thing, which is why I find myself …" she looked around, "here."

"Now I am confused."

"No Sir, you are drunk and I have a habit of letting my ideas fall out of my mouth without putting them in a proper order first. Forgive me if it all sounds jumbled.

Please I beg you to hear me out, I'll try to speak slower. I wish to save the King's life but I can't do it alone. That is why I am here and what I am seeking your assistance for. If you were to secure the role of executioner, you would know what parliament's intentions are first hand. They will undoubtedly need a scaffold and seeing as you have an unrivalled talent for such things. What if you then offered to build the very apparatus parliament would require ? Only you could transform a simple scaffold into an elaborate stage. One that would enable you to suspend the crowd's perception of reality. I've seen a great many of your stages Sir and I remember everyone left me bewildered at the feats you achieved. Could you construct a stage that would allow us to switch the King in a way that no one would see or suspect, allowing him as the axe came down to escape unnoticed, unharmed ?"

"So, let me get this straight, We, that is I, I find some good men, willing to offer their services and act as the Kings executioners. I then put myself forward to construct the scaffold, building one fit for a King. I dare say with the right mechanisms, I could make a trap door that opened efficiently and quietly. Then you suggest that the King escapes through the crowd. Such a stage would need to be high and big, high enough to suspend one's beliefs and big enough to allow people to be underneath and black. We would need lots of black drapes and curtains. Yes, it would need to be all black, hides all manner of things you know. It certainly sounds like a daring plan."

"Daring, yes, but would it be possible?"

"Anything is possible if the will is strong." Inigo mused as Jane continued.

"If you were 'the executioners', you could take charge of the whole debacle, setting the stage, as you envision it, with the necessary and required scenery or props. As no one else has come forth or is likely to, you currently have an advantageous opportunity to put yourselves forward. Obviously, you would need a disguise, in fact you'd probably all need to be disguised, which is not implausible or even unusual for men who undertake such work, is it ? Besides I'd imagine the Queens men will have many costumes. Sir, I fear this to be the only hope left to us, admittedly a hazardous one but if we truly believe it is a worthy cause, to save the King's life," she paused to wipe her eyes. "Let us be the ones to bring this awful chapter to a close, with your designs. Let us give the King his freedom and give these power hungry men of parliament, the spectacle they want. Then these poor and wretched ordinary folk, so weary of war, will have an end to these terrible times and Cromwell will get what he desires ~ a head."

There was a long silence while Inigo called for more ale and considered Jane's words carefully.

"Then what ? What life do you envision the King to have, when the world assumes him to be dead ? And what of our friend, Mr Shirley ? What part will James be playing in this… escapade ?"

Jane sighed, for she now felt she ought to explain everything. She realised she was asking a lot of Inigo so thought it only right for him to know the whole truth.

"I believe the King would be happy just to live, peacefully and quietly. As for Mr Shirley, James has already been playing his part, really rather well, exceptionally in fact. You see he is the very King we are trying to save. It is he that parliament has prisoner, he has been acting as His Majesty for the best part of a year, hence why you have not seen him."

"What ? Well I'll be damned. The old devil, how in God's name ?"

"The true King's life was in terrible danger, much like how James now finds himself. The King and James swapped places last November when the King left Hampton Court. At that time, we believed James, as the King, would make his way swiftly to France, but sadly he was betrayed and apprehended before he could cross the channel. The true King is safe and far away, so it is James that is parliament's prisoner and it is he that they wish to do away with."

"Are you telling me the old rogue has been living like a King, this whole time ?" Inigo burst into peals of belly laughter.

"Yes Sir, he has and it's fair to say he's made a good time of it, but now that they wish him great harm, his guard is heavy and fierce so there is no other way we can help him escape now. It feels to me that this idea is the only opportunity we would have to free him, to save him. Unless you can think of a better one ? I feel we have this one final opportunity and there is no one else, no one who would even consider such a thing. It is only you who could imagine the design or have the brilliance to implement it."

Jane sat back satisfied with this explanation although she knew that whenever she got excited about something it was always so hard for her to put it into the right words and then put them in the right places. She hoped it sounded better and clearer and more plausible than even she imagined, there was a long painful silence, her satisfied smile drooping as she patiently awaited the great man's response. She ran her fingers in circles over the grooves in the sticky table top, feeling such internal conflict, ridiculous yet powerful, sure but with creeping doubts. What she couldn't see were the dusty cogs of Inigo Jones' mind clicking back into gear as he contemplated the idea.

"James, you old dog. Yes, I'll do it. I am at your service madam, of course we must do all we can to save him, we are his family ! I trust His Majesty is fully aware of all this, this plan ? And he is in alignment with these designs of yours, more to the point he will be happy living as a dead man ?"

"Yes Sir, I believe he will, he is born again. He knows as well as any of us, that in Cromwell's England we are all as good as dead anyway. It is James who needs us now."

"Then we have not a moment to lose, my lady," he took a last swig of the dregs of the bottle, confidently rising from his seat and took the purse Jane had placed before him.

"Come with me Madam. We have much to do, firstly we shall seek to employ the Queens men but I warn you, they are… rough round the edges and have since fallen on hard times, their abode is perhaps one that might shock … a lady such as yourself."

With his sense of duty and purpose revived he gallantly took great strides and his leave. Jane excitedly followed Inigo from the tavern, wrapping her cloak around her.

James was beginning to sense the gravity of his performance with the feeling of an impending finale. He was left mostly alone, Firebrace and the other servants were left behind on the Island, the guard now more serious and less amenable which had taken the fun out of it all. The one saving grace was Sir Thomas Herbert who became his new groom of the bedchamber. He was a gentleman traveler who distracted and captivated James with exotic tales from India, Persia and Arabia transporting him to far flung tropical places. He shared the beautiful poetry of Rumi which James hoped one day to whisper to Jane. He was now painfully aware that he hadn't seen her for months, his thoughts were constantly upon her. Her beauty, her grace, her hair, her mouth, he was so consumed by thoughts of her that time thankfully passed quickly. There were letters that came and various people requesting visits but these had to be declined, much as James would have adored the opportunity to perform, he thought these people would have known the King too well, putting him at greater danger. Other requests came of a most dubious nature from people that James had not heard of, who now wished to pray with him ? James found these ungracious and sent them all away. He would certainly not allow those who had been absent this whole year come and pray with him now !

♛

James was moved in the dead of a winter's night to the new army headquarters at Windsor Castle and it soon became startlingly obvious that these guards were serious, deadly serious. James felt a deep sadness as he walked through the great halls that had been stripped of their splendour. Although he had never seen them as they had once been, they were now bare, hard, cold and nothing of what James had known or remembered the Royal houses to be. He kept visits to an absolute minimum but was aware through letters and whispers that he or rather the King did have some friends left who were doing their best efforts in an attempt to free him. Then there was Jane, brave, daring, beautiful Jane. James had absolute faith in her for he knew she loved him, the very thought of her transported him far away from the walls that contained him for his heart was free. Sir Herbert encouraged James to add meditation to his prayers and focus his mind in the ways of the Persian sages, this encouraged feelings of such love, such depth and devotion, he began to enjoy the meditations and he sought to pray more and more, which he thought, would be most becoming of a King anyways.

The puritan guards of Windsor were dull, miserable and trying their hardest to ignore that it would soon be Christmas so James decided the very best thing for him to do was to embrace it. He committed to celebrate in the most splendidly sumptuous way possible and available to him as King, in his castle. These desires and designs were begrudgingly obliged to him for he was, after all, still the King. James was in his element, insisting on extravagantly beautiful decorations and many excellent musicians, who were brought to play continuously while a wonderfully lavish festive feast was prepared. He revelled in the fun and frivolity of it all, not just the delicious food and fine wines but especially how much it irritated those who were his captors.

Christmas came to the castle in the most outrageously opulent and magnificent style, James spent his days as if they were his last, in a constant state of celebration. He demanded that every corridor be filled with the beautiful sound of lutenists who played from dawn till dusk. The fires were full, heaving with warmth, as the snow softly fell outside. His cup was never empty and he regularly raised it to all those that served him, thanking them for all their efforts, which made the serving girls giggle and infuriated the stiff and rigid guard all the more. Letters and messengers flew out of the castle speedily to General Cromwell, reporting on the audacity of the King who was behaving, well, like a King and flagrantly ignoring the new regime. James laughed with a great deal of satisfaction as he raised a glass to the good people of England and wished them all, good health, happiness and most of all their Liberty.

Back in Glastonbury, the former King who was now known simply as Brother Harry was comfortably tucked away in the Mendip hills, embracing the peace and serenity of his new life with Good Wife Gollop. They shared silence and long walks together, played chess and prayed for the world they hoped to see.

When they received the grim news they feared from London, that executioners were being sought, it shocked them both to the core, could this really be what the world had come to ? Who would have considered such a thing possible ?

Ma Gollop was seriously troubled, Harry equally so but able to contain and control his emotions far better. His thoughts were with his family and the poor man offering his life in place of his.

Harry had not said a word since reading the grave news the messenger had brought into the Bluebell with the packet of letters from the day's first, and because of the winter weather only, coach.

Ma Gollop poured him a warm cider from the fireplace, shaking her head in disbelief.

"What is the world coming to ?"

Joseph soon came in through the swing doors with the wind behind him, all eyes turned to him but their thoughts were in London and the unfortunate events unfolding there.

"Welcome Joseph, have ye heard ? It's awful and you just as well hear it from me. They are scouting the streets of London seeking a henchman to cut off the King's head. Can you believe it ?"

"No, I can't believe it Ma, they want to do away with the King ? Well I'll be damned, that's treason that is ? Them damn puritans really don't like Christmas do they ?" He said, as shocked as the rest of the room. Harry nodded to him from his quiet corner, touched by his show of support. Joseph took off his hat and shuffled over to the fire and the cider.

"Help yourself Joseph," called Ma Gollop as she went to the kitchen to fetch bread and cheese, after all it was Christmas and although all celebration had been stamped out and forbidden, Ma Gollop had a rebellious streak and loved the spirit of sharing and hosting and nothing not even that ' bloody Oliver Cromwell,' would be stopping her.

After a long silence and loosened up by the cider, the laughter returned to the little Inn. Harry remembered many magical and fantastic Christmases but now he was far happier to live simply. He was thankful to be amongst good and honest people, a luxury he became aware had been denied him most of his life. The honesty of simple folk restored his faith in human nature more so now he was watching from afar, the destructive and deceptive nature of those given powers over the rest.

They sang, told stories and shared food by the roaring fire well into the early hours before Joseph took his leave and they raised their mugs.

"May God bless us all and may God save the King."

Things were not going well for Cromwell who was driven to despair. Deeply frustrated with his promiscuous daughters who were devious, seething with jealousies and consistently dissatisfied despite their father moving them into palaces and sleeping in the King's beds. They persistently whined and demanded more, running rings around their father and driving him almost psychotic. He needed somewhere to assert his authority so he called a council of commissioners enabling him to divert all of his wrath elsewhere. He was outraged that the King would do something so…blatant, so offensive, so.. he was lost for words. Transferring all of his frustrations and focusing all of his hatred at the King who had dared to hold Christmas celebrations at Windsor. He was furious at the boldness of the man who was behaving like the King of his castle. Cromwell was hopping mad and boiling with fury, that the King had so greatly disrespected him and of course God with this flagrant display of … well, Kingship. He took it upon himself to set wheels in motion of a most deadly nature.

"Only God sits upon a throne, not man, not he !"

Ireton's eyes flashed with a wicked darkness, gleefully encouraging Cromwell's words and thoughts.

"Yes, General ?" He sneered.

"Remove the crown from this man and take his head with it if you have too, he has committed treason against God and treason against the people of this good nation."

Cromwell paced like a madman around the silent room, which was now in shock at his words and the implications of his desires. There had been whispers but until then no one had heard them uttered by the man himself. After a long eerie pause, one man found the courage to stand up to him.

"This is insanity, surely we can all see that ? There is not a court in the land that could charge a King with treason. The very act of treason is a crime against the King, this is utter madness."

Cromwell, who was not used to having anyone disagree with him, especially when in such momentous rage cast a deadly glare and screamed at him to get out.

"As you wish Sir. But I want it known that I'll not have any part in this murderous campaign and I suggest to all of you here that you guard your conscience against this evil design." He gathered his effects and promptly left the room.

Thus the news was out and had reached all corners of the country, the King was to be brought to trial. These were dark days indeed.

James, however, was happily continuing with his flamboyant performance, in total denial of their evil designs. He found it ridiculous and almost laughable that such a monstrous thing should come to pass.

Cromwell set a date for the trial, even though every Englishman knew there was no court in all the land that could try an ordained King, one was nevertheless, hastily contrived, coerced and constructed in Westminster. James prepared for the performance of his life. He had had various notes and letters from the King advising him on everything from his words to his composure. The whole thing felt absurd, this was no court of law, it was pure theatre. James had a simple script, to ask upon whose authority he had been called.

It was a cold January day when a coach came to take James into London, he was still enjoying himself and the wines far too much to notice the sober mood of the guard. He was taken to St James palace and was thankfully escorted to his quarters for not having been there before James had no idea which way to go. He was glad to be back in town and found himself greatly looking forward to the morning when his performance would begin. He dined well and slept well and ensured that the

King's finest clothes were laid out for him, deciding to wear the George the King had sent him as a mark of honour and hopefully protection. He chose a wide brimmed hat that would hide his features but his hair and beard had grown so long it would be doubtful if anyone would question him. James had refused all offers of a shave, not trusting any army men with his elegant neck.

♛

The next morning following a brisk walk to Westminster, James took to the stage. After being so long in solitude, James was thrilled to be in front of such a large and captive audience. Despite the dark, ugly miserable faces of the so-called jury, there seemed to be great support for the King with cries of 'God save the King' from the corridors rebounding all the way up to the rafters, which only incensed the 'jury' more. They were unprepared for James, who was behaving as if in a comedy, flatly refusing to acknowledge them or their authority, which brought peals of laughter from the crowds and fury to his self appointed judges.

♛

Meanwhile, the former King being far away from the madness, sequestered away in Glastonbury devoted himself to prayer. At the rare times he did leave the safety and relative comforts of Good Wife's Gollop's Inn he made straight of the ruins of the Abbey to surround himself with Saints and the company of older Kings. Here he could lament and feel heard throughout the corridors of time. He prayed to and with King Arthur, Queen Guinevere, Joseph, Mary and Jesus imploring them all to come to the aid of James, the people and the country, for he felt nothing less than a divine intervention could help them now.

♛

James was in his element, finding great humour in the unfolding chaos, he repeatedly denied the judges their authority and therefore their control of the situation. He was thoroughly enjoying their flustered attempts to regain order, there were screams from the stalls of their treacherous, treasonous behaviour which did nothing to aid their feelings of hopelessness which James found hilarious. He didn't have to say very much at all, he simply observed the raucous comedy and laughed quietly to himself. It was however too much for a red faced Cromwell and his new puppet Bradshaw, a meek solicitor who had been forced to lead proceedings. They were visibly distressed, Bradshaw called for people to be removed from the court and when one of the jurors was heard supporting the King, Cromwell promptly escorted him out too. Lord Fairfax was conspicuously absent and women were jeering from the gallery that at least he had the wit to stay away. It was becoming fascial and more and more ridiculous. Outside the courthouse came rallying cries for the Royalist cause and over everything else could be heard constant chants of, "God save the King."

It was too much for the parliamentarians, James was soon removed from the court as they deemed it unnecessary for the King to be party to their proceedings. And why not, they had after all smashed and crushed every other aspect of the Kingdom so they might as well make a complete mockery of its laws as well. Behind closed doors, the court rolled out their new concept of what they had convinced each other of as justice, while outside of those doors the people awaited their conclusions.

♛

The mock jury soon came to a mock conclusion of their mock trial and recalled the King for sentencing. As James walked through the silent and serious crowds he scanned them for Jane. For her hair, for her cloak, for any part of her he could pull towards him, for all his bravery and conviction, his resolve was now flagging. He recalled that night in London when he begged her for this opportunity that now burdened him. Remembering the wild times they had on the Isle of White, the boundless joys and laughter, feeling such heights of ecstasy just being near her, he now wanted more than anything else to see her face, to touch her, to taste her, to make love to her. Even with the severity of the situation he could think of nothing else other than being wrapped around her body and kissing every part of it. In fact this is how he had made all of this dreadful situation bearable, with these wild imaginings and fantasies which were becoming more and more illicit and passionate. So lost in these daydreams, he didn't notice some of the people were crying and sobbing.

Bradshaw stood and called for silence. "The court, being satisfied that he, Charles Stuart, was guilty of the crimes of which he had been accused, did judge him, tyrant, traitor, murderer and public enemy to the good people of the nation, to be put to death by the severing of his head from his body." The jurors then rose to their feet as a deathly and horrible hush surrounded everyone present.

It was not how James had envisioned his end would come about but then he hadn't honestly given it much thought, he loved his life and was so enthralled in the living of it, especially lately. When the court passed their judgement James did request to speak but it was denied him, this confirmed to James that these were no gentlemen.

James was in shock, he never believed it would come to this, that this terrible fate would befall the King. How could this be ? He tried hard to show no emotion as the words rebounded in his mind. With every ounce of valour he could muster James left the courthouse with half a mind to reveal himself and expose their incompetence but as a man of honour, he could not embarrass the King besides he would rather die than live amongst them, despicable scoundrels every one.

♛

James bravely composed himself and heavy heartedly made the slow walk back to St James palace with elegance and grace. He returned to his rooms to be alone, sending even the bishop away. Pouring himself a large glass of wine, he sunk into a bottomless sorrow. All the strength and confidence he had been so used to had now left him, he was defeated, lost and frightened.

He collapsed in absolute grief, the unbearable weight of the sentence passed upon him crushed his very soul to pieces, his lament was unconsolable. The grim realisation that death awaited him was all encompassing and he couldn't think or see clearly, he couldn't escape, he could do nothing but face the horrors his mind conjured of what lay in the day's before him. He couldn't pull himself out of it or even bring himself to think of Jane as he felt ashamed as if he had somehow failed her and failed to save the King's life, forgetting that he had already done so.

♛

Jane had been amongst the women jeering from the gallery's, her heart ached for the man she loved. He was so daring, seeing him bravely standing fearlessly in the face of such depravity only endeared him to her all the more. She wanted to call and reach out to him wishing nothing more than to kiss those lips that spoke to her in her dreams and had done for most of her life. She was however under no illusions that one wrong move could jeopardise the plans she had so perfectly and brilliantly devised with Inigo and the rest of the Queens men. Jane watched from a distance with utter pride and total adoration for the man she loved as herself. For she was him and he was her, they were as one and she thought of nothing else but him, every waking moment.

♛

So it was that the date was set on the 30th January which was just three days away. Luckily an executioner had been found, which disgusted the townsfolk of London as it was inconceivable that anyone would step forward for such a dastardly deed. The Queen's men who so gallantly volunteered their services for the grotesque job were invigorated and thrilled to be acting again, especially in service to the King and their friend. Miraculously a scaffold builder had also come forward, who even convinced parliament to use the Banqueting House for the hideous event and was paid most handsomely for it. Inigo Jones would construct a stage, scaffold worthy of any masque, the King and Queen would have been astonished, Inigo applauded himself knowing neither of them would ever see it.

♛

The next morning James had regained his composure and restored himself as regent. He carried on as he imagined the King would do with resolve and dignity. When he had no word from Jane he knew the only way to get a message to her was send a ring to Elizabeth Wheeler's house in Westminster. The ring was a message in and of itself, James entrusted Sir Thomas Herbert with it and told him to wait for a reply.

♛

Lady Elizabeth was startled when Sir Herbert called at her home. She greeted him kindly albeit suspiciously, when he instantly handed her the ring from the King. Elizabeth calmly invited him in and showed him to a room where he could wait, which he was expecting. Quietly shutting the door behind her, she then bolted like a colt up the stairs to the top of her house where Jane had been staying. Jane was most surprised when Elizabeth breathlessly flew into the room.

"Sir Thomas is here, downstairs, now."

"Who ?"

"Sir Thomas Herbert of the bedchamber, he's down stairs and he gave me this."

Elizabeth handed Jane the King's ring which she immediately recognised.

"Oh," she sighed as her heart sank and her face crumpled as she knew this to be the signal that he was ready for the end. She wanted so much to tell him everything, to comfort him, to reassure him.

"Poor soul. He must be mad with grief and horror and hatred and… poor man, Jane what can we do? What can we do ?" Elizabeth howled.

"Where is Sir Herbert now ?"

"Downstairs, in the drawing room, what does it mean ?" sobbed Elizabeth.

"It means I must quickly write a message to James, I don't want him to think I have abandoned him," she whispered hastily, writing him a letter.

"Elizabeth, remember that time I asked you to look after something for me ? Where did we put it ?" Jane knew that James now needed his instructions as to how he was to play out this final chapter, she was touched by his courage. They quickly found the old cabinet the King had given her in long ago in Oxford. It had remained hidden in Elizabeth's house since Jane placed it there. She blew the dust from it, and opened it for the first time. Seeing it filled with trinkets and broken pieces of jewellery she smiled to herself realising it had been a test rather than a favour. Into the back of the cabinet she placed the two letters, one with the last words from the King and one from her. When she was satisfied they were well enough hidden she passed the whole cabinet to Elizabeth holding onto her hands.

"We need your strength now, more than ever," she said as she looked determinedly into Elizabeth's eyes which only made her cry more.

"I love you Lizzy and I know you have done everything within your powers to be of assistance to me, to James and to the King. This is it, this is the last time your loyalty will be called upon, you have served us all well and you will be rewarded in life and in heaven. I praise and thank God for you every day, I couldn't have done any of this without you."

Elizabeth was overcome and could hardly speak.

"I don't want this to be the end, I want things to be better for His Majesty, for James, for all of us. Especially for you." The two friends embraced lovingly around the small wooden cabinet, then Jane kissed her friend and gave her a reassuring nod.

Elizabeth wiped her eyes, blew her nose and took a deep breath before heading back down the stairs to where Sir Herbert was waiting.

"Thank you for your patience Sir, here please give this to His Majesty along with my deepest.." She began to cry, Herbert placed a kindly hand upon her shoulder.

"Forgive me, Sir, but what have we come too ? .. How ? .. I mean I'm not sure what to say or how to say it but, I never in all my days thought we would see one as dark and despicable as this, this is a sad day for us all Sir. For what it's worth, please would you tell him that I'll be praying for him."

"I certainly will, may God bless you Madam."

"May God bless the King," said Elizabeth as Sir Herbert left, wrapping his cloak around his consignment and making his way quickly back to the palace. The guard didn't check his person as it was a cold night and they had no reason to suspect him of anything. Sir Herbert hastened to James and gave him the cabinet of broken jewels but James knew the real treasure to be concealed in it somewhere and waited till he was alone to find it.

♛

Having found the letters and seeing one in Jane's hand, he opened it straight away. It read,

Dear heart, please forgive me, you must know that I have been there with you these past days. I am astounded by your bravery. My heart and my thoughts have never left you. I pray you share the faith that I have, truly the Lord holds you in his hands, trust that we will come for you.

James read and reread the words but he felt so wretched and hopeless he had no faith. He cried as he kissed the words she had written him and resigned himself to his or rather, the King's fate and the executioner's axe.

The other letter was from the King and James knew very well what this would be, it was heavier and weightier that the other for it contained exactly what the King wished to be said and done in his last days and hours, he was after all a meticulous man. James was resistant to open it, it felt so final as this was when the curtain would close, not just upon his performance but upon his very life. With one hand he felt around his neck, he had always enjoyed his body and loved how wonderfully it all worked together. Now it seemed he had a particular fondness for his neck and how it held his head up so perfectly. He let out a belly laugh that turned into roars of laughter either from the wine or from the hysteria of his great peril. It was whilst he was in this state of joyful resignation there came a knock to the door. James at once composed himself and was thankful they hadn't come just a few moments earlier, putting the letters into his pocket he turned to see who wished his attention. Parliament, either through cruelty or concern, were bringing the King's youngest children, Henry and Elizabeth to see him one last time. James in his hysterical cynicism believed it to be the former but nonetheless he agreed to this visit alone and sent all the other scavengers and vultures away. The children unsurprisingly did not recognise him, James said it was due to them being so overcome with tears and sadness as he tried to help them in their grief and console them as a father would. The King had given him no instructions as to what to say to his children so James hastily improvised and did the best he could to impress upon their minds loving and lasting memories of the man they thought to be their father, he sincerely hoped that he had in some way soothed their sorrow. He then gifted them with the jewels from the cabinet and hugged them tightly before they were led away leaving James even more wretched, devastated and alone.

♛

That evening passed painfully slowly, thankfully the wine was good and James heartily drank, requesting a further bottle after eating little of his evening meal. He then paced the room restlessly in between vain attempts to rehearse the King's words but he was in turmoil, Sir Herbert encouraged him to be still and meditate but he could do neither, his thoughts constantly turned to Jane. James licked the wine from his own lips and raised his glass to her, "Jane, my Joan of Arc .. to the love we will ever know." He downed his glass and called for another bottle, nothing could fill the hollowness.

♛

In the meantime Jane and Inigo had been feverishly busy planning with the Queens men. They were a fun bunch of rogues with poetic hearts and a love for chivalry, beauty and most of all freedom. Inigo had devised a most ingenious performance and had made a working model of the stage stroke scaffold set up so as to convey his directions fully as there could be not one inch of error. The Queens men who thankfully were at their very best when preparing for a performance were once more captivated and inspired by Inigo's brilliance. The stage was to be draped in black velvet and he had insisted that it be raised and that the King would have to step out on it from one of the upper windows.

"Like this," he placed his working model next to an upturned chest playing the part of the Banqueting House.

"What, you're having the King climb out of a window ? That's ridiculous, they'll never go for it, they will never agree to that."

"Well actually," remarked Inigo with the twinkle in his eyes that spoke well before the words had left his mouth.

"Well I'll be blown," said Jono, who earlier in the week had volunteered his services as Axe man and already been paid handsomely for it, hence the many flagons of ale the men had been enjoying since.

"So, come on then Jones, how in God's name, how did you convince them of such a canny idea?"

"Actually it was Jane and the King's inspired idea. I just suggested it, as it would be the most degrading for him and he would then be up high and out of reach.

Firstly so everyone in the crowd could see and secondly as a deterrent should any one be plotting to free him. I used their own fear against them and told them the truth, if you tell them the truth in jest, people don't believe it. I then told them that the guards would find it far easier to keep the crowd at bay, if they were in place along here, keeping the people as far back as possible, you see. They are scared to death of their own actions but even more frightened of a possible uprising. Oh and I told them that having the King walk under the great ceiling, would be crushing and painful for him, which clinched it. Sick to their bones these men are and cruel, the lot of them." Inigo shook his head.

"So, I've told them that the scaffold, our stage," he looked around for effect, making sure all eyes were fixed firmly on him and his every word.

"Will be here," he said, positioning it on the corner.

"Isn't that a bit awkward ?"

"Aye, for them maybe, but for us it's perfect and here's why, look with all the crowd out the front here, you'll be able to get away easily and unseen out the back here and make your way to the riverside down here. See ? Now where were we, ah yes so the King has walked through the house, then he comes here, to the very last window and steps out of it onto the stage, like so. I've told them that given the height and haste with which the scaffold has been built, only one or two men may accompany him. Fortunately those roundheads think it belittling to be climbing out of a window, so maybe only the Bishop, Juxton, who is by all accounts a good man and possibly our good friend Sir Herbert, will join him. John, you and Fred will be here." Inigo pointed to their position.

"Good friend ? I thought Sir Thomas Herbert was a parliamentarian ?" Asked Jane surprised.

"Aye, indeed he is but things and especially people are not always as they seem my dear. Sir Thomas is a man of the world, I met him many years ago when we were both travelling. He spent a great deal of time with the mystics of Asia and Persia, he can perform feats of such magic that we could only dream of. Sir Thomas is a dear and trusted friend."

"I didn't know, he came to the house but I didn't meet him…"

"More's the pity, he is an excellent man, like us, a lover of all things beautiful. He has been charming young James with tales of the orient and the poetry of the Ottoman, assisting him with meditation and focus. We are indebted to him for he has a certain flair for the magical, which my dear will be invaluable."

"I had no idea someone so close to James was on our side." Smiled Jane.

"A gambler tends not to reveal his cards, especially if he is holding aces," winked Inigo.

"Now where's my henchmen, ah .. here and here, Jono this is you and this is you Freddy." Inigo moved corks about setting the scene and indicating where everyone should place themselves.

♛

Jono had enjoyed his interview for the would be King killer enormously. He had found those that were seeking to employ an executioner easily, in the very same tavern where Ireton had written his remonstrance, these puritans were creatures of habit. Jono and Freddy had covered their heads with sacks so that just their eyes could be seen. In hushed discussions, Jono performed with perfection the cruelty they expected from one who would undertake their dastardly plans, easily convincing them he was indeed their man. Telling them that the burden of committing such a terrible, heinous act, the killing of a King, demanded absolute anonymity and he would therefore never reveal his face or his name. It was all too easy, he said he required a second, beckoning Freddy. Together they acted so convincingly, they made the executioner seekers nervous, but having finally secured what they had thought to be impossible, they were delighted, Cromwell would be pleased. Jono then demanded half of his fee up front and the same for his second, who was prowling, silently lurking in the shadows. They left the tavern with full pockets and applauded each other's performance.

♛

"Miss Ryder, this is you, you will be here," Inigo continued, looking around then smiling as his eyes found hers.

They all glanced over at Jane as she blushed but returned their smiles.

"What about you Jones, where will you be?"

"Aha, I was just getting to that, here. Henry, Nicholas, Robert and me will be underneath here," he lifted up the black velvet showing under the platform.

"But first let's get to the business at the top, Jono and Freddy this is where you'll be, we will carry the coffin there first light and you boys must stay with it. You let no one near it and you're not to leave, not even for a piss. You must stay in your cloaked costumes and wait, there is absolutely no room for error boys … none … so we must all be in alignment with perfect timing," Inigo looked at each of them dead in the eyes.

"The King, our James, will climb out the window here and then of course not wanting to miss an opportunity to act, he will no doubt command the crowd. I believe the King has sent a script of his last words, which, knowing James, will be said beautifully. Then he must take his place here, before the block, which I've insisted on being very low. This gives us the advantage of blocking the view from the crowd and those gawpers inside as long as you Fred, position yourself here, with your back to them, then spread out your cloak like this. Make sure you've pushed the Bishop or whoever it is, well back over here and behind you, Sir Thomas will instinctively know his best position. The coffin is to go here, but we will of course be on hand with the set. John, when you are satisfied that everyone is in position you are to raise the axe. Jane this is the signal for you to cause a howling hullabaloo, screech and scream make as much commotion as you can." No one dared take a breath as they focused every part of themselves upon the makeshift stage.

"And then ?" Begged Jono.

"Well," smiled Inigo, "that's the clever part."

The day came much quicker than the people of London had anticipated, many were in despair and some were hopefully awaiting a reprieve that wouldn't come. The Prince of Wales had sent desperate pleas from the Netherlands and many of the commissioners who had previously sat in on the King's trial were now fearful and absent. The mood was thick with angst, disbelief and uncertainty.

There hadn't been many who slept well that night, even Cromwell had been awake for most of it. He had risen and shamelessly left London early. It appeared that even he wanted to be far away from this terrible turn of events he had coerced and orchestrated.

Inigo had slept little these past days spending all his time securing the stage into exactly the position he wanted it. Whitehall was heavy in guard and atmosphere. He and the executioners however, had free movement as even the guard who had witnessed the horrors of war, were fearful of men who would so willingly perform such a task. Jono and Freddy very much enjoyed being disguised but in plain sight and it humored them greatly, which only unnerved the guard all the more.

At the Palace, Sir Thomas Herbert came in early following maids, whose eyes were wet with tears as they brought breakfast but James, who had not slept, refused the food and sent them all away. He stared out of the window watching the dark clouds move across the grey sky and barely noticed Sir Thomas preparing his last outfit or heard the incantations he whispered. James had memorised the last words the King had sent him and thought them worthy and dignified. He hoped he would be able to extend and command those virtues upon the scaffold and above all, do the King justice.

Jane and Elizabeth had stayed up most of the night together and spent the morning in prayer. Jane knew that is where James would be and she hoped to reach out to him on the winds of the divine. How she wanted God to hear her and watch over the man she loved and all of those brave men that loved him.

"Please protect them, please, Lord, I implore you."

Far away in the little town of Glastonbury, it was also a somber morning. The news had reached them just the day before so there was no time to digest or think about the unfolding and unfortunate turn of events. No one could quite believe it had come to this or that such a thing was possible, even those that had swayed towards grievances and parliament were as shocked and as saddened as those that were true Royalists. What would this mean for them, for England ?

Harry had been fasting and at prayer, since news of the trial had reached them. Good Wife Gollop would every time her mind was still enough for the terrible thoughts to creep in, shake them out in disgust.

"No good will come of this, you mark my words, terrible, terrible business," she said to the young girl who was helping her and who couldn't stop crying for she was at an age when emotions tended to be out of control.

"That Cromwell, who does he think he is ? You can't just go round taking the heads off Kings, he's the devil himself," Ma Gollop carried on talking mostly to herself as the poor young girl, recoiled in shock, then returned to her sobbing.

"The world's gone mad and none more madder than him, if he thinks he'll gain anything but curses for the rest of his days, what a to do."

It had snowed heavily during the night and the whole of Glastonbury and as far as the eye could see, was covered in a blanket of perfect white. As nothing and no one could get through or wished to be about on this most terrible of days, all was still and silent, not even the birds disturbed the perfect peace. Ma Gollop kept the fires of the Bluebell lit and every corner was clean. She had food cooking although she knew no one would be eating and she didn't expect to see a soul either. When they had finished their chores they sat quietly by the fire, fixing their gaze upon the flames, all of their thoughts were in London and the goings on there. Thankful for the comforts they had and quietly praying for all those poor souls whose lives were about to change forever, they waited for this day to be over. Ma Gollop was most surprised when Joseph made his way through the snow and her door.

"Bless my soul, whatever has happened ? How come you've dragged yourself here Joseph ?"

"Thirst," he smiled.

"Aye, I thought as much," she laughed as she went to pour him a warm cider and pulled another chair to the fire.

"Bless you Ma Gollop, you are a fine woman and it's on days such as these that I find myself wanting to tell you so and remind myself," he raised his glass and drank to her good health and to the young lady who sat with them, then lost his thoughts to the fire alongside them.

It wasn't long before she was surprised again, when Harry came slowly down the stairs to join them.

"Ah, here comes the monk, I wondered when you'd be joining us, come pray for the King and for what was once England." Joseph said half smiling up at him. He was still none the wiser to Harry's true identity but him having been a guest and by all accounts kin to Ma Gollop, Joseph had made it his business to befriend him. They had struck up a friendship of sorts, both being men of few words and both with a talent for chess, the game of Kings as Joseph called it and the man who everyone had come to call Harry had agreed. Ma Gollop smiled and stood up to get more cider and another chair.

No one knew when the dreadful event was to take place and deep down they all hoped that it never would, that at the last moment news would come of some reprieve. Everyone except Harry, who knew too well that the outcome was now inevitable.

♛

Inigo Jones peered out at the guarded crowd from his vantage spot underneath the scaffold. Henry, Nicholas and Robert were under there with him sitting on the back of a barrow. Robert had that morning already played the part of undertaker, scouring the streets and slums for someone of similar height, features, etc but in the end had to settle on simply finding someone freshly dead. He was so pleased with himself when he found the ideal candidate, even punching the air with relief and satisfaction much to the bewilderment of the poor fellows grieving family. It must be said that every one of the Queens men were beyond thrilled to be performing once more and had regained their sense of purpose and of living.

♛

It was a dismal, dark day, bitterly, biting cold, Jane was restless, impatiently and nervously moving about in the crowd to keep warm and to keep her thoughts at bay. The crowd was restless too and constantly being pushed back by the guard, they'd been kept waiting for so long. Finally at 2 o'clock in the afternoon, in the distance could be heard the dire sound of a singular drum. Jane kept her eyes to the scaffold and her breathing steady as a small boy ran through the crowd shouting, "The King cometh."

This was it, the final act, the moment they had all been waiting for, each of them knew their part and had acted it out so meticulously, they were keen and confident. The Queens men locked eyes with each other without saying a word, preparing themselves for the performance of their lives, for they knew their very lives depended on it all going to plan. There would be no applause and no one would ever know, which made it all the more daring and delicious.

Jono and Freddy however were enthusiastically over performing to the shouts, boo's and hisses as they stood centre stage, dressed in the garb of the most horrid. It had been years since they had enjoyed so much attention.

With a heavy guard, James, Bishop Juxton and Sir Herbert were walking slowly from St James palace through the masses of people, many wanting to kiss him, many shouting, 'God save the King,' some shouting profanity. James focused on his footsteps with a cane and Sir Herbert at his side to steady him. He pretended he was preparing for a great masque and there would be a roaring applause as he sang his finale. It was these thoughts and fantasies that filled his mind as he approached the great Banqueting House, once home to pure revelry, fun, magic and wonder, where he had enjoyed some of the best days of his life. He turned for one last look at the crowd which, held back by guards, had become a mixture of taunts and devotion, a cacophony of such that it was impossible to hear anything but noise. He desperately wanted to see Jane, scanning the sea of faces for hers, was he stalling ?

Was he afraid ? Was he really about to die ? Was this to be his last look at life ? So many thoughts rolled around his mind, then like a divine apparition, there she was.

He stopped and mouthed her name silently, unable to believe it or to speak.

She forced her way through the guard and pressed herself against him, knowing she had only the briefest moment to whisper,

"I have always been yours, I have loved no other more…remember ? We have a son ! " She kissed his cheek before she was wretched away and swallowed up by the crowd.

James was stunned with both elation and disbelief as he put his hand to his cheek where she had kissed him. He was struck by the strangest recollection of a passionate dalliance some years ago, he remembered the sound of her voice as those words echoed around him, her whisper drowning out the sound of everything else. She has loved no other more, had they loved each other before, they had a son ? A vague memory flashed through his mind as he held his heart, in a daze he stumbled but fortunately Sir Herbert was there to catch him.

James entered the Banqueting House, totally unaware that his dearest friends were concealed and concocting a most fantastically daring escape. He was as if in a dream as he took to the stairs with unswerving gallantry. Jane had stirred his soul and every step was now a dance as love poured into him and filled him so completely that he no longer felt any fear. There was simply no room in his being for anything other than pure joy. Realising he was a father, James couldn't help but smile to himself, almost laughing which unsettled those angry puritan men who were expecting him to be otherwise. He entered the great hall Rueben had painted that he knew so well and was at once transported back to those happier times. He imagined the sour stern faces of those puritans men to be softer, kinder folk resembling an audience of others he knew and loved before. It was as if he had stepped back in time and everything was as it once gloriously was. A splendid vision of loveliness, he saw the King and Queen with their beautiful family applauding him and everyone joyfully cheering his performance. As he was led to the window which he was to step out of, he turned to give his audience one of his tantalising bows he was so famous for, then he bade them all a good night and adieu as he climbed through the dazzling light of the window, jarring his senses back to the cruelty of that sad and numbing January day.

As the icy air hit his face it took his breath away and brought him back to the savagery of the dreadful scene that awaited him below. There were gasps from the crowd as an inconceivable silence fell like snow about those who had come to witness this awful and harrowing ultimatum.

Bishop Juxton began reciting prayers while James looked into the crowd, making him instantly hyper aware of the gravity of the situation which narrowed his focus. He suddenly had the strangest feeling that he knew the men who stood in stupid disguises before him. As he surveyed his surroundings he noticed little tell-tale nuances that reminded him of none other than that great man of theatre and production Inigo Jones. The whole scaffold was draped rather tastefully in beautiful black velvet and even the axe looked unreal. He questioned himself as he flipped between realities. Was this some kind of a production ? Was he now in a somewhat strange altered state, was this hysteria ? Was he hallucinating ? He noticed there were different levels to the scaffold, much like a stage and that the block was incredibly low, it would require him to almost lay completely flat on the floor. As he looked from the block to the executioner, who apparently had brought a friend along, it seemed to James as if they were sniggering. He did a double take at the coffin for although that too was draped in black velvet he was sure he saw a body already inside it, which one of the henchmen swiftly covered. James looked back at Bishop Juxton who was in full flow with his eyes skyward as if he was opening up the doors of heaven for him. It all seemed so unreal. Sir Herbert brought him back into the moment, looking into his eyes and holding his hands giving him the confidence to address the crowd, eloquently and precisely as the King had wished him to do. Unsure he had been heard as the crowd seemed so far away James then turned to Juxton and Herbert, repeating the words he had practiced and just shared.

"Remember," he said to himself echoing Jane's words. He couldn't help but smile as he was overcome by the strangest feelings of courage and hope. Slowly, James undressed, handing over his jackets and tying back his hair, unaware that beside and beneath him were his dearest and most loved friends and the great man himself. Inigo Jones was making the final and necessary last minute preparations and adjustments to their daring plan. If there was even the slightest error they would all end up without their heads.

As the King had instructed, James made it known that he forgave those that had brought him here and those that were about to end his life. He thanked Bishop Juxton and Sir Herbert for their service to him, then told the executioners he wished to pray and would signal when he was ready to meet his maker by holding out his hands, the executioners, who were still sniggering, silently nodded in agreement. James fought back the most awful sense of foreboding and fragility as he touched his cheek where Jane had last touched him with her lips. All was still.

Remember.

James looked about him, taking his last taste of life with a deep breath. Bravely and with great dignity, he got down onto his knees and prayed. Freddy then moved to his position as Sir Herbert joined him, holding out their cloaks to obstruct the puritan's view from the windows, just behind them the Bishop was still facing up to the heavens, deep in prayer. When James was satisfied he had said all he could, he laid flat and put out his hands, Jono then slowly lifted the heavy axe into the air. Jane upon seeing her signal, screamed so violently loud it plucked at the very nerves of everyone in and around the crowd. Simultaneously Elizabeth, on the other side of the road, let out a shriek so awful and shockingly shrill that all attention was turned to them, everyone being so on the edge of their senses anyways. At that precise moment Jono, in perfect timing with the swing of his axe, kicked a lever next to the block where James had rested his head, which then opened and dropped James through a trap door before instantly snapping shut again. At the very same instant, Freddy kicked the coffin triggering a side opening, out of which rolled the cadaver procured by Robert that morning. James, who felt the floor move beneath him, had in a moment of terror believed himself to be sliding into hell. He tried to resist his descent but instead he landed safely into the arms of Nicholas and Henry who were in prime position to catch him. James regained his senses and quickly realised them not be devils, demons or the hounds of hell but his friends and fellow Queens men. He was startled, initially panicked but then so relieved to see them and be in their arms, he smacked Nicholas fully and firmly with a kiss on the lips.

"You beauty," he panted.

They all cast their eyes above at the thud of the axe as it fell, upon the Great British Monarchy and a dead man's neck. It didn't make it any less of a task, Jono had closed his eyes and hoped it had been a clean cut. Freddy then swiftly stepped forth and held up the head of the poor chap, throwing it quickly into the crowd as agreed, making it indistinguishable once the frenzy of relic hunters had had their way with it. Inigo sighed with an enormous sense of pride mixed with relief as Robert wrapped a filthy stinking cloak around James, causing everyone to recoil, "What ? No one will stop you if you're covered in shit."

The silence that was at first all consuming became a groan from the people that was almost unearthly. Jane froze, spine chillingly shocked to her core when the axe finally fell, while those around her screamed in horror and anguish as they accepted their part in the killing of their anointed King. The sickening and deplorable sight of a head being held up then thrown into the hands of the King's subjects, spurred wild cries and shouts, pushing and shoving as folk began grabbing, scratching and clawing at the head of the man whom they thought to have been their sovereign. The macabre sight let Jane know that James had to be alive, safe and hopefully far from this maddening crowd. With a pounding heart she backed her way out of the heaving throng and slipped away with one single thought. Thank God !

And so it was, the horrific deed was done. The inevitable scramble for the King's head, blood or hair provided the most excellent and opportune diversion for James, Nicholas and Henry to make their way out the back of the scaffold, down the side of the Banqueting house and on to the river bank, out of the fracas undetected and unnoticed.

♛

Meanwhile Jono and Freddy, who were well used to quick scene changes, were swift in their movements. With impeccable dexterity they cleared the stage and lifted the remains of the body into the waiting casket. The two men then placed the lid on top and lowered it via pulleys so cleverly devised by Inigo Jones down on to the same barrow that had bought it there and had been since tucked away under the stage and in the wings as it were. Robert fixed it securely, whilst Inigo retrieved the head of the poor fellow who now looked nothing like himself let alone the former King of England. Parliament had its head, the army its sport and the people their spectacle but the very air in Whitehall was serried with disgust and gloom. Heavily cloaked Inigo, who had already dismantled any sign and all evidence of the swinging doors, made his way with Robert wheeling the barrow with a guard escort through the dispersing crowd back to St James Palace.

♛

Jono and Freddy, still wearing their disguises, climbed back through the Banqueting House window and proudly accepted the heavy purse laid out for them. The parliament man who had secured their service was visibly shaken and muddled his words. Jono intentionally held out his blooded hand, offering to shake the upright, uptight puritan but he recoiled in horror, hastily dropping the purse and putting a handkerchief across his quivering mouth.

"God bless you sir," said Jono, catching the purse while pretending to doff a hat he wasn't wearing.

"God saved the King," whispered Freddy under his breath but he saw the puritan shudder, signaling that he had indeed heard. They were the only men in good spirits as they took their reward and bowed out of the rooms fleeing down the stairs, waiting to be far from prying eyes before removing their disguises. Jono and Freddy then bolted off in the opposite direction to the others, the plan was to meet again on the following Friday. The sun had not shone that day, it was bone chilling cold, damp and icy as the last of the Queens men dispersed. Simultaneously, diplomats and envoys from all over Europe scattered like rats back to their princes with the awful news while Jane and Elizabeth made their way back to Elizabeth's home in Westminster.

♛

In Somerset, safely by a roaring fire, the former true and rightful King of England moved his Queen across the chess board with sweeping grace.

"I do believe it's checkmate," he said as he placed his hands together and under his chin surveying his easily won victory.

"Well I'll be," said Joseph, moving his eyes about the board for although not a novice he really had not seen that move coming.

Harry smiled, for like every man, he enjoyed winning.

♛

The deathly silence had not left the streets of London, there was much troubling the minds of the men who had been party to one of the worst days of English history. The coffin along with the morbid remains were placed on a public display of sorts, inside the palace. Selected persons could come and view the body in a dimly lit room for a number of days while those wicked commissioners thought of what to do with it. It was thankfully deemed inappropriate to be buried in Westminster Abbey so the poor chap was taken quietly to Windsor Castle to be unceremoniously tossed inside a vault within the crumbling chapel of St George, long since ruined and ransacked by the parliamentarians.

♛

Jane was never more thankful when Friday eventually came, she had been fretting, wild with anticipation and fantasies all week at the thought of seeing James again. She had stayed quietly hidden away with Elizabeth, while keeping a close eye on the outcomes around Whitehall and Westminster but now Jane was finding it hard to hide her excitement. She had spent her days taking great care in choosing an outfit for her reunion with James and had thought of little else. She was so looking forward to seeing him and all of the Queens men who had so bravely risked their lives for him. The memory of that day amused her no end knowing that their daring plan had been a success. The sun shone brightly that Friday as she made her way through the quiet streets. She wandered past the wall where she would sit waiting for her father, thoughts of him flashed through her mind so she looked up to the sky knowing he was watching over her and blew him a kiss. She made her way to the meeting place, a tavern that was the usual haunt for out of work actors. Everyone there was well used to seeing theatrical outbursts from those unable to practice their art or flaunt their talents. Jane made her way to the back rooms where they had agreed they would all meet. It was such a wonderful sight seeing the Queens men so happy to be in each other's company. Their energy flew around them, making Jane feel as if she was on a magic carpet as she floated into the room upon their ecstasy's, Inigo noticed her first and threw his arms in the air.

"Aha ! Here she is," he warmly embraced her and brought her further into the room as everyone greeted her. She was so very pleased to see them all but she couldn't hide her desperation to see James.

"Pour this lass a drink young Fred and we will sing to the good health of the King."

Jane took the mug of ale gratefully but she was obviously distracted, searching for James amongst the joyful crowd.

"He's been waiting for you, over here lass," smiled Inigo, his ruddy cheeks shimmering the light of the fire, his eyes bright and alive. He began to laugh as Jane had clearly not recognised the clean shaven James, who coyly stood behind the wild and excitable others.

"Would the Lady care to join me in a glass of wine ?"

He smiled as he held out a glass to Jane and their eyes met for the first time in a long time, suddenly it was as if there was no one else in the room. Jane nervously giggled and without taking her eyes from him, curtsied. Placing the mug on the table, she raised her other hand to take the glass he offered her. He looked remarkably different now as James, the James she remembered, the actor she had adored her whole life, the bravest and most noble of gentlemen who not only was willing to stand for the King but had so bravely laid down his life for him.

Inigo saw their need to have a moment alone so led the crowd away singing. James wrapped his fingers over Jane's hand and around her glass as he filled it with rich red wine, the finest found in London, paid for with the puritan's purse.

"Well, well well, what do we have here ? A gift from the heavens ? A sprite ? You must be a fairy, a fairy with fairy dust, the queen of the fairies ? Do you remember me, My Lady ?" He whispered through her hair so sweetly, his words dripping once more like honey into her soul. She blushed and couldn't help but smile, as she vividly remembered the last time he said those words to her. He remembered.

"Yes, I do, I remember you," she tittered, stumbling for words and taking the glass to her lips. Without taking her eyes from his and with his hand still wrapped around hers, she drank the wine he gave her as James took up her other hand and playfully caressed her fingers.

"We are each other," he said, gently kissing her hand with those perfect lips Jane craved so much. She dared not move as James took his kisses to her wrist, sensing his breath upon her skin made her tingle with delight and anticipation. He kept his eyes locked with hers as he took his kisses from the inside of her arm to the crease of her elbow, where the sleeves of her dress stopped him from devouring her. Jane gasped, she found herself swaying defenceless to his advances and what's more she willingly welcomed them. Thankfully Inigo returned, snapping them out of it and pulling them back into the revelry of the moment, they burst into playful laughter and rejoined the celebrations. James raised his glass and wrapped his arm around Jane's waist, pulling her close to him while they joined in with the song, looking at each other longingly, happily anticipating the inevitable passions that awaited them.

Epilogue ~ Afterwards

The Cromwellian nightmare that followed, continued to scar the people and the times. The fanatical puritans destroyed all that was good and great about Britain and every bit of beauty that adorned her. The face of Albion was changed forever. Particularly in Ireland where, Cromwell driven mad by his insatiable daughters and by Ireton's relentless pestering, massacred the poor people there. All those that valued peace and beauty had no place in the republic he gave them and taxed them heavily for. They were dark days, Ireton was soon slain leaving Cromwell free of his possession but on returning to England having made himself king in all but name, the usurper ruled cruelly. He went to great lengths to besmirch the Stuarts, using Milton to produce pamphlets saying shameful things about King Charles and salaciously smearing the good names of King James and the Duke of Buckingham forever. As William Blake once said, Milton was "a true poet but …of the Devil's party without knowing it." Even those puritans who initially saw potential in Cromwells ideals, took their leave of him and the country, sailing west to the Americans, taking their shame with them.

♛

Harry was a world away content in his comfortable room at the Bluebell Inn. He committed himself to becoming the town's hermit Saint, in perpetual prayer, praying for the souls of everyone and for the town itself. He played chess and found great joy in seeing his beautiful daughter blossom and flourish and fall in love in the simplistic way of country folk. Ever thankful for the charmed and peaceful way he was able to live out the rest of his life. Jane, being so knowledgeable, well connected and now adept at facilitating escapes, was able with ease to spirit Princess Elizabeth, the King's daughter from the Isle of White, where she too was held captive. Feigning her demise, Jane's network of helpers switched her with the body of a young maid who had succumbed to fever, then Jane led her to the safety of Glastonbury. Declared dead to the world, Princess Elisabeth would now be known as Temperance and was able to live out the rest of her natural life in peace with her father. Likewise when Jane's son Broome begged her to free him from the constraints of the Whorwood household, he too mysteriously died to the rest of the world upon the Isle of White. He was then able to live out his days freely known as Daniel in Glastonbury, where he fell in love with Temperance. Ma Gollop would bequeath the keys of the Bluebell Inn, (by then affectionately known as the Mad House) to them and their children. Knowing full well that her life's purpose was fulfilled, Ma stepped back into the corridors of time to patiently wait until her service was required again.

The King's eldest son Charles intent on claiming his inheritance was initially crowned King in Scotland but following a defeat after a Battle at Worcester found himself fleeing in disguise to the safety and sanctuary of his Father in Glastonbury. Harry was able to advise and prepare him as they walked and prayed together within the Abbey grounds. Harry encouraged his son to be joyful and to wait, for patience leads to courage. The time will come.

Harry took great pleasure in the coronation of his son as Charles the second. He was as they had envisioned, eventually invited back to wear the crown of Great Britain and lead the fortunate Isles in a glorious restoration, the republic having failed so miserably. There were certain terms and conditions which Charles had to agree to but he had one stipulation of his own. He insisted that his Father be made a Saint which he duly was, the week before Charles was enthroned. Harry was honoured to be known forevermore as King Charles the Martyr, to this day he remains the only Saint within the Anglican Church. Harry keenly observed his son's merry reign although he never sought to intervene.

Queen Henrietta, lately the Queen mother found it harder to bear. Knowing her husband to be alive yet so far removed and out of reach. She took great comfort knowing that he and their daughter were safe, happy and above all in the arms of each other. Whenever a letter came from her, Harry would lock himself away for days meditating upon her words, her scent, her memory and her love.

When Harry died peacefully in his sleep the town kept vigil for their living Saint who had always prayed for them, blessed them and often beat them at chess. His funeral though a simple affair was worthy of a man who was well respected by all of the towns folk and a great many strangers. No one noticed the King's presence, he was disguised under a heavy woollen cloak with his Duke of Buckingham at his side. No one except his younger sister Temperance recognised him to be her brother. Surprisingly the tomb was a rather grand one for such a simple man, ornate and fabulously adorned with carvings of fine craftsmanship, a testament to the man and regality placed within it, made by none other than Inigo Jones. In recognition of his loyalty and service the new King had given Jones lands upon which he had built himself a fine house at Butleigh, five miles south of Glastonbury, so he could be near to his old friend and patron. The Queen had intended to stay in England with her son but the heartbreak was too great for her, upon hearing the news of her husband's natural death she fled back to France, she would never recover. Without the King she was half the person she once was. She stumbled through life a few further years, relying heavily upon doctors becoming a recluse. Distraught and heartbroken she died, asking that her heart be taken to be buried with her husband which it secretly was, in a silver casket.

As for Jane and James they spent every moment together blissfully in each other's company, joyfully in love. So deeply, truly and perfectly did they adore each other that they continue to chase each other throughout all of time, so they may always and forever more, live happily ever after.

I was totally disoriented as I opened my eyes, seeing the old lady smiling back at me. It took a few moments for me to remember where I was and when I was !

"I've just had the strangest dream," I uttered as I wiped my mouth worried I'd been dribbling. I sat up taking in my surroundings, the fire was still roaring and the wind was still howling outside. The old lady carried on smiling as I got myself together.

"I must have fallen asleep, I'm so sorry."

"Aye, that you did but no bother you were only asleep for a moment, if that."

"What ? A moment, but .. wow, I had this huge, amazing dream. I saw .. I mean I was there but not there, it was as if everything was unfolding before my eyes like, like an epic film. It was so …real."

"Aye, that'll be that quantum photon entanglement we mentioned. Maybe you slipped into a portal and flipped into another slice of time."

"But, I saw lifetimes, the King's life, we were, it was the civil war, we were here in Glastonbury, but," I tried desperately it find the words to make the dream fit in to this reality as I looked about me and outside the windows, vividly remembering it as it was in a different time.

"Aye, time, it's not what you think it is, you know. What was it that the wise fella said, spooky action at a distance ? You saw Glastonbury did you ?" She smiled.

"Yes, I've sat here before and I saw you … but a different you, you were running a hotel .. an Inn, at the top of the High street .. it was called, now what was it called ?"

The old lady smiled as if straight from her heart, sitting back in her chair as I frantically flicked through the images of my mind, trying to hold the dream that was so clear but was now like smoke.

"It's gone but I saw it all. It was an epic, so detailed, so real. I was there but I overlooked it all and was able to skip along with them. They, the Queens men, I mean they were there and there was a lady with flowing auburn hair, but she was always hidden in a great green cloak. What was her name ? Gin...Jane, that's it, Jane and she loved the King only it wasn't the King.. and he didn't die ..no one died !"

"Well that is good news." Chuckled the old woman.

I carried on trying to fit the fragments of the dream into something coherent.

"Dear heart, don't even try, you can't fit the expanse of a dream into mere words, I believe you, you see Glastonbury did have a role to play in that time although no one knew of it, until now that is, seems like you've tapped into something...spooky." Her kind eyes sparkled, "come with me I'll show you something," she got up and waved her hand encouraging me to do the same.

"I'll just pay for this," I said, reaching for my bag.

"Ah, don't worry about that, Paul will take care of it, won't you Paul dear ?" Paul magically appeared and nodded silently to the old lady, as he cleared the cups and bowls away.

"Now, come with me dear."

I followed her as she floated out the back of the pub, under the low ceilings and along the cobblestone floor which is obviously where the wagons used to come. I recognised it all, although differently, as it had once been, it was like walking through time, as flashes from the dream flew through my mind.

We came out onto the car park and the 21st century, taking a sharp right past the rows of shiny electric cars. The storm had given way to fast moving clouds and rays of sunshine although it was still blustery and cold. We made our way to the church of St John's which dominates the little town's High street and climbed the steps that led us in through a side door although it felt and I remembered it to have once been the main door. It all seemed weirdly familiar. I followed the little old lady into the church as she stopped to speak to a tall elderly man who welcomed her fondly. He then produced a bunch of huge old iron keys and led the way to another side door. Above it was the royal crest, the lion and the unicorn of King Charles, the second. They had been placed in churches as an act of loyalty to the crown after the restoration, although this one was rather special, the old man whose name was Bill pointed out. He was a tall willowy chap with a kindness about him that he shared with the lady who had led me here. He promptly opened the door, dipping his imaginary hat to her as she walked through and to me as I followed. The door opened out on to a sparse graveyard covered in lush green grass vibrant and glistening from the earlier rains. There directly in front of the door was a huge ornate, white and weathered tomb. It was wonderfully carved and decorated and obviously ancient. The old lady made straight for it and stood in reverence next to it.

"This, it was once in the Abbey you know, been moved around a lot since then, some believe it to the tomb of Joseph of Arimathea, others believe it to be of some wealthy merchant."

I walked around it, admiring the incredible artistry that was still visible, someone had put a lot of effort into it, it looked and felt strangely familiar.

"And what do you think it is ?" I asked, intrigued as to why she had brought me here and why I had followed. I really was having such a bizarre day.

"Aha ! Well you see dear heart, I know what it is," she smiled as I ran my fingers over it which seemed to spark my imagination as suddenly I remembered I had seen it before, in my dream, it was shining pure white and it was indeed in the Abbey ruins. I remembered the men on horseback, the King and the Duke in disguise. The ladies gathered there comforting each other. Jane was there, with James, the man who played the King, the old lady was there too. There was a great crowd gathered listening to the priest reading from a prayer book as they laid an old man who was once the true and rightful King to rest amongst the Saints and older Kings of England.

"I know what this is or rather what it once was. I dreamt about this, this was the tomb for the King, the real King .. Charles .. he wasn't beheaded at all, they saved him. You all saved him. He came to live here, with you, well someone a lot like you. He died peacefully and was buried here, in Glastonbury."

The old lady reached out placing her hand gently on the top of the tomb without saying a word, her eyes filled with tears as she looked over at me.

"It's been said he was a troublesome King, who didn't know how to rule but wheels were set in motion long before he came to the throne. You were right, you already knew. Trust yourself dear one. The renaissance happening in Europe was a threat to the authority of the Catholic Church so they came and destroyed everything, again, much as they did to the Cathars of Southern France. Instigating 30 years of war that raged throughout Europe wiping all traces of wonder, beauty and magic from the minds of men. After 30 years of senseless war no one dared look back or remember. King Charles' sister was indeed the Queen of Bohemia and their father regularly made trips to Stuttgart to meet with alchemists. It was these events that led directly to the downfall of the Stuarts. They knew too much. Charles was a good man, a kind man and one with such high hopes for England, for humanity. He, like his father, believed in peace and they knew that beauty would save the world, alas the world wasn't ready, but maybe it is now."

Bill called kindly from the door saying he was locking up the church so we turned to head back to the door we had come through. He had great strength for an old man as he heaved the heavy door shut and turned the giant keys locking it behind us. We walked silently out through the porched entrance that led out onto the high street. It all looked so different now that I had the dream to compare it with, we walked out of the iron gates as Bill closed and locked them behind us, bidding us a good night. The street lights came on as the old lady turned to me with both hands outstretched and we hugged.

"Well, wasn't that nice, it was lovely to see you again, thank you for sharing today with me. Maybe now you can write a different story, a different history for folks to remember, one with a better ending. We always find each other, you can be sure of that, until we meet again, good night dear heart and a fond farewell." She smiled as she looked up and down the street, ready to cross the road.

I was so disoriented I laughed out loud as I called after her.

"Thank you, It was lovely meeting you … again ? Oh please wait, it's been such a strange day. Forgive me, I do remember meeting you down there, today and I remember us going to the George for something, which I don't remember paying for but I'm still trying to make sense of that dream, trying to put it into words, these memories, they're old but feel new, I remember you, but a different you, you ran this little ...."

"The Bluebell Inn." She called over her shoulder without looking back, leaving me dumbfounded as she glided across the road, down the alleyway past the Labyrinth book shop and out of sight.

♛

With never ending love to my Parents and Beautiful Children.

Huge Thanks and Heartfelt Gratitude to Scribbler Steph and Dr Tim.

Thanks also to everyone who contributes to Wikipedia.

These are the books that have inspired me in the writing of this one.

The King's Smuggler by John Fox

Merchants of Light by Betty J. Kovacs

The Three Musketeers and Twenty Years After by Alexandre Dumas

The Stuart's in Love by Maurice Ashley

The Chemical Wedding of Christian Rosenkreutz

Grey Eminence by Aldous Huxley

The Dreamland Trilogy by Mrs Hills and Dan Thompson

The Glastonbury Grail by The Gnaughty Gnome

For Angela.

27th March 2025, 400 years after King Charles inherited the throne from his father James.